Gersonides on Providence,
Covenant, and the
Chosen People

SUNY Series in Jewish Philosophy
Kenneth Seeskin, editor

Gersonides on Providence, Covenant, and the Chosen People

A STUDY IN MEDIEVAL JEWISH PHILOSOPHY AND BIBLICAL COMMENTARY

by
Robert Eisen

STATE UNIVERSITY OF NEW YORK PRESS

Published by
State University of New York Press, Albany

For information, address State University of New York Press,
State University Plaza, Albany, N.Y., 12246

Production by Cathleen Collins
Marketing by Bernadette LaManna

Library of Congress Cataloging in Publication Data

Eisen, Robert, 1960-
    Gersonides on providence, covenant, and the chosen people : a
study in medieval Jewish philosophy and biblical commentary / Robert
Eisen.
        p.   cm. — (SUNY series in Jewish philosophy)
    Includes bibliographical references and index.
    ISBN 0-7914-2313-1. — ISBN 0-7914-2314-X
    1. Levi ben Gershom, 1288–1344.   2. Jews—Election, Doctrine of.
3. Philosophy, Jewish.   4. Philosophy, Medieval.   I. Title.
II. Series.
B759.L44E38   1995
296.3'11—dc20   94-9215
                                                            CIP

10 9 8 7 6 5 4 3 2 1

To My Parents

Contents

Preface

The present work is an outgrowth of my doctoral dissertation, which examined Gersonides' interpretation of the exodus story in his *Commentary on the Torah*. My research on this theme spurred me to think about the larger question of how Gersonides comes to terms with the whole notion of Jewish chosenness. It also forced me to consider the overall relationship between Gersonides' philosophical and exegetical writings. These issues are essentially the two foci of the present study.

This book should appeal primarily to specialists in medieval Jewish philosophy and biblical exegesis. Yet I have made every attempt to make it accessible to a wider audience. I devote an entire chapter to basic concepts in Gersonides' philosophy that are necessary background for the rest of the study. I also make a point of consistently reviewing ideas dealt with in earlier chapters when they are alluded to in subsequent discussions, so that the reader who is unfamiliar with this material will not have to rely on memory alone to keep abreast of my arguments. I offer my apologies to the specialists who may find that my efforts render portions of this study superfluous or repetitive.

My interest in Gersonides was kindled a number of years ago when I was a graduate student at Brandeis University searching for a dissertation topic. My graduate adviser Marvin Fox at one point suggested that I take a look at Gersonides' biblical commentaries as a potential avenue for research. I reacted with lukewarm interest, perhaps more out of ignorance than out of any concrete objection. Sensing my reluctance, Dr. Fox made another suggestion, one that, I believe, exemplifies the quality of the guidance that I received from him throughout graduate school. He asked me to take two weeks to prepare any section in Gersonides' *Commentary on the*

Torah as thoroughly as I could, and that he and I would then spend an af-
ternoon taking up the portion I had chosen. In those two weeks, it became
clear to me what Dr. Fox had wanted me to discover. By the time we sat
down to review a section from Gersonides' commentary on Exodus, I had
found Gersonides' biblical commentaries to be an unusually rich body of
writings both philosophically and exegetically—though, surprisingly, one
that for the most part had been neglected by scholars of medieval Jewish
thought.

To Marvin Fox I owe my deepest gratitude, not only for this initial en-
counter with Gersonides and for directing the dissertation that resulted
from it, but also for his involvement at every stage of the present project.
Aside from his innumerable insights and suggestions that have been in-
corporated in my work, his whole approach towards Jewish philosophy
and exegesis informs the present study. It is he who taught me to appreciate the importance—and complexity—of the relationship between these
two disciplines. But Dr. Fox's role in my development has gone well beyond purely intellectual concerns. He has also taught me that integrity and
decency are as important to being an academic as the scope of one's learning. I hope to continue benefiting from his wisdom for years to come.

I was privileged to have the guidance of other accomplished scholars
who assisted in my initiation into the world of Gersonides' thought.
Nahum Sarna and Seymour Feldman, who served on my dissertation committee, were instrumental in this process. Dr. Sarna proved to be a most
valuable resource for me, not only for his knowledge of the biblical text for
which he is renowned, but also for his command of medieval Jewish exegesis. Dr. Feldman, one of the foremost experts on Gersonides, contributed
greatly to my knowledge of Gersonides both through his written work and
personal communications.

I could not have produced the present monograph without the help
of a number of other teachers who have influenced my development as a
student of medieval Jewish thought. I would like to thank Jaroslav Pelikan
and Jonathan Boswell, who were responsible for first exciting my interest
in medieval studies when I was an undergraduate at Yale. I also owe a
great debt to Alfred Ivry who, while I was a student at Brandeis, instilled
in me an appreciation for Jewish and Islamic philosophy, and provided
guidance in the study of the Arabic language. I owe a similar debt to
William Johnson of the Philosophy Department at Brandeis, who played a
central role in my education and personal development while I was a graduate student.

The present monograph has greatly benefited from the careful reading of a number of colleagues. Menachem Kellner's insightful comments

forced me to refine and recast a number of my central arguments. He also provided me with moral support and encouragement for the duration of this project. Charles Manekin offered valuable suggestions and encouragement. I also benefited from the insights of my colleague at George Washington University, Max Ticktin, who read the manuscript with great care. Max has served in any number of roles in my life, including those of teacher and adviser, to name but two. I do not know where I would be without the support he has provided in helping me become acclimated to the life of academia.

I also want to acknowledge my other colleagues in the Religion Department and the Judaic Studies program at George Washington University: Harry Yeide, Dewey Wallace, Abbie Ziffren, Sonya Quitslund, S. H. Nasr, Alf Hiltebeitel, Paul Duff, Howard Sachar, Bernie Reich, Eva Jospe, Judith Plotz and Yael Moses. Their contribution to this project was in providing a receptive environment for me to conduct my research and grow as a scholar.

I should also make mention of my colleague at the University of Maryland, Susan Handelman, whose friendship and professional advice have been invaluable to me in the last two years.

I would like to thank the Mellon Foundation and the Memorial Foundation for Jewish Culture for their generous financial support while I was doing my doctoral work. My thanks also go to George Washington University for providing similar support as the present project was nearing completion.

I am indebted to the Hebrew University of Jerusalem and the Biblioteca Medicea-Laurenziana in Florence for granting me permission to make use of their microfilms, which are cited in this study. It is here that I should also express my gratitude to Eli Freiman of Ma'aleh Adumim, Israel, who generously and patiently shared his research on manuscripts and printed editions of Gersonides' *Commentary on the Torah* while I was doing my doctorate and throughout the duration of this project. His assistance allowed me to conduct my research with a scholarly accuracy that would not have otherwise been possible.

I also want to thank the American Academy for Jewish Research for granting permission to include in this study an appendix on the *pinnot hatorah* in Gersonides' thought. This appendix is an edited and revised version of my article "Reason, Revelation and the Fundamental Principles of the Torah in Gersonides' Thought," *Proceedings of the American Academy for Jewish Research* 57 (1991): 11-34.

Finally, I would like to thank my parents to whom this book is dedicated. If I were to try to express what their love and support have meant to me over the years, I could only fall short of capturing the full scope of my feelings. A simple statement of gratitude will have to suffice. Besides, if I were to say more, I know that it would embarrass them.

Robert Eisen
Washington, D.C.
December, 1994

List of Abbreviations

AJS Review	*Association for Jewish Studies Review*
BT	Babylonian Talmud
CCAR Journal	*Central Conference of American Rabbis Journal*
C. Chron.	Gersonides' *Commentary on Chronicles*
C. Dan.	Gersonides' *Commentary on Daniel*
C. Esther	Gersonides' *Commentary on Esther*
C. Josh.	Gersonides' *Commentary on Joshua*
C. Kings	Gersonides' *Commentary on Kings*
C. Neh.	Gersonides' *Commentary on Nehemiah*
C. Prov.	Gersonides' *Commentary on Proverbs*
C. Sam.	Gersonides' *Commentary on Samuel*
CT	Gersonides' *Commentary on the Torah*
EVE	Emended Venice edition of Gersonides' *Commentary on the Torah*
F	Manuscript Or. 42, Gersonides' *Commentary on the Torah*, Biblioteca-Medicea Laurenziana, Florence, Italy
Guide	Maimonides, *Guide of the Perplexed*, Shlomo Pines, trans. (Chicago: University of Chicago Press, 1963)
HUCA	*Hebrew Union College Annual*
JQR	*Jewish Quarterly Review*
JT	*Jerusalem Talmud*
MH	*Milḥamot ha-Shem* (*The Wars of the Lord*)

NJPS	New Jewish Publication Society translation of the Hebrew Bible (1988)
PAAJR	*Proceedings of the American Academy for Jewish Research*
REJ	*Revue des études juives*
Touati	Charles Touati, *La pensée philosophique et théologique de Gersonide* (Paris: Les Editions de Minuit, 1973)
WL 1 & 2	*The Wars of the Lord*, vol. 1 and 2, translation of Gersonides' *Milḥamot ha-Shem* by Seymour Feldman (Philadelphia: Jewish Publication Society of America, 1984)

ONE

Introduction

Levi ben Gershom (1288–1344)—also known as Ralbag[1] or Gersonides[2]—is regarded as one of the intellectual giants of the medieval Jewish world. What is perhaps most impressive about Gersonides is the number of disciplines at which he excelled. In academic circles, Gersonides is known primarily as a philosopher whose stature in the Middle Ages was second only to that of his great predecessor, Maimonides. His philosophical works include an original treatise, *The Wars of the Lord,* and a number of super-commentaries on Averroes' expositions of Aristotle.

Philosophy, however, was only one of many pursuits. In the medieval Jewish community, Gersonides was perhaps best known as a biblical commentator. He authored an extensive body of exegetical writings, many of which are still printed in standard rabbinic Bibles (*Mikra'ot Gedolot*). Indicative of his popularity as an exegete is that his *Commentary on Job* was one of the very first Hebrew books to be printed. We also have evidence that Gersonides was a talmudic authority of some stature, an expertise that is evident in his discussion of halakhic issues in his *Commentary on the Torah.* Gersonides was also a renowned astronomer and mathematician. It was in these areas that he exerted his greatest impact outside the Jewish community. A number of his astronomical and mathematical works were translated into Latin.[3]

Gersonides was in many ways the best representative of the culture in which he lived. He spent his entire life in Provence, an area that in his period witnessed a remarkable flowering of Jewish intellectual life. Provence was located at the crossroads between Jewish communities in France to the north which excelled in talmudic learning, and Jewish communities in Spain to the south which were renowned for their accomplishments in phi-

1

losophy, mysticism, and poetry. The intersection of these two worlds in Provence allowed this region to produce one of the most vibrant Jewish cultures of the Middle Ages.[4]

Soon after his death, Gersonides became a controversial figure. The views expressed in his philosophical work, *The Wars of the Lord,* and in his biblical commentaries tended towards the unorthodox and thus aroused the ire of the more traditional elements of the Jewish community. As a more conservative strain in Jewish thought began to develop in the century after him, Gersonides' writings were attacked. Prominent Jewish thinkers such as Crescas, Arama, and Abravanel severely criticized his views. These attacks would dampen interest in Gersonides' writings among Jewish thinkers until the modern period. It is only in contemporary academic circles that Gersonides has again been fully revived as a subject of study.[5]

The present project is a study of Gersonides' views on the concept of the Chosen People. There is perhaps little need to justify the value of exploring this issue. If Gersonides is regarded as one of Judaism's greatest philosophers, the concept of Jewish chosenness has consistently been one of its principle doctrines. We therefore have as the subject of our study both a philosopher and a theme that are of central importance in the history of Jewish thought.

Yet, there are several reasons that an analysis of the issue of Jewish chosenness is of particular importance in the study of Gersonides. The first has to do with the nature of his philosophical system. Gersonides grapples with the same tension between the world views of Aristotle and the Bible that had characterized the philosophy of Maimonides and would continue to be a focus of concern for Jewish philosophers until the end of the Middle Ages. But unlike most other Jewish philosophers in his period, Gersonides was willing to adopt key elements of Aristotelian metaphysics that were in conflict with the thought-world of the Bible and its rabbinic interpreters. The central feature of Gersonides' philosophical system is a highly Aristotelian conception of God—one that betrays the strong influence of Averroes. Like Aristotle's First Mover, Gersonides' God is an impersonal Being. He is a Deity who has limited knowledge of events in the world below, is unable to experience a change in will and cannot interact directly with human affairs.

The challenge which therefore characterizes much of Gersonides' philosophy is in interpreting the central doctrines of the Bible so that they conform to this conception of an impersonal God. With great creativity and ingenuity, Gersonides recasts all the major biblical categories—such as creation, prophecy, providence, and miracles—in order to bring them into line with his philosophical principles.

It should be clear why a study of Gersonides' views on Jewish chosenness is important for an understanding of his philosophical thought as a whole. It is with the concept of the Chosen People, as much as with any other major doctrine in Judaism, that the conflict between Gersonides' Aristotelianism and his loyalty to the tenets of classical Judaism is most evident. How can the Jewish people have a special covenantal relationship with God if God is an impersonal Being? How can there be a Chosen People if God does not directly interact with human affairs? The coherence of Gersonides' synthesis of Aristotelian philosophy and traditional Jewish doctrine is therefore very much dependent upon how well he handles the issue of Jewish election.

We may also mention here that if Gersonides' Aristotelianism posed a challenge to the notion that the Jewish people had special standing in God's eyes, the Christian environment in which he lived would only heighten that challenge, albeit in a very different vein. How acquainted Gersonides was with Christian theology and philosophy is not easy to determine. Gersonides' contacts with Christian clerics appear to have been prompted primarily by his expertise in astronomy.[6] Nevertheless, he surely must have been aware—as Jewish thinkers in Christian Europe generally were—that one of the central doctrines of the Church was the repudiation of Jewish chosenness.

Another reason that a study of Gersonides' views on the concept of the Chosen People is important is that it provides an opportunity to explore a much neglected portion of his writings: his biblical commentaries. Specialists in Gersonides' philosophical thought have tended to focus their energies almost exclusively on his major philosophical work, *The Wars of the Lord*, a work that explores six topics: the immortality of the intellect, prophecy, divine knowledge, providence, cosmology, and creation. It is characterized by detailed and systematic philosophical argumentation in which Gersonides carefully weighs the views of his predecessors before deciding on his own position. At the end of each section, Gersonides also demonstrates that his views are in harmony with biblical doctrine.[7]

Far less attention has been paid to Gersonides' exegetical writings. It is difficult to make generalizations about these works, since they exhibit wide variation in content, style, and structure. Yet one feature they have in common is that, to one degree or another, they all draw from the philosophical material in the *Wars*. Some of the commentaries are thoroughly philosophical. In his *Commentary on the Song of Songs*, for instance, Gersonides utilizes his philosophical views in the *Wars* in order to read the Song of Songs as an extended allegory about the intellect. The *Commentary on the Torah*, which is perhaps his most important exegetical work, incorporates a mixture of philosophical material and more purely exegetical exposition. Others commentaries, such as those on the historical books in the Prophets, are more exegetical than philosophical. The philosophical element, however, is never entirely absent.

The feature which is perhaps most indicative of the philosophical character of Gersonides' exegetical works is the *to'aliyyot*, or 'lessons,' which appear in most of his commentaries.[8] In these *to'aliyyot*, Gersonides reviews the major philosophical lessons gleaned from the portion of the biblical text upon which he has just commented. These lessons offer philosophical insights in one of three areas that are described in his introduction to the *Commentary on the Torah*: the commandments, moral and political philosophy, and theoretical philosophy that includes metaphysics and natural science.[9]

Given the wealth of philosophical material in these commentaries, it is surprising that they have received so little attention from scholars of Jewish philosophy. One prominent scholar has questioned whether these writings are of any value at all as a source for Gersonides' philosophical views. In a brief statement in his *Philosophies of Judaism*, Julius Guttmann claims that the philosophical positions expressed in the biblical commentaries deviate significantly from those expressed in the *Wars*. Guttmann's assessment is that Gersonides altered his philosophical positions in the commentaries in order to appeal to a more traditional audience.[10] Guttmann, however, offers no evidence for his far-reaching claim. Moreover, he is the only scholar, to my knowledge, who holds this view.

Charles Touati was the first scholar, at least in recent times, to highlight the significance of the biblical commentaries as sources of insight into Gersonides' philosophical thought. Before the appearance of much of the scholarship on Gersonides in the last few years, Touati had already called attention to the wealth of philosophical material in Gersonides' exegetical writings and urged scholars to take a closer look at this portion of Gersonides' corpus.[11] Touati himself followed up on this suggestion in his major work, *La pensée philosophique et théologique de Gersonide*, the most comprehensive study to date on Gersonides' philosophical thought.[12] In this monumental study, Touati made extensive use of Gersonides' exegetical writings alongside the material in the *Wars* in explicating his philosophy.

But despite Touati's efforts, the scholarship on these works is still very much in a preliminary stage. Touati's work still focuses primarily on the philosophical issues dealt with in Gersonides' *Wars*. Other scholars have produced only a handful of studies on the philosophical material in Gersonides' biblical commentaries.[13] Thus, there is much that still remains to be explored about the role of Gersonides' exegetical works in the development of his philosophy.

We may also add that it is not just the philosophical material in Gersonides' commentaries that has received inadequate attention. There are, for instance, no studies on the exegetical method that Gersonides employs in these works. Gersonides' commentaries exhibit a remarkable blend of exegetical styles. He often adopts Maimonides' philosophical method of biblical interpretation, but he is just as much influenced by the French and Spanish tradition of Jewish exegesis which emphasized *peshat*, the plain meaning of Scripture, over *derash*, the homiletical meaning. Gersonides often draws from the great commentators in this tradition—Rashi, ibn Ezra, and Rashbam—even though he often does not cite them by name.[14] Gersonides also makes highly creative use of rabbinic aggadah throughout his commentaries, even though, once again, he does not often cite his sources.[15]

Another virtually unexplored area in Gersonides' biblical commentaries is his treatment of halakhah. We find in Gersonides' *Commentary on the Torah* lengthy halakhic discussions whenever he encounters legal sections in the biblical text. In these portions of his commentaries, Gersonides develops and applies a highly original method of interpretation in an attempt to connect the teachings of the oral Torah with those of the written Torah.[16]

The present study is designed to offer at least a partial corrective to the imbalance in the scholarship on Gersonides by examining a major philosophical theme that is developed primarily in Gersonides' biblical commentaries. Our analysis of Gersonides' views on Jewish chosenness must certainly begin with an examination of some of the principle doctrines in the *Wars*. Some of the issues discussed in this treatise—such as prophecy, divine knowledge, and providence—are very much relevant to the question of Jewish chosenness. However, the bulk of the material for our study is to be found in the biblical commentaries. For the most part, it is in these writings that Gersonides develops his views on God's providential relationship with the Jewish people and attempts to formulate a philosophy of Jewish history. Most of our effort, therefore, will be devoted to this section of his corpus.

Our study will also attempt to make a more general assessment of the relationship between the philosophical material in the *Wars* and that which is found in the biblical commentaries. If the commentaries do indeed contain philosophical insights not found in the *Wars*, as we will argue, we must then ask the following questions: Why would Gersonides choose to divide his philosophical views between two very different genres of literature? Why would he insist on expressing some philosophical views in the *Wars*, and others in his exegetical writings? The significance of these questions is underscored if one notes that Gersonides is the only major medieval Jewish philosopher, aside from Saadiah, who produces both a major philosophical work *and* a body of biblical commentaries.

This is one issue that Touati does not address in his major study. Throughout his book, Touati brings together the philosophical material in the *Wars* and the commentaries as if it is all extracted from one large work. No attempt is made to evaluate the distinctive contributions of these respective portions of Gersonides' corpus to the development of his philosophical thought.

One possible approach is to argue that the *Wars* and the biblical commentaries simply represent different stages in Gersonides' intellectual development. Since the commentaries were written, for the most part, at a later stage of Gersonides' career than the *Wars*,[17] he was bound to come up with new philosophical insights in the course of composing his exegetical writings that are not represented in his earlier work. While there is certainly some truth in this assessment, there may be more to the differences between the *Wars* and the biblical commentaries than the chronology of composition. What needs to be investigated is whether Gersonides consciously chose to deal with some issues in the commentaries rather than in the *Wars*, and if so, why.

We must, of course, recognize our limitations here. A comprehensive evaluation of the relationship between the philosophical material in the *Wars* and that found in the biblical commentaries is well beyond the scope of our project. The present study deals with only one issue in Gersonides' thought that straddles the boundary between philosophy and biblical commentary. There are certainly many other such topics. Still, by focusing on an issue as important as the concept of the Chosen People, we will get some insight into how philosophical material is apportioned by Gersonides between his philosophical and exegetical writings.[18]

There is one other limitation that we will have to impose upon our study. In the course of our discussion, we will be dealing with some of the non-philosophical aspects of Gersonides' commentaries. An analysis of any philosophical theme in these writings inevitably forces us to confront such issues as Gersonides' exegetical method and his use of rabbinic aggadah. However, it is important to emphasize that our focus will be on the philosophical material in Gersonides' commentaries and that we will not be able to explore these other issues in any detail. It is not that the latter are unimportant or uninteresting; on the contrary, they are of sufficient significance and complexity that they are best left for separate study.

To summarize, the purpose of our project is twofold. First, an analysis of Gersonides' views on the concept of the Chosen People will provide important insight into his philosophical thought. It will enable us to see how Gersonides interprets a doctrine that is both central to Judaism and at the same time is a formidable challenge to his Aristotelian principles. Second, our study will allow for a careful examination of the much neglected philosophical material in Gersonides' biblical commentaries. We hope to highlight the value of these writings as sources of insight into Gersonides' philosophical system and to provide a better understanding of the relationship between these works and his major philosophical treatise, *The Wars of the Lord*.

We begin our study in chapter two with a survey of the philosophical material in the *Wars* that is relevant for our project. Of interest to us will be Gersonides' views on divine providence, an issue that is dealt with in a number of places in the *Wars*. We will demonstrate that while the *Wars* provides essential philosophical concepts for an understanding of Jewish chosenness, it does not offer a philosophical framework to account for the ongoing relationship between God and the Jewish people throughout history. The key element that is missing in the *Wars* is a philosophical interpretation of the covenant idea, perhaps the central concept for any interpretation of Jewish chosenness.

The rest of our study will focus on Gersonides' biblical commentaries and show that it is only in these writings that Gersonides fully develops an interpretation of the covenant idea. We will proceed in a historical manner by tracing Gersonides' interpretation of the covenant concept in each of the major phases of Jewish history, from the time of Abraham onward. The main thread running through our entire analysis will be the centrality of the Patriarchal covenant in Gersonides' reading of history. We will show that Gersonides equates this covenant with a special form of providence that is inherited from one generation to the next, and that it is this expression of providence which, in turn, accounts for the unique relationship between God and the Jewish people.

Chapters three and four will discuss Gersonides' philosophical interpretation of the Patriarchal covenant and its role up to the conquest of Canaan. In chapter three, we will examine Gersonides' exegesis of Genesis 15, in which the Patriarchal covenant is first formulated. It is here that Gersonides first identifies the Patriarchal covenant with an inheritable form of providence. In chapter four, we will see how Gersonides utilizes his understanding of the Patriarchal covenant to explain events in the rest of the Pentateuch, and, in the process, refines his philosophical views about the nature and function of the covenant.

Chapters five and six will focus on Gersonides' philosophical understanding of the Sinaitic covenant. In chapter five, we will discuss the two major issues that are essential in Gersonides' understanding of this covenant: the ascendancy of Mosaic prophecy and the role of the Torah as a guidebook for philosophical perfection. Chapter six will assess Gersonides' views on esoteric discourse and whether he in any way supports Maimonides' esoteric method of reading Scripture. This latter subject is important both for an understanding of Gersonides' views regarding the role of the Torah as philosophical guidebook and also for gaining insight into Gersonides' attitude towards his own philosophical writing. In these chapters, the centrality of the Patriarchal covenant in Gersonides' thinking will continue to be evident. We will see that Gersonides understands the covenant at Sinai as an outgrowth of the Patriarchal covenant.

In chapters seven and eight, we will look at Gersonides' philosophical views on Jewish history from the time of the conquest to the messianic period. Most of our analysis in these chapters will concentrate on the Patriarchal covenant which, according to Gersonides, continues to play a central role in God's relationship with the Jewish people up to the end of history.

Chapter nine will shift from the content of Gersonides' philosophical views regarding the Jewish people to the style in which these views are expressed. We will attempt to explain Gersonides' tendency in the biblical commentaries to describe God's providential activity in terms that seem more appropriate for a personal God than the Aristotelian God depicted in the *Wars*. This issue is important not only for evaluating Gersonides' views on Jewish chosenness, but also for assessing the character of the biblical commentaries as a whole. Chapter ten is our concluding chapter in which we will make final assessments of the issues that have prompted our study.

TEXTS AND TRANSLATIONS

The Hebrew text of *The Wars of the Lord* (*Milḥamot ha-Shem*) that was used for our study was the Leipzig edition of 1866 (*MH*). Despite numerous errors, this text is the best Hebrew edition available.

Seymour Feldman has undertaken the ambitious project of translating the entire treatise into English. So far, two volumes have been completed (*WL* 1 and *WL* 2), which cover the first four of the six books in the *Wars*. For English translations of passages in books one through four, we have cited Feldman's translation. This translation has the advantage not only of providing a faithful rendering of a difficult text, but also of affording us corrected readings in the Hebrew, since Feldman consulted three manuscripts that correct the errors in the Leipzig edition. In some instances, I have deviated from Feldman's translation. In such cases, I have indicated that I have made some adjustments to his reading of the text.

Feldman has not yet translated books five and six of the *Wars*. Translations of passages from these books are therefore my own. Professor Feldman has been kind enough to offer his assistance by reviewing my translations of these texts, and, where necessary, correcting them in light of the manuscript material in his possession.

Gersonides' biblical commentaries present more of a problem. All of the commentaries have been published. However, due to the general neglect of these writings, none has ever been published in a critical edition, nor have any been translated into a Western language.[19] For the Hebrew texts of the commentaries, we have therefore relied, as have other scholars, on standard published editions. The specific editions used in this study are identified in my bibliography, along with the forms of citation that appear in my notes. All translations from the commentaries are my own.[20]

The exception was our treatment of Gersonides' *Commentary on the Torah*, his largest and perhaps most complex commentary. Of Gersonides' exegetical works, this commentary was the most important one for this study, since it yielded many of Gersonides' central positions and insights regarding our topic. In this case, therefore, we looked beyond the printed editions in order to ascertain the most reliable readings of the text.

The resources that were used to ensure accurate readings of this commentary will require some explanation. The *Commentary on the Torah* has been printed several times: in Mantua (before 1480), Venice (1547), and Amsterdam (1724). Scholars have generally relied on the 1547 Venice edition, which has been reprinted in New York (1958) and Jerusalem (1967). The problems with this edition are evident; even with a superficial reading of the text, one finds a multitude of errors.

A group of Israeli rabbinic scholars at Yeshivat Birkat Moshe in Ma'aleh Adumim have begun working on a critical edition of the *Commentary on the Torah*. Their preliminary research on the manuscripts has brought additional problems to light regarding the reliability of the printed editions. They have found evidence that a substantial amount of material from the original commentary was not included in the Venice edition.

I have been in touch with Eli Freiman, one of the principal scholars in this group, who has been kind enough to share his work with me.[21] Freiman and his colleagues have discovered thirty-five extant manuscripts of the *Commentary on the Torah*, which can be divided into two distinct families. The manuscripts in one of these families contain substantially more material than those in the other family. The problem with the printed editions of Mantua and Venice is that they are based on the family of manuscripts with incomplete texts. Freiman's group believes that the longer version is, in fact, the more authentic of the two. They therefore intend to publish their critical edition on the basis of the more complete family of texts.[22]

This edition has not yet appeared in print.[23] However, Freiman has shared important information with me, that has given me access to a more accurate reading of the commentary than that of the printed editions. First, Freiman has identified for me the manuscript upon which his group is basing its critical edition: Or. 42 from the Biblioteca Medicea-Laurenziana, in Florence, Italy. I was able to obtain a microfilm of this text through the Institute for Hebrew Manuscripts of the National Library, at the Hebrew University in Jerusalem.

In the course of his research, Freiman has also come across an interesting phenomenon that is highly relevant to our concerns. It would appear that the discrepancies between the Venice edition and the more complete version of the text did not go unnoticed by earlier scholars. Freiman has located several old copies of the Venice text that contain handwritten corrections based on the more complete family of manuscripts. These corrections are most often written into the margins. In some copies whole pages of lengthy handwritten passages have been inserted into the binding.

Freiman discovered one remarkable edition of this kind which was originally from the Etz Ḥayyim Library of Amsterdam and is now in the National Library at the Hebrew University in Jerusalem. According to Freiman, the corrections and additions in this text appear to have been based on a large number of manuscripts. This corrected edition provides, in his estimation, a highly accurate reading of the commentary. I was also able to obtain a microfilm of this text from the National Library.[24]

These two texts, the Florence manuscript (F), and the emended Venice text from the Etz Ḥayyim Library (EVE), were used throughout this study to ensure accurate readings of the *Commentary on the Torah*. Discrepancies between these texts were settled in favor of the emended Venice edition, which, in the absence of a critical edition, is perhaps the next best thing. However, on some occasions, the reading in the Florence manuscript was adopted when it was clear that it presented a far superior rendering of the text.

In the course of this study, I discovered that while this manuscript material was helpful, its impact on the project was actually rather minimal. Most of the material that appears in the more complete version of the commentary, but which was wholly excluded from the Venice text, was not relevant to our concerns. This material deals mainly with philosophical explanations of the biblical commandments or technical halakhic issues. The Florence manuscript and the emended Venice edition were helpful mostly for correcting small errors in the printed edition of the commentary. Only in rare instances did these corrections make an important difference in the reading of a passage.

We should mention that an edition of Gersonides' *Commentary on the Torah* is also in the process of being published under the auspices of Mossad ha-Rav Kook in Jerusalem. The first volume that includes the commentary on Genesis appeared recently.[25] However, it is not a critical edition. The editor made use of the Venice printing and a limited body of manuscript material in the private library of Mossad ha-Rav Kook.[26] Our preference in this study was therefore to rely on the resources suggested by Freiman and his group.

One final note on translations of biblical passages. All English translations of biblical quotations are from the new edition of the Jewish Publication
Society (NJPS). I will, however, deviate occasionally from this translation
when it differs significantly from Gersonides' own understanding of the
biblical text.

TWO

The Philosophical Background

PROVIDENCE, MIRACLES AND INHERITED
PROVIDENCE IN *THE WARS OF THE LORD*

Since *The Wars of the Lord* is Gersonides' major philosophical treatise, an analysis of Gersonides' views on the Chosen People must certainly begin with this work. While there is no separate discussion in the *Wars* devoted to Jewish chosenness, there is extensive treatment of the subject of divine providence—and it is within the context of this general philosophical category that Gersonides' views on Jewish chosenness must be understood.

This chapter will therefore be devoted to an elucidation of Gersonides' theory of providence. We will first look at the fourth book of the *Wars*, in which Gersonides maps out his central positions on this issue. We will then examine Gersonides' treatment of miracles, which is taken up in a separate discussion in the closing chapters of the *Wars*. Finally, we will turn to a cryptic passage in the final pages of the *Wars*, in which Gersonides suggests that providence can be, in some sense, inherited from generation to generation. The intention here is not to conduct a thorough investigation of Gersonides' views on providence—a task well beyond the scope of this study—but rather to summarize this aspect of Gersonides' philosophy so as to provide the background necessary for the central theme of this study, Jewish chosenness. We will devote extended discussion only to those issues that have not been adequately clarified by previous scholars and that are also key to our subject.[1]

PROVIDENCE

We noted in the introduction that the entire character of Gersonides' philosophical system hinges on his highly Aristotelian conception of God. Before we discuss Gersonides' position on providence, it is therefore imperative that we become better acquainted with Gersonides' views on this central issue.

A number of Aristotelian premises lie at the basis of Gersonides' conception of God.[2] The first is that God is the source of all essences that descend into the world below through a chain of emanations or Separate Intellects. Second, God controls all events in the celestial and sublunar realms through His self-intellection. By perpetually contemplating His own essence, God powers all motion and change in the universe. Finally, God's thought process cannot undergo change; the activity of self-intellection is an entirely static one.[3]

These premises have important implications for divine knowledge that are worked out by Gersonides in the third book of the *Wars*.[4] Gersonides reasons that if God's thought cannot change, His knowledge of the world is necessarily limited. Through self-intellection, God can have cognizance of the essences that are responsible for all that exists, since these are immutable objects of knowledge. However, God cannot have knowledge of particulars, because they are in constant flux. Nor, by corollary, can He have knowledge of historical events, since these by their very nature also undergo constant change.

Yet, despite these observations, Gersonides is not satisfied with God's complete ignorance of particulars and temporal events. Gersonides goes on to argue that God does have some knowledge of particulars, but not in the same way that human beings do. While human beings know particulars in their particularity, God knows them only insofar as they are ordered within the unified scheme of the divine mind.[5] Gersonides also includes in God's knowledge some awareness of historical events. While human beings have direct cognizance of events in the temporal order, God knows them only through the immutable laws that are responsible for all motion and change in the sublunar realm. In summary, Gersonides argues that God has perception of the changeable world of particulars and temporal occurrences, but only through the immutable essences and laws contained in His own mind.[6]

Closely connected to the question of divine knowledge is the issue of free will. If God has knowledge of future historical events—even if only through the medium of immutable laws—does this mean that all human action is foreordained? Gersonides follows the logical implications of his theory of divine knowledge by asserting that human beings for the most part follow the course of events determined by the order in the divine mind. Their actions, like everything else in the sublunar realm, are controlled by laws within God's thought process. But Gersonides also emphatically upholds the principle of free will[7], which he claims is both mandated by philosophy and is a fundamental principle of the Torah. Gersonides therefore asserts that man can occasionally contravene the predetermined order, particularly when prophetic communication has warned him of oncoming disaster.[8]

Most audacious is Gersonides' claim that in instances in which man exercises free will, God is entirely ignorant of his course of action. This conclusion follows from the notion that God is able to see only that which has been determined in the divine mind. Due to this limitation, God cannot have any perception of human action that has contravened that order. Do the limitations on God's knowledge in any way compromise God's perfection? Gersonides answers this question firmly in the negative. God knows that human actions are by their very nature contingent. Thus, there is no imperfection when God does not know the actual outcome of those actions; in recognizing their contingency God knows the nature of human actions as they truly are.[9]

Perhaps the most significant feature of Gersonides' conception of God is that He is unable to experience any change in will. Therefore, whatever knowledge God does or does not have with regard to events in the sublunar realm, He certainly cannot be involved personally in the natural order; God cannot directly intervene in human events, nor can He spontaneously respond to human need.[10]

In summary, while Gersonides sees God as very much in control of the universe, he also places crucial limitations on Him. God has knowledge of all events in the world, but it is a static knowledge that does not encompass human actions that contravene the predicted order. Furthermore, God experiences no change in will, and therefore in no way interacts personally in human affairs.

Let us now turn to Gersonides' views on divine providence as developed in book four of the *Wars*.[11] Gersonides posits two basic forms of providence that protect the human species: general providence and individual providence. General providence is embedded in the thought process of God, which has just been described. The order in the divine mind that is activated by God's self-intellection is the best of all possible worlds. Thus, the motions of the heavenly bodies that implement the laws in the divine mind act to preserve the various species in the sublunar realm in the best possible manner. The human species receives the greatest degree of protection from general providence because of its rank and nobility. The heavenly bodies regulate all of man's thoughts and actions for maximum possible benefit.[12]

General providence, however, does not safeguard human beings from all forms of harm. Even with the protection afforded by this type of providence, man is still subject to harmful chance events—which are unavoidable by-products of the divine plan. The influences of the celestial bodies produce the best of all possible worlds in the sublunar realm, but on rare occasions these benevolent operations will converge in a manner that produces events deleterious to human welfare.[13]

To be protected from these chance events, man must acquire individual providence. This type of providence, unlike general providence, operates only in select individuals who have achieved some degree of intellectual perfection. The more perfect a man's intellect, the more able he is to avoid oncoming danger.[14]

How does individual providence manifest itself? In his major discussion of providence in book four of the *Wars*, Gersonides deals with two expressions of individual providence: prophecy and providential suffering. A third expression of this type of providence is miracles, a subject that Gersonides leaves for a later discussion in book six of the *Wars*.

At this point of our discussion we will focus on the first two manifestations of individual providence. How prophecy confers individual providence requires little explanation. Through the prediction of the future, the prophet can successfully avoid harmful chance events that have been determined to befall him. Those who are not worthy of prophecy but have enough intellectual perfection to warrant some form of individual providence can still receive protection from chance events through providential suffering—a phenomenon that Gersonides identifies with the talmudic concept of *yisurin shel 'ahavah*, or 'afflictions of love.' In this case, the Active Intellect does not provide information for the recipient, but arranges for a painful obstacle to thwart him from encountering oncoming danger. An example that Gersonides uses to illustrate this type of providence is that of a man who finds himself unable to travel on a voyage because a thorn has become stuck in his foot; the man then finds out that the ship on which he was supposed to travel has sunk. Alternatively, a man is unable to travel on a voyage for a similar reason but then experiences great fortune because he remained at home.[15]

Later on, Gersonides takes this idea one step further by arguing that not only does providential suffering preserve the righteous man from physical calamity; it also guards him from potential spiritual injury as well. A man may experience suffering because he has begun to stray from the path of intellectual perfection. In this case, providential suffering can serve as a warning to stop the righteous man from severing his ties with the Active Intellect.[16]

The major problem that Gersonides must deal with here is to explain these two forms of providence in light of his conception of an impersonal God. If God provides prophetic communication and inflicts providential suffering to help one avoid oncoming disaster, it would appear that God is indeed responding to human need and directly intervening in human affairs—activities that should be impossible in Gersonides' metaphysical system.

With regard to prophecy, Gersonides responds to this problem by referring back to book two of the *Wars*, where he has already dealt extensively with this subject.[17] Prophecy occurs when a person has achieved a high degree of intellectual perfection and is therefore able to receive emanations from the Active Intellect during sleep. These emanations provide knowledge about the future because they impart information about essences and laws in the divine mind that control the operations of the natural order.

For these essences and laws to become predictions about actual events, the prophet's imagination must also play a role. The imagination provides the particulars that embody the general communications from the Active Intellect in concrete images. It is due to the input of the imagination that the prophet will inevitably prophesy about his own fortunes and those close to him, because the imagination of the prophet is always preoccupied with events and concerns related to his own immediate environment.[18]

The quality of prophecy is not uniform. The prophet with greater intellectual perfection and a more developed imagination will experience clearer, more accurate prophecies. One who has less perfection will experience prophecies that tend to be in parables and riddles that require interpretation. If properly deciphered, prophecies of this sort also yield valuable information about future events.[19]

Furthermore, the Active Intellect cannot impart to the prophet any more knowledge than that which is contained in the divine mind. That is, a prophetic prediction only dictates what *should* occur according to the laws governing the sublunar realm. Consequently, there is no guarantee that events will actually follow a given prophetic prediction. Free will can always contravene the order determined in the divine mind. It is for this reason that in the Bible God can issue warnings that are later nullified if man decides to repent.[20]

The important point to draw from all this is that, according to Gersonides' theory, prophetic communication can occur without any need for a personal God. The prophet taps into the emanations he receives from the Active Intellect in order to retrieve valuable information about future occurrences and uses this information for maximizing his own well-being.

All the while, God continues to contemplate His own essence without any awareness of or concern about whether prophetic communication has actually taken place. Prophecy is, in effect, a process whereby the prophet reads over the divine shoulder.[21]

Norbert Samuelson suggests an effective analogy to explain this process. Samuelson compares the Active Intellect to a radio transmitter perpetually emitting signals, while the perfected intellect is analogous to a properly tuned receiver that picks up these signals. Just as the receiver is able to pick up signals not available to other receivers that have not been properly tuned, so too a man who has perfected his intellect is able to receive emanations from the Active Intellect that are unavailable to ordinary intellects. Moreover, in the same way that the transmitter is in no way 'aware' of whether its signals have been received, so too the Active Intellect does not 'know' that its emanations have been communicated to the intellect of the prophet.[22]

Providential suffering presents more of a problem. With prophecy, the Active Intellect imparts information to the prophet about the future that the prophet then utilizes to circumvent imminent harm. With providential suffering, the process is entirely different. Here, the Active Intellect *itself* intervenes in human events by providing a physical obstacle against oncoming danger, a process that would appear to involve direct divine interaction in human affairs.

Gersonides responds to this challenge in a statement that is all too brief but nonetheless illuminating:

> This [kind of providence] emanates from God because it is its nature to reach *anybody* who is prepared to receive this kind of providence, just as the Agent Intellect works upon anything that is prepared to receive its activity, although it does not possess knowledge of the individual as individual.[23]

What Gersonides is arguing here is that providential suffering operates in the same impersonal manner as all other actions performed by the Active Intellect. The Active Intellect makes available at all times the full range of emanations that control processes in the natural order. What determines which specific emanations will be instantiated in the sublunar realm at any moment depends solely on which material subjects are prepared to receive those emanations. But, for its part, the Active Intellect has no concern or knowledge about which of its emanations have actually become operative. The same process occurs with events that produce providential suffering. Such events are also controlled by emanations from the Active Intellect that are available at all times. These emanations become operative only when a particular man is at the requisite level of intellectual perfection which allows him to be subject to their influence. There is again no need for personal divine involvement, since the Active Intellect remains entirely ignorant of whether its providential laws have actually become operative.

Thus, what Gersonides appears to envision are alternative providential systems. All people are protected by the general providential order, but when a man perfects his intellect, he can, in effect, 'graduate' from this general providential determinism and become subject to a higher, more protective determinism—one that provides obstacles to oncoming harmful events. Thus, what responds to an individual who experiences providential suffering is not a caring, personal God, but an alternative series of impersonal laws that have become activated on his behalf.

There are a number of ambiguities and difficulties in this theory which Gersonides does not confront. Perhaps the biggest problem is Gersonides' failure to clarify the metaphysical mechanism that allows the more protective providential laws to become instantiated. For instance, it is unclear how the perfection of an individual's intellect causes the higher order of providence to become operative and affect events in his vicinity.

Even more problematic is the role that the celestial system plays here. It must be kept in mind that according to Gersonides, the general providential order is controlled by the precise coordination of the motions of the heavenly bodies and the essences that stream down from the Active Intellect. Therefore, if an alternative series of providential laws becomes operative—even for a single individual—one would have to assume that the motions of the heavenly bodies would be altered to bring these new laws into effect. But what would provide the impetus for such an alteration in the celestial system if not a change in divine will—a possibility unacceptable to Gersonides? Moreover, any alteration in the finely honed movements of the celestial system would presumably have serious, and perhaps harmful, effects on the entire sublunar realm. While a single individual would experience providence, the rest of the natural order would be completely thrown out of kilter. Gersonides at no point confronts these issues.

Touati gives a rather different reading to the doctrine of providential suffering than what has been presented here, a reading which should be briefly discussed.[24] Touati argues that the notion of providential suffering, if understood literally, contradicts basic positions in Gersonides' philosophy: first, God would be the direct cause of evil and, second, God would have to have particular knowledge of the individual who receives this form of providence. Touati therefore proposes that providential suffering is not really a manifestation of individual providence at all. Rather, it is a chance event in the general providential order that has turned out to be 'providential' by warding off some greater harm. Understood in this way, providential suffering does not imply that God is the direct cause of evil, nor does it assume that God knows particulars.

The major problem with Touati's reading is that it is hard to justify from the text of the *Wars* itself. Gersonides clearly identifies providential suffering as a form of individual providence, not general providence. Moreover, our own interpretation circumvents the problems Touati raises without reading Gersonides in so non-literal a fashion. Providential suffering does not make God the source of evil. On the contrary, Gersonides is trying to argue that this form of pain is in every sense good, since it protects one from greater harm. Nor does God have to know particulars. As we have explained, what is responsible for this form of providence is a series of impersonal providential laws that are activated only when an individual has achieved the proper level of intellectual perfection.[25]

A most important point for our concerns is Gersonides' assertion that both general and individual providence can operate for national entities in a manner analogous to the providential care that affects a single person.[26] This point emerges in a discussion at the end of book four of the *Wars*, in which Gersonides attempts to explain biblical passages that appear to contradict basic principles in his philosophy. Of particular concern to Gersonides are those instances in the Bible, such as the closing chapters of Leviticus, in which God threatens the Israelites with direct physical punishment. These passages would indicate that God can be directly responsible for evil, a conclusion that is in conflict with Gersonides' conception of God as a benevolent Being.[27]

Gersonides responds to this problem by arguing that such punishments need not contradict the notion of God's goodness because they are invariably an expression of providential suffering. Gersonides explains that God may threaten and inflict suffering on an entire righteous nation when some of its members have begun to 'sin'—that is, when they have started to sever their ties with the Active Intellect.[28] In such instances, a divine warning is issued so that they avoid impending spiritual harm.

Gersonides goes on to explain that a whole nation can experience individual providence in much the same way that a single person can. This conclusion follows from an analogy with general providence. If the stars control the fate of national entities in a manner similar to that of individuals, there is every reason to assume that individual providence can be operative for a nation as well. Thus, both general and individual providence can affect either a single person or an entire nation.[29]

Gersonides makes another important observation about providential suffering that applies to individual and nation alike. Providential suffering will operate only as long as there is hope that an individual or nation will repent and return to a state of intellectual perfection. However, once the recipient becomes hopelessly mired in sin, providential suffering no longer exerts its influence, and the individual or nation then becomes subject to chance events. Gersonides links this state of affairs to the biblical conception of *hester panim*, whereby God "hides His countenance" from the Israelites.[30]

Gersonides also argues that God's benevolence is not compromised by biblical references to divine punishments inflicted on nations other than the Jewish people. These afflictions are invariably the result of divine providence on behalf of the Jewish people itself. Gersonides' chief illustration for this contention is the miracles in Egypt.[31]

There are a number of other issues in Gersonides' treatment of divine providence in book four of the *Wars* that should be mentioned. Gersonides devotes a separate discussion to the problem of the suffering of the righteous. Much of this discussion draws from material that we have already dealt with. One reason the righteous suffer, according to Gersonides, is that they may have temporarily severed their connection with the Active Intellect by allowing themselves to be distracted by material concerns. In such moments, even the righteous are vulnerable to harmful chance events. Another reason for the suffering of the righteous is that they may be experiencing providential suffering. As we saw earlier, providence can sometimes express itself in the form of a painful malady or obstacle that protects an individual from even greater physical or spiritual harm.

A third explanation is based on entirely new speculations on Gersonides' part. Gersonides argues that the righteous sometimes suffer because their ancestors have sinned and have been punished. It is not that the righteous person is being held accountable for the sins of his ancestors; rather, he has simply inherited the material misfortunes of his ancestors, who have proven to be unworthy of providence.

Gersonides' intent here is clarified in an illustration that draws from the contemporary experience of the Jewish people. Gersonides claims that the Jews in his own day are not in any way responsible for the exile and hardship they have endured. They are in exile merely because their forefathers had incurred divine punishment many generations earlier. Gersonides goes on to explain that the exile will be perpetuated as long as the operations of general and individual providence do not counteract the present state of affairs.[32]

One other issue that needs to be dealt with briefly is immortality. Gersonides' treatment of providence in book four of the *Wars* focuses almost exclusively on this-worldly happiness; both primary manifestations of providence—prophecy and providential suffering—are seen as means for increasing the material well-being of one who has achieved intellectual perfection. But it is important to point out that for Gersonides the most important reward consequent upon intellectual perfection is immortality. Along with a number of other medieval philosophers, Gersonides believes that by perfecting the mind, one fills the intellect with intelligibles that can survive the demise of the body. Thus, immortality is providence in its most exalted form.

The identification of immortality as the highest form of providence is made briefly in an important passage in book four of the *Wars*, where Gersonides attempts to deal with inconsistencies in his theory of providence. Gersonides is particularly troubled by the fact that according to his theory, the righteous can sometimes suffer while the wicked prosper. Several solutions are proposed for this difficulty. One answer—and the one that interests us here—is that the inequities of this life are of no great consequence, since the true goal of human happiness is not material benefit but "spiritual felicity" (*haẓlaḥah nafshit*)—an allusion to immortality. Here it is clear that the material rewards of providence in this life are of secondary importance to the reward achieved in the afterlife.[33]

To sum up thus far, Gersonides envisions two types of providence which confer material well-being on individual persons or nations: a general form by which the heavens afford basic protection to all members of the human species, and a higher form that affects only those who have achieved intellectual perfection. This form of providence safeguards a person or nation from the threat of chance events in two ways: through prophecy and providential suffering. With the first, the prophet receives information which allows him to avoid oncoming danger. With the second, a person circumvents harm by experiencing a painful obstacle. Yet, the highest form of individual providence is spiritual well-being, or immortality, by which the rational soul survives in the afterlife.

Most important, one does not need to posit a personal God to explain these forms of providence. The phenomena of prophecy and providential suffering that appear to require God's direct involvement in human affairs are, in fact, controlled by impersonal laws that respond to the individual who has perfected his intellect.

MIRACLES

There is one other manifestation of divine providence in addition to prophecy and providential suffering. Individual providence can also express itself through miracles, a topic that is dealt with by Gersonides in a separate discussion in the last book of the *Wars*.[34] Since this is a more complex issue than the other elements of Gersonides' theory of providence, we will follow Gersonides' lead in according it separate treatment.[35]

The question of miracles is one of the most formidable challenges faced by Gersonides. On this issue, the Aristotelian and biblical elements in Gersonides' thought clash head-on. How is it possible for God to perform miracles if He cannot experience a change of will and cannot directly intervene in the natural order?

Before Gersonides tackles this question, he makes a number of important preliminary observations which need to be reviewed.[36] Gersonides begins his discussion with remarks about the nature of the enquiry. He informs us that since he has never actually seen a miracle, all the data for his treatment of this subject must necessarily be drawn from the biblical sources which provide firsthand accounts of miraculous events. There is, in Gersonides' opinion, nothing wrong with this approach. Secondary observations, he claims, are often used in constructing scientific theories when immediate observations are not available.[37]

Gersonides follows through by listing several characteristics of miracles that are inferred from the biblical text. First, miracles can occur in substances or accidents. Second, a prophet is always present when a miracle occurs, though his exact function may vary. The prophet either performs the miracle himself, or the miracle occurs spontaneously for his benefit. Sometimes, the prophet is able to predict the advent of the miracle. At other times, the prophet brings about the miracle by praying for it or by commanding its arrival. A third characteristic of miracles is that they always exhibit a providential function. Thus, miracles invariably result in the acquisition of a physical or spiritual good, or the avoidance of some spiritual or physical harm.[38]

Gersonides then attempts to determine the agent of miracles. There are only three possibilities: God, the Active Intellect, and the prophet. After a lengthy discussion, Gersonides concludes that the Active Intellect is the agent of miracles.[39] But it is important to point out that in this discussion Gersonides is attempting to identify only the *proximate* agent of miracles. Gersonides never questions that the ultimate or remote cause of miracles is God Himself. As with all other processes in the sublunar realm, the Active Intellect can perform its actions only through emanations that originate in God. Gersonides informs us that it is for this reason that miracles in the Bible are often attributed to God. Since God is the remote cause of these events, it is as if He has directly performed them Himself.[40]

With these preliminary points in mind, we can now look at Gersonides' solution to the central dilemma regarding divine will. Gersonides formulates the problem as follows: If God is the cause of miracles, one of two alternatives must follow.[41] One possibility is that God undergoes a change of will. For Gersonides this alternative is obviously unacceptable, since it violates basic premises in his metaphysics. The other possibility is that all miracles are built into the natural order from the time of creation. This alternative is also rejected by Gersonides for two reasons. If miracles are programmed into the created order, it would follow that the presence of a prophet would not be needed; miracles would occur on their own, regardless of whether a prophet was present. Yet we know from the biblical sources that a prophet is always present when miracles occur and that he must therefore serve some important role in these events. Another problem with the notion that miracles are built into creation is that they would be necessary events. This too cannot be correct, since free will in human affairs would have to be entirely nullified in order for miracles to fulfill their predetermined function at the proper place and time.[42]

Gersonides solves this dilemma by proposing that miracles function in the same manner as other forms of providence. That is, they are the result of impersonal laws that become activated on behalf of an individual who has achieved intellectual perfection. The only difference between miracles and other forms of providence is that miracles are controlled by a special order of laws in the divine mind that are rarely implemented but are capable of producing unusual events in the sublunar realm.[43]

Gersonides does not provide much information about how these special laws of miracles actually function. We have only one passage in the *Wars* in which this issue is discussed in some detail. However, there is enough information here to make sense of Gersonides' position on the matter. The passage to which we are referring specifically describes how substances can be created by miracles. With this kind of miracle, Gersonides explains, the Active Intellect causes a whole series of events in an instant of time that should have taken far longer. Thus, for example, there is no reason why a stick could not turn into a snake, given a long enough duration of time. This process would normally require the elements of the stick to rearrange themselves so that a snake would finally be produced. What makes the event a miracle is that the whole process occurs instantaneously:

> . . . the turning of a stick into a snake can be accomplished by natural processes over an extraordinarily long period of time by the stick acquiring its form [i.e., of the snake] and relinquishing [its own] form until it becomes a snake. The miracle is thus in its being generated [i.e., the snake] without intermediary steps which normally occur in the course of nature. . . . Nothing can be generated miraculously if it cannot also be generated by natural process over an extended period of time.[44]

What emerges here is that miracles contravene the natural order to the extent that the Active Intellect speeds up a number of intermediary steps in producing a new substance.[45] But we are also told that in the performance of miracles the Active Intellect can utilize only those pathways that are in conformity with the laws of nature. The special laws controlling miracles are therefore distinct from the laws of nature but at the same time are a variation on those laws.

Touati provides an illuminating analogy to explain what Gersonides has in mind. Touati compares the Active Intellect to a chemist who can produce the same substance through two different chemical reactions, one of much shorter duration than the other. Similarly, when miracles occur, the Active Intellect is not completely circumventing the law-like operations of nature; like the chemist, it is simply using an alternative pathway to produce the same result in a more efficient way.[46]

There are also indications in a number of passages in Gersonides' writings that miracles can occur in a manner that renders them practically indistinguishable from natural events. This idea is implied in Gersonides' interpretation of the hardening of Sihon's heart at the end of book four:

> In regard to the story about the hardening of the heart of Sihon, it exemplifies either divine providence on behalf of Israel [so that] Sihon suffers evil in order that Israel inherits his land, and this would be a case of divine intervention by a miracle; or this evil was intended to happen to him, and the stubbornness that was determined by the heavenly bodies was one of the instruments by means of which this evil was about to befall him.[47]

Note that Gersonides is unsure here about whether the punishment of Sihon was a miracle or simply the result of normal influences from the constellations. There appears to be no way to distinguish between the two.[48]

But regardless of how one understands the precise mechanism of miracles, what is important to realize is that Gersonides has ingeniously circumvented the difficulties spelled out above. Miracles do not require a change of divine will or God's personal intervention in the sublunar realm any more than other providential events do. Miracles are the result of a special series of impersonal laws that are available at all times but function only on behalf of an individual who has perfected his intellect and who therefore acts as a substrate to activate those laws. Put another way, miracles function in a manner similar to providential suffering. With providential suffering, the individual becomes subject to an alternative series of general and impersonal laws that create painful obstacles to protect him from even greater harm. Miracles operate in the same way—but instead of using a painful obstacle to ward off harm, a series of unusual laws are in-

stantiated that produce miracles. As Touati accurately puts it, the occurrence of miracles constitutes the replacement of a "natural determinism"
with a "miraculous determinism."[49]

With this theory, there is also no need to posit that miracles are foreordained in creation. It is only the *laws* of miracles that are built into the
natural order; *specific* miracles occur when an individual who is at the
proper level of perfection requires one. Miracles are therefore contingent
events that are dependent on the worthiness of the individual and his circumstances at the time that the miracle is required.

Other features of miracles can now be explained. It is clear why a
prophet must always be present when a miracle occurs. Only someone
with a high degree of intellectual perfection can serve as a substrate for the
special laws that produce miracles. It is also apparent why miracles can be
predicted by the prophet. Because miracles are controlled by laws within
the divine mind, they are subject to prediction in the same way that all
other law-like events in the natural order are. By communicating with the
Active Intellect, the prophet will therefore receive information about any
miracles that might be in store for him.[50]

Finally, we should mention a few restrictions that Gersonides places
on miracles. Gersonides is careful to point out that only the laws of nature
are affected by miracles but not the rules of logic or mathematics. Thus
God can never miraculously create a triangle the angles of which would
not add up to a hundred eighty degrees.[51] Second, a miracle cannot result
in a permanent alteration in the sublunar realm, because it would imply
that there is some essential deficiency in the sublunar order. Therefore,
miracles bring about only a temporary correction in the sublunar realm.[52]
Finally, the motions of the celestial bodies do not participate in the production of miraculous occurrences in the sublunar realm, as is the case
with all forms of natural generation. Instead, miracles are the result of emanations flowing directly from the Separate Intellects to the Active Intellect.[53] Nor can the motions of the celestial bodies themselves be objects of
miraculous events. Thus, the miracle in Joshua 10 did not in any way involve a cessation of the sun's motion.[54]

Gersonides' ingenuity notwithstanding, his theory of miracles is certainly not free of difficulties. In fact, the major problem is the same as the
one raised in connection with providential suffering, a form of providence
that, as noted above, operates in a manner similar to that of miracles. Once
again, Gersonides does not give us sufficient information about the metaphysical mechanism which causes the higher order of providence to be instantiated. As was the case with providential suffering, it is unclear, for
instance, how a perfected intellect can cause an alternative series of providential laws—in this case miraculous laws—to become operative.

To his credit, Gersonides does appear to deal with the role of the celestial system in the production of miracles, an issue that he did not address in his discussion of providential suffering. We saw earlier that with
respect to the latter form of providence, Gersonides never explains how an
alternative providential determinism could be implemented without the
motions of the heavenly bodies being altered, and that an alteration of this
sort is extremely difficult to square with Gersonides' metaphysics. A
change in the motions of the celestial system, it would seem, would have
to involve a change in divine will and would also have a harmful effect on
the rest of the natural order.[55] Now the same question can be asked about
miracles, since these events also require the instantiation of an alternative
providential determinism; here again, it would seem that the motions of
the heavenly bodies would have to be altered to implement the new laws.
But in this case Gersonides tries to confront the difficulty. As we just noted,
Gersonides simply excludes the heavenly bodies from participating in the
production of miraculous events—and though Gersonides does not explicitly make the connection, this move seems deliberately designed to
grapple with the questions that arise if the heavenly bodies have a role to
play in the occurrence of miracles.[56]

The problem is that Gersonides' solution is more of an attempt to bypass the difficulty than to confront it. How can Gersonides by simple fiat
exclude the heavenly bodies from the process of producing miracles? If all
events in the sublunar realm involve the participation of the heavenly bodies, how can miracles occur without their assistance? Miracles are, after all,
law-like events just like natural occurrences. All that Gersonides tells us is
that miracles are caused solely by emanations that come from the Active
Intellect—a process that has no analogy with other events in the sublunar
realm. Thus, despite Gersonides' efforts, the nature of the mechanism that
produces miracles remains unclear.

Menachem Kellner offers an account that differs from the one given
here.[57] Kellner argues that Gersonides sees miracles as events that are built
into the natural order since creation. Miracles achieve their importance
only when a prophet can predict their arrival and thus receive benefit from
them. An example which Kellner uses to illustrate his interpretation is that
the splitting of the Red Sea would have occurred even if the Israelites had
not been there. What made the event miraculous was that Moses was able
to predict that event and was therefore able to make use of it for a providential purpose.

Kellner's analysis runs into difficulties on a number of points. First
and foremost, Kellner is suggesting an interpretation that Gersonides has
explicitly ruled out. Kellner is arguing that not only are the laws of miracles built into the natural order, so are the specific miracles themselves. We

saw that Gersonides rejects this possibility, because it implies that the prophet's presence at the site of the miracle is superfluous and that contingency is negated.[58] Second, Kellner's interpretation hinges on the notion that miracles must be predicted in order to be of any use for providential purposes. Gersonides sets no such condition. In his opening remarks, he makes clear that miracles are sometimes predicted, but at other times they are not. Moreover, in one passage, Gersonides suggests that on some occasions a person may experience a miracle even if he is not a prophet at all. This point is made in connection with a discussion regarding the miraculous deeds reported in rabbinic literature that were performed by sages who were not prophets. Gersonides explains that in such instances the sages had achieved a high enough level of intellectual perfection to warrant such providence.[59]

To summarize, miracles occur as a result of a special series of laws in the divine mind that become implemented for an individual who has achieved a high level of intellectual perfection. Again, there is no need to posit a personal God in this process. What responds to a person who experiences a miracle is not a God who spontaneously and willfully intervenes in the natural order, but a series of impersonal laws which that individual has activated as a result of his superior intellect.

At this point of our discussion, we can discern the overall strategy in Gersonides' approach to providence. The principle underlying his entire treatment is that in all cases where it would appear that God is communicating with man, the truth of the matter is that it is man who is communicating with God. By perfecting his intellect, man is able to tap into ever-present potentialities in the divine mind and make use of them for his own benefit. Such an individual can become a prophet by retrieving valuable information from God that concerns future events. He is also capable of bringing providential laws into effect that directly affect events in his immediate vicinity. These laws produce providential suffering, or in rare instances, miracles. In all these cases, man is the one who initiates action, not God.

INHERITED PROVIDENCE

The final concept from the *Wars* that we will analyze in this chapter is an important variation on Gersonides' overall theory of providence. In the closing passages of the *Wars* in his discussion of miracles, Gersonides intimates that in certain instances individual providence can, in effect, be passed on from one generation to the next. That is, the individual providence that a particular person experiences will, in some cases, confer benefits on his descendants—even after his death—simply by virtue of their blood relationship with him.

The doctrine of inherited providence[60] is more difficult to explain than the issues we have dealt with thus far, for a number of reasons. Almost nothing is said about it in the *Wars*; Gersonides refers to this concept only in passing while trying to solve another problem regarding miracles. Moreover, Gersonides' brief remarks on the subject are far from clear. Finally, there has been little scholarly analysis of this concept. To my knowledge, Touati is the only one who even takes notice of it.[61]

We will therefore have to analyze the issue of inherited providence with some care. It will also be necessary for us to make reference to passages from the biblical commentaries that will help clarify Gersonides' position. At this point in our discussion, we will deal only with material from the commentaries that helps explain the brief statement about inherited providence found in the *Wars*. The rest of the material in the commentaries pertaining to this doctrine will be analyzed in the coming chapters.

The issue of inherited providence crops up during Gersonides' attempt to make sense of a biblical passage that appears to refute his position on miracles. Gersonides is troubled by the incident in II Kings 13, in which a dead man is brought back to life when his body is placed in the same grave as that of the prophet Elisha. According to Gersonides, there are a couple of reasons why this miracle should never have occurred. First, miracles can happen only when there is a prophet in the vicinity whose intellect is at the proper level of perfection to merit this kind of providence. Second, a miracle must serve some providential purpose. In this case, neither condition is fulfilled. Elisha is no longer alive when the miracle occurs, and presumably, all communication with the Active Intellect would have ceased with his death. Moreover, the miracle appears to serve no providential function, given the fact that Elisha—the presumed beneficiary of the miracle—is no longer alive when it takes place.

Gersonides attempts to solve these problems by introducing the notion of an inherited form of providence:

> In solution to [the question of the man's resurrection], we will say [as follows]: It would seem that just as there are two types of providence due to the celestial bodies—one, preservation of the individual, and the other, preservation of a group [of people generated from him][62]—similarly, there are two types of providence due to conjunction with the Active Intellect: one type being preservation of that individual, and the second,[63] preservation of the group [of people] that is generated from him, such that there

is providence also in that which is generated from him [me-'inyano] after death.

In this manner, you will find that God made a promise to Abraham regarding divine providence over his offspring when He said, "but I will execute judgment on the nation they shall serve";[64] God thus told him about the miracles that He would bring to punish the Egyptians that were due to divine providence resulting from conjunction of the chosen forefather [Abraham] with Him.[65]

In this manner divine providence might have still attached itself to Elisha with the result that this miracle occurred to him after his death for the sake of his honor. For this is not any more peculiar[66] than providence over one's [very own] possessions. It is also possible that there was someone there [near Elisha's grave] who was worthy of performing this miracle, even though this is not explicitly stated.[67]

What Gersonides means in this difficult passage can only be clarified by first taking note of a crucial piece of information that he provides in his biblical commentary on the original episode in II Kings 13:21. There Gersonides explains that the dead man was brought back to life to safeguard Elisha's honor. That is, it was not fitting that an ordinary man be buried with a prophet of Elisha's stature. The man was therefore revived in order to find a more suitable resting place.[68]

With this in mind, Gersonides' remarks in the passage cited above can be clarified. Gersonides claims that one can explain the miracle that happened to Elisha by referring to instances in which individual providence is passed on to one's descendants. As evidence that the inheritance of providence is possible, Gersonides refers to the miracles that occurred to the Israelites in Egypt. Those miracles, he claims, were the direct result of Abraham's providence, even though he had lived several generations earlier. Gersonides goes on to reason that if providence can be operative after the death of an individual for the sake of his descendants, it is not hard to imagine that providence will continue to function after a person's death in order to safeguard his honor. This is precisely what happened to Elisha.[69]

What interests us most here is not the incident with Elisha, but the notion that individual providence can be passed on to one's descendants. While this concept appears to be novel and important, Gersonides is painfully brief in explicating its meaning. Let us try to get a better understanding of this idea by first taking a careful look at the reasoning which Gersonides uses to prove the existence of this phenomenon. Gersonides seems to justify the notion that individual providence can be inherited on the basis of an analogy with general providence, which, he claims, can also be passed on to subsequent generations. This point is made at the beginning of the passage from the *Wars* that we cited earlier:

> . . . just as there are two types of providence due to the celestial bodies—one, preservation of the individual, and the other, preservation of a group [of people generated from him]—similarly, there are two types of providence due to conjunction with the Active Intellect: one type being preservation of that individual, and the second, preservation of the group [of people] that is generated from him, such that there is providence also in that which is generated from him [me-'inyano] after death.

The same position is more clearly expressed in a passage in the *Commentary on the Torah*. In his commentary on Genesis, Gersonides tries to account for the fact that in one of God's dialogues with Isaac, God promises good fortune to Isaac's descendants by virtue of Abraham's merit and without any mention of Isaac's.[70] Gersonides concludes from this formulation that Isaac had not reached a degree of perfection equal to that of Abraham and that the providence to be experienced by future generations of Israelites would therefore be inherited from the latter. Gersonides then adds the following explanation:

> It is evident from here that it is possible that divine providence over those conjoined to Him can continue in their descendants after them. This is similar to providence over the [human] species which is due to the pattern of the stars; that is, from it [i.e., the pattern of the stars] success will continue in the descendants of the man who has experienced success. It is also possible that this [benefit] will continue for a long time. This was explained in its entirety in the book, *The Wars of the Lord*.[71]

Here the analogy between the inheritance of individual providence—that is, "providence over those conjoined to Him"—and the inheritance of general providence is drawn once again, but with much greater clarity than in the *Wars*.

One major difficulty in both these passages, however, is that Gersonides does not explain how general providence can itself be inherited. What Gersonides is probably alluding to is a concept that he discusses in book four of the *Wars* during his treatment of the suffering of the righteous, an issue we have already dealt with.[72] One will recall that of the many reasons Gersonides offered to account for the suffering of the righteous, one explanation was that misfortune can be passed on simply by circumstance. A person with intellectual perfection may suffer as a result of inheriting the material misfortunes of a wicked ancestor who was not deserving of providence. Gersonides illustrated his point by reference to the lowly condition of the Jewish people in exile. The Jews in Gersonides' own period are not responsible for their suffering. The exile is due to the sins of earlier generations who were unworthy of providence and invited punishment that would affect the Jews of subsequent periods.

What we did not mention but is now relevant is the corollary which Gersonides draws from this reasoning. Gersonides goes on to explain how a wicked person can prosper by similar circumstances. If a righteous person may suffer misfortune bequeathed to him by his forefathers, a wicked person, conversely, may inherit the material benefits which have accrued to a righteous ancestor. Thus, for example, if a person has become wealthy as a result of individual providence, that wealth will be passed on to his descendants, regardless of the latter's state of perfection. Furthermore, Gersonides adds, those inherited benefits will tend to be perpetuated for a long time by the operations of the constellations, since the constellations generally function for man's benefit:

> It is evident that something like this happens with the sinners who receive benefits [simply] because they are born with them. And these benefits continue to be enjoyed by sinners so long as the misfortunes coming from the heavenly constellations do not displace them.[73]

In all likelihood, it is this passage that Gersonides has in mind when he refers to the inheritance of general providence. General providence can be passed on to one's descendants in the sense that the normal workings of the constellations will tend to perpetuate for an extended period the material fortunes a righteous man has earned during his lifetime. It is by analogy with this phenomenon that Gersonides postulates the existence of an inherited form of individual providence as well.

Our interpretation is borne out by a passage from the commentary on Genesis that we cited above:

> This is similar to providence over the [human] species which is due to the pattern of the stars; that is, from it [i.e., the pattern of the stars] success will continue in the descendants of the man who has experienced success. It is also possible that this [benefit] will continue for a long time.[74]

Here Gersonides states clearly that general providence can be inherited, in that the patterns of the stars ensure the perpetuation of the material fortunes of a righteous ancestor for an extended period of time.

There is another passage in the *Commentary on the Torah* which also draws an analogy between the inheritance of individual and general providence, but gives a somewhat different explanation of how general providence is inherited. During an extensive exposition of providence in his commentary on Exodus, Gersonides makes the following comments:

> . . . it is thus clear that this [individual] providence attaches itself to the righteous who are conjoined with Him. It is also clear that it attaches itself for their sake to their descendants in a manner similar to that of general providence which is found in people in the same two forms [i.e., in an individual and in his descendants]. This is the case [i.e., that general providence exists in both forms] because when a man is born, his particular affairs are determined by the constellations, and from them are determined in a general manner the affairs of his descendants who come after him.[75]

Gersonides is reiterating the claim that individual providence may be passed on to one's descendants just as general providence may. He then explains that general providence can be passed on to one's offspring, because the stars, in determining the course of events in an individual's life, also determine the course of affairs for his descendants. That is, the fortunes of a man and his descendants are causally linked through the determinations of the stars.

The explanation offered here to justify the inheritance of general providence is somewhat different from that expressed in book four of the *Wars*. There it was suggested that general providence merely sustains the material benefits of the ancestor for his descendants. Here it is the actual providence determined at the birth of the ancestor himself that affects his descendants.

Now that we have a better idea of what Gersonides means when he says that general providence can be inherited, let us now take a closer look at the inheritance of individual providence. As we have seen in the passages cited from the *Wars* and the biblical commentaries, Gersonides repeatedly argues for this phenomenon on the basis of simple analogy; if general providence can be passed on to one's descendants, so can individual providence. While this form of argument may seem somewhat unsatisfying, it is important to point out that this is not the first time Gersonides employs this method of reasoning. We made reference earlier to the notion that individual providence could be operative for entire nations, not just individuals. Gersonides justified this claim by simply pointing to a similar phenomenon with general providence.[76] Gersonides seems to have assumed that in a number of respects the characteristics of individual providence could be deduced on the basis of a symmetry with general providence.

What benefits does the inheritance of individual providence confer? Again, Gersonides does not say much to help us; but in the one passage in the *Wars* where this doctrine is mentioned, Gersonides does provide one example of inherited individual providence by informing us that the miracles experienced by the Israelites in Egypt were due to providence inherited from Abraham. It would seem, therefore, that the inheritance of individual providence allows for the direct transfer of providence itself. That is, it presumably enables the descendants of the righteous man to enjoy the same manifestations of providence which the righteous man himself experiences: prophecy, providential suffering, and miracles.

If we are correct in this assessment, the crucial difference between the inheritance of individual providence and general providence also becomes clear. What Gersonides means when he refers to inherited general providence is that a descendant is able to take advantage of material possessions bequeathed to him by a righteous ancestor. The inheritance of individual providence, in contrast, is the actual transfer of providence itself.

We should mention one other point of information about inherited providence that emerges in the biblical commentaries. In his commentary on Deuteronomy, Gersonides hints that individual providence can be passed on only when the ancestor has experienced this type of providence in its strongest form: ". . . just as general providence extends success to a man such that he and his offspring are protected by it for a very long time, so does this occur with individual providence *when it is perfect*."[77] Here Gersonides interjects an important condition. It is only when individual providence is "perfect" that it can be passed on to one's descendants. Thus, not every righteous man can bequeath providence to his descendants.

We can gain a richer understanding of Gersonides' views on the inheritance of individual providence by noting that this is not the only instance in which individual providence extends beyond the person who has actually earned it. In several passages in his biblical commentaries Gersonides discusses other similar phenomena. For example, individual providence will guard over those who are in the geographic vicinity of the righteous man, even if they are not at all related to him. This idea plays a prominent role in Gersonides' reading of the dialogue in Genesis between Abraham and God regarding the destruction of Sodom and Gomorrah. The mere presence of a minority of righteous men, Abraham argues, should ensure the well-being of the entire community.[78]

Also, Gersonides informs us in some passages that relatives and friends of the righteous man certainly do not have to wait for the latter's death to be protected directly by his providence; they are also protected during his lifetime. Thus, Lot, who would not have normally been the recipient of individual providence, was accorded great wealth by virtue of his association with Abraham.[79] Hagar experiences prophecy only by virtue of her association with Abraham.[80] There are also instances in which one may experience providential suffering by virtue of one's closeness to a righteous individual.[81]

The point that becomes clear from all these examples is that inherited providence is only one instance of a larger phenomenon by which providence can extend to those who are in some way or other associated with a righteous individual. Inherited providence is unique only in that it continues to function even after the righteous individual has died.[82]

Most illuminating is the rationale Gersonides offers in a number of passages to account for the providential protection accorded to relatives and friends of the righteous man during his lifetime. Gersonides reasons that providence protects these people because the righteous person will obviously be gladdened by the good fortunes of those about whom he cares and saddened by their misfortunes.[83] Gersonides therefore extends the notion of providence in a highly original manner by arguing that providence protects the loved ones of the righteous man in the very same way that it guards any of his cherished possessions.

This reasoning can easily be applied to justify the inheritance of individual providence as well—even though Gersonides never explicitly makes this connection. Inherited providence can be seen as another means by which providence protects the people about whom the righteous man cares. Just as providence can extend in space to protect the loved ones of a righteous individual during his lifetime, so can it extend ahead in time to include his loved ones in generations to come. Again, the only unique feature of inherited providence is that it continues to function even after the righteous man's death.

Yet even with the help of these insights, there is much about the transfer of individual providence that Gersonides fails to explain. The central problem is similar to the one we encountered in discussing providential suffering and miracles; Gersonides provides no information about the metaphysical mechanism that would account for this phenomenon. In the case of inherited providence, this deficiency is especially serious, since it is hard to imagine a mechanism that would confer providence long after the death of the individual who has actually earned it.

One last point is in order regarding inherited providence. It should be noted that this concept betrays the influence of rabbinic sources on Gersonides' thinking. As Touati mentions, Gersonides' notion of inherited providence is essentially a philosophical version of the well-known rabbinic doctrine of *zekhut 'avot*, or "merit of the fathers." This concept is frequently cited in rabbinic sources as the factor responsible for God's redemption of the Israelites from Egypt and their subsequent protection from other calamities; it is due to the merit of the Patriarchs that the Israelites receive such privileged treatment.[84] There are other examples. For instance, we have a talmudic source in which it is reported that R. Eleazar ben Azariah is appointed head of the rabbinical academy because his blood relationship with Ezra the Scribe is seen as conferring divine protection.[85]

To sum up this portion of our discussion, inherited providence adds an important dimension to Gersonides' overall theory of providence. General providence can be inherited in the sense that a descendant can share in the fortunes of a righteous ancestor by acquiring the material wealth that ancestor has earned through providence. Individual providence can also be inherited, in that providence can be directly transferred from a righteous person to his descendants. The inheritance of individual providence is justified by Gersonides on analogy with general providence. Yet, it is probably best understood as an extension of a broader phenomenon in Gersonides' thinking by which providence can watch over the loved ones of the righteous individual in much the same way that it guards any of his possessions.

Gersonides' major philosophical treatise, *The Wars of the Lord*, provides an impressive range of philosophical concepts with respect to divine providence. General providence confers protection on the human species as a whole by means of the influences of the celestial system that creates the best of all possible worlds. Individual providence provides an even higher degree of protection for those who have achieved intellectual perfection. This form of providential care manifests itself in the form of prophecy, providential suffering, and miracles. The most exalted form of providence, however, is immortality, which is also consequent upon the perfection of the intellect. Finally, an important variation on Gersonides' theory of providence is the concept of inherited providence. Not only do general and individual providence affect the recipient; these forms of providence can also have an influence on his descendants as well.

Key to understanding Gersonides' views on providence is his insistence that, whatever its manifestation, providence does not involve a change of divine will nor God's personal intervention in human affairs. What brings about providence is really man's initiative, not God's. By perfecting his intellect, an individual is able to tap into the potentialities in the divine mind in order to retrieve information about the future or to bring laws into effect that influence events around him.

If there is one major difficulty with Gersonides' views on providence, it is that he does not provide enough information about the metaphysical mechanisms that make the various forms of providence possible. The only exception, perhaps, is his theory of prophecy. Here Gersonides is quite explicit in explaining how the prophet is able to receive communications from God about future events and circumvent oncoming danger without there being any personal involvement on God's part. But for those manifestations of providence in which actual events in the sublunar realm are affected—providential suffering, miracles, and inherited providence—Gersonides is far less generous to his reader. In all these cases, the perfected individual graduates from the general providential determinism to an alternative, more protective providential determinism. Yet, Gersonides never adequately explains how the perfection of the intellect allows for such a process to occur, nor does he clarify the precise role of the celestial system in implementing these forms of providence. The problem is especially evident with the concept of inherited providence that not only subsumes the other manifestations of providence but affects individuals who themselves may not even be worthy of providential care.

We are now in a position to offer some reflections regarding the central theme of our project: providence over the Jewish people. In the course of developing the various aspects of his theory of providence in the *Wars*, Gersonides has obviously provided ample information to account for God's providential relationship with the Jews. This should come as no surprise. After all, the method Gersonides openly adopts in the *Wars* is to prove at the end of each book that his philosophical positions are in conformity with the biblical text. Therefore, Gersonides' treatments of prophecy, providential suffering, and miracles all lead inevitably to an explanation of the relationship between God and the Jews as described in the biblical history. This is especially true of Gersonides' treatment of miracles, which is based entirely on biblical evidence. We should also make special mention of Gersonides' notion that both general and individual providence can affect an entire nation as if it were a single individual. This conception, in particular, seems designed to justify God's unique relationship to the Jewish nation as a whole.

However, despite the extent of Gersonides' treatment of providence in the *Wars*, it is clear that there does not emerge from this work a truly comprehensive theory for the special status of the Jewish people. What Gersonides offers in the *Wars* are discussions that account only for individual instances of divine providence in the biblical narrative. There is no separate discussion tying these elements together into an overarching theory of Jewish chosenness.

The key ingredient missing here is a treatment of the concept of covenant. It is the covenant idea which, in the biblical and rabbinic traditions, serves as the underpinning for the special relationship between God and the Jewish people from the time of Abraham onward. It explains God's ongoing association with the Jewish people throughout history, one that remains unshakeable even when they are disobedient to Him. If Gersonides is to offer a successful theory of providence for the Jewish people, he must therefore account for this concept. He must explain in philosophical terms what it means for God to be not only the source of providential care but the God of Jewish history as well.

We might suspect at this point that the doctrine of inherited providence provides Gersonides with the basis upon which to build a theory of covenant. This form of providence, as we have seen, allows for the continuity of God's providential care from generation to generation. However, this concept is not well developed in the *Wars*. Gersonides' remarks are so brief that we had to call on passages in the biblical commentaries to make sense of this elusive concept.

This last observation, in a sense, sets the stage for the rest of our study. If the *Wars* does not provide adequate philosophical justification for God's covenantal relationship with His people, we must then delve more deeply into his biblical commentaries to see whether these writings provide an account for the covenant concept. We will therefore begin in the next chapter with Gersonides' interpretation of the covenant with Abraham in Genesis 15.

THREE

The Covenant with Abraham

GERSONIDES' INTERPRETATION OF GENESIS 15

The doctrine of the Chosen People has its roots in the first verses of Genesis 12, in which Abraham is summoned by God to settle in the land of Canaan and informed that he is to become the father of a nation destined for greatness and blessing. After Abraham's arrival in Canaan, God formalizes His promise in the covenant "between the pieces" in Genesis 15 and with the covenant of circumcision in Genesis 17. In subsequent dialogues with the other two Patriarchs, God repeatedly reaffirms His covenantal relationship with Abraham's descendants.

It is the covenant in Genesis 15 which is particularly important in the early biblical history, for it is this covenant that ultimately guides the course of events throughout the rest of the Pentateuch. The slavery of the Israelites in Egypt, their redemption from bondage and conquest of the land of Canaan are all a fulfillment of the terms of the covenant laid out in Genesis 15. Our analysis of Gersonides' exegetical works will therefore begin with a careful examination of his commentary on this central chapter in the biblical text. What we will discover is that it is here that Gersonides begins to formulate a philosophical interpretation of God's covenantal relationship with the Jewish people, an interpretation that lays a foundation for all of Gersonides' further speculations on the subject.[1]

We should first make note of the philosophical problems that the biblical concept of covenant presents for Gersonides. In its simplest terms, a covenantal relationship between man and God presumes that God on His own initiative enters into a contractual agreement with human beings. This conception is in obvious conflict with basic principles in Gersonides'

39

metaphysics, for as we have continued to emphasize, Gersonides does not believe that God can willfully intervene in the sublunar realm or interact personally with human beings. It therefore makes little sense in the context of Gersonides' philosophy for God to enter into a covenantal agreement of any kind.

The covenant with Abraham is particularly problematic because it is a covenant that is, in modern scholarly terminology, unconditional. God's promises of blessing to Abraham and his descendants are made without asking for anything in return. Thus, in this case Gersonides not only has the problem of explaining God's personal involvement in human affairs; he must also deal with the added difficulty that all activity in the implementation of the covenant is apparently from God's side alone.

The difficulties the notion of covenant presents for Gersonides are evident in his interpretation of the biblical narrative which first makes reference to that concept. We are alluding here to the flood story, where the covenant idea is invoked in two passages—first at the beginning of the narrative and then at the end. While the flood episode is not directly relevant to our study, it is instructive to take a brief look at how Gersonides handles the covenant concept in this portion of the biblical text. Gersonides' approach here in many respects anticipates his interpretation of the covenant with Abraham in Genesis 15.

According to Gersonides, the world was destroyed by flood for two reasons. First, it was an act of divine providence on behalf of Noah, because he was saved from the influence of moral corruption in his generation, an influence which threatened his high level of intellectual perfection. Second, it was an act of providence for the human race as a whole. In their state of moral degeneration, human beings, with the exception of Noah, were unable to attain any level of perfection whatsoever. The world was therefore destroyed and then regenerated through Noah's offspring so that man would have the opportunity to achieve the exalted state of perfection for which he was created.

For these reasons, God instructed Noah to build an ark to save himself and his family and advised him to preserve male and female members of each animal species. This latter imperative was a manifestation of divine providence over mankind as a whole in that animals are necessary for the well-being of man and would therefore serve the needs of Noah's offspring once the flood was over.[2]

The first reference to the covenant concept in the flood story appears at the very beginning of the narrative. After informing Noah that He is about to destroy the world, God adds the following remark:

... I will fulfill [*ve-hakimoti*]³ My covenant with you, and you shall enter the ark, with your sons, your wife and your sons' wives. And of all that lives, of all flesh, you shall take two of each into the ark to keep alive with you; they shall be male and female.⁴

Now it is important to point out that along with the philosophical problems this passage raises for Gersonides, there is also an exegetical difficulty. While God promises to "fulfill" His covenant with Noah, there is no mention in the biblical text of any previous covenant.

Gersonides attempts to address both difficulties with the following interpretation:

... this covenant which is referred to [here], is according to my opinion, that which God made on the seventh day to sustain the world in such a way that there would not be any more need for the kind of creative activity with which He created the world in six days, as we have explained in the portion of *va-yekhulu*.⁵ This covenant [with creation] was fulfilled with Noah in His commanding him to make the ark according to the reported description and that he should enter the ark with his sons and their wives, and that he should also bring in with him at the very least every species of animal that walks and flies, male and female, so that all the species of animals would continue to exist. Or perhaps God made a covenant with Noah before this occasion, even though it was not mentioned. The first explanation is, however, the better one, according to my opinion.⁶

In order to appreciate fully what Gersonides is saying here, we must first be reminded of the philosophical assumptions that would inform his reading of God's dialogue with Noah. According to Gersonides, God never actually speaks to anyone. The prophet may envision a conversation with God, but only because his imagination has embodied the impersonal information imparted by the Active Intellect in the form of a dialogue. It is thus only in this sense that God converses with Noah.⁷

It is also important to recall that, in Gersonides' thinking, the images appearing in the prophet's vision are often metaphors conveying important theoretical and practical truths when properly decoded.⁸ This appears to be the operative principle in Gersonides' interpretation of the covenant in Noah's prophetic vision. Gersonides sees the covenant as a metaphor produced by the prophet's imagination that conceals a deeper philosophical content. In Gersonides' reading, the covenant is a symbol representing God's static, non-creative posture towards the natural order since the first six days of creation. God has a "covenant" with creation in that He sustains the created world by perpetually implementing the fixed laws which control all natural processes. God "fulfills" this covenant with Noah in the sense that Noah is being charged with the obligation of ensuring that no new creative activity on God's part will be needed after the flood. For this end, Noah is commanded to build an ark to preserve the various species of animals from destruction.

What is important to note is that Gersonides has interpreted the covenant in a way that suits his metaphysical premises. He carefully construes the covenant in a manner that avoids any suggestion that God is somehow interacting with events in the sublunar realm in a personal manner. In fact, the covenant here is defined in such a way as to underscore God's very *lack* of involvement in the affairs of the world. If Noah does participate in this covenant, it is only to the extent that he helps preserve God's static relationship with the natural order by following through on the divine directive to build an ark.[9]

The fact that Noah is called upon by divine command to ensure the continuity of the covenant may appear to complicate matters by implying that the covenant involves divine intervention in human events. But we must again keep in mind that the conversation between God and Noah would be viewed by Gersonides as a product of the prophet's imagination. God's instruction to Noah would be seen as the result of impersonal providential laws that have been concretized in the prophet's imagination as a divine commandment.

Gersonides has also solved the exegetical difficulty mentioned above as well. The biblical text seemed to assume that God would confirm a covenant with Noah despite there being no indication of any previous agreement between God and Noah. Gersonides' reading solves this problem by suggesting that there was, in fact, a prior covenant—one that pertained to the created order, not to Noah.

Gersonides' interpretation comes in handy once again at the end of the flood story, when God promises Noah that He will never again bring a flood to destroy the world.[10] Here again Gersonides interprets the covenant to refer to God's relationship with nature. God is informing Noah that after the destruction, the laws governing natural processes will continue to operate in an uninterrupted fashion.[11]

The approach Gersonides adopts to explain the covenant concept in the flood story anticipates a similar strategy in his commentary on Genesis 15, which will occupy us for the rest of this chapter. Let us first recount the events in this chapter. Genesis 15 begins with God appearing in a vision to Abraham and reiterating earlier promises of blessing and reward for Abraham and his descendants. Abraham answers by expressing his fear that God's repeated promises will not be fulfilled, given that he has no heir. God attempts to ease Abraham's worries by showing him a star-filled sky and by telling him that his offspring will be as numerous as the stars. God also repeats his promise that Abraham's descendants will inherit the land of Canaan. Abraham seems to insist on greater assurance when he asks, "Oh, LORD God, how shall I know that I am to possess it?"[12] God responds by commanding Abraham to participate in a covenant ceremony. Abraham is asked to prepare five animals, four of which are split in half. After Abraham scares away birds of prey which are apparently attracted by the carcasses, a deep sleep falls over him. God then informs Abraham that his offspring will be slaves in a foreign land for four hundred years. At the end of that period, He will execute judgment upon their oppressors, and they will leave with great wealth to claim their inheritance. A flaming torch then passes between the pieces of the animals to seal the covenant.

In his interpretation of this episode, Gersonides discusses a range of philosophical issues. Of particular importance to Gersonides is Abraham's question, "Oh, LORD God, how shall I know that I am to possess it?" Gersonides sees this query as stemming from philosophical perplexity. What concerns Abraham about God's promise is whether his offspring will be worthy enough to merit divine providence so that they will be able to inherit the land of Canaan. Abraham reasons that this reward will no doubt be conditional upon their achieving the requisite state of perfection, a condition that is by no means guaranteed. Gersonides points out that this condition is implied by God's own words later on in Genesis 18:19, in which He makes clear that Abraham's offspring must "keep the way of the LORD by doing what is just and right, in order that the LORD may bring about for Abraham what He has promised him."[13]

Gersonides interprets God's response to Abraham as an attempt to allay these fears. According to Gersonides' rather novel reading, the purpose of God telling Abraham about the events in Egypt is to inform him that his descendants will acquire providence by witnessing the miracles that will bring an end to their slavery. By seeing God's wonders, they will believe in Him and dedicate themselves to His service so that they will then be worthy of inheriting the land of Canaan. Symbolic of this prediction is Abraham's confrontation with the birds of prey that attack the animals he has prepared. The birds of prey represent the Egyptians and other nations who will try to destroy God's covenant with Abraham's descendants but will not succeed.[14]

These are the major points in Gersonides' commentary on Genesis 15 relevant for our purposes. Let us now take a closer look at what Gersonides is saying here. In order to comprehend fully Gersonides' interpretation, one must first be aware of the special status of the land of Israel in

Gersonides' thought. In an earlier passage in the commentary on Genesis, Gersonides explains that God promised the land of Canaan to Abraham and his descendants because that geographic location is particularly receptive to "divine overflow" (*shefa' 'elohi*). By settling in this land, Abraham and his offspring would therefore experience divine providence more easily than in any other location.[15] It is for this reason that, according to Gersonides, Abraham is so concerned about whether his offspring will be worthy of inheriting the land of Canaan.

Gersonides' interpretation of the actual dialogue between God and Abraham in Genesis 15 appears to be fairly straightforward. However, a closer examination reveals that much of Gersonides' reading can be properly understood only by referring to information in the *Wars*—material to which Gersonides makes only vague allusion in his commentary.

Let us begin with Abraham's initial concern about the worthiness of his descendants to receive divine providence. The nature of Abraham's worry becomes much clearer with the help of remarks made by Gersonides in book six of the *Wars* regarding the fallibility of prophetic predictions. There Gersonides makes the point that all future rewards consequent upon individual providence cannot be reliably predicted by the prophet. In such cases, there is always a built-in condition that the recipient have the proper level of intellectual perfection to be worthy of the providence he is about to receive. This condition cannot be guaranteed, since the recipient has the choice at any time to contravene the determined order, and he may therefore fail to merit providence at the proper moment.[16]

There is an important corollary to this point which is alluded to here, but is more clearly expressed in passages in the *Commentary on the Torah*. Gersonides informs us that all divine promises that guarantee benefits over an indefinite period of time are also not reliably predicted by the prophet. Such promises by their very nature are due to individual providence, for as Gersonides argues, it is highly improbable that such rewards could be guaranteed over such a duration simply by the effects of general providence; and like all other instances of individual providence, rewards predicted for an indefinite duration will come about only if the recipient is worthy.[17]

These philosophical insights help illuminate Gersonides' interpretation of Abraham's concerns in his dialogue with God. Abraham is justified in being fearful that God's promise regarding the inheritance of Canaan will not be fulfilled, since this promise is obviously of indefinite duration and therefore can be only the result of individual providence. The inheritance of Canaan, in consequence, will be very much dependent upon the worthiness of Abraham's descendants—a condition that cannot be reliably guaranteed.

The crucial information from the *Wars* is alluded to in one of the *to'aliyyot* at the end of Gersonides' exposition of Genesis 15:

> ... beneficial promises which God promises to a prophet that are not delimited by time or place will not be fulfilled unless those about whom the prophecy was made are worthy of that promise. Therefore, Abraham asked for a sign regarding God's promise that his offspring would inherit the land.[18]

Gersonides' interpretation of God's response to Abraham can also be better understood in light of information in the *Wars*. According to Gersonides, God promises Abraham that his descendants will merit the divine providence necessary for inheriting the land of Canaan because they will witness the miracles in Egypt which will convince them to believe in God and devote themselves to His service. The same interpretation is given a more rigorous philosophical treatment in a passage in the *Wars* to which we alluded in the last chapter.[19]

The issue of the exodus comes up in a discussion at the end of the fourth book of the *Wars*. There Gersonides expresses perplexity over those sections of the Bible that speak about divine punishment coming directly from God. Direct divine punishment contradicts a basic premise that God is never the source of evil.[20] In his solution to this problem, Gersonides first takes up those instances of punishments in the biblical narrative experienced by the Israelites. Such punishments, Gersonides explains, are merely examples of providential suffering. God will inflict providential suffering on an entire righteous nation to encourage repentance when some of its members have begun to sever their ties with the Active Intellect. Thus, in these cases, suffering is certainly not the result of evil coming from God but is rather due to God's goodness.

More problematic are examples in the Bible of direct divine punishment involving the enemies of Israel. In these cases, Gersonides cannot invoke the notion of providential suffering, because these nations would presumably not warrant such providence. To solve this difficulty, Gersonides proposes that suffering inflicted on these other nations is also due to God's goodness. In these instances, Israel's enemies are punished as a result of divine providence over the Israelites themselves. Gersonides reasons that if the righteous are themselves afflicted with suffering for providential purposes, there is certainly nothing wrong with the wicked suffering for the same reason. Thus, even here, God's actions are for the good.[21]

Gersonides' major illustration of this point anticipates his interpretation of Genesis 15. Gersonides adduces the biblical story of the ten plagues in Egypt as evidence that providence over the Israelites can result in the suffering of another nation. Gersonides explains that God hardened Pharaoh's heart so that miracles could be performed for the sake of the Israelites. The ultimate purpose of these miracles was to bring the Israelites to intellectual perfection by convincing them of God's existence and strengthening their belief in Him:

> The miraculous story about the hardening of Pharaoh's heart leading to additional troubles for Israel is also an instance of providence, for in this way the people acquired a firm belief [in God]. For when Pharaoh became liable for punishment—and since it was possible for some good to accrue to Israel by means of this kind of punishment to him such that Israel would become convinced of God's existence and of His power by means of these many miracles—God brought it about that Pharaoh [himself] hardened his heart, so that His miracles would be multiplied and that the true belief would be spread throughout Israel.[22]

Gersonides finds proof for his interpretation in the biblical account itself. Gersonides cites the following passage from Exodus, in which God commands Moses to confront Pharaoh:

> Go to Pharaoh. For I have hardened his heart and the heart of his courtiers, in order that I might display these My signs among them, and that you may recount in the hearing of your sons and your sons' sons how I made a mockery of the Egyptians and how I displayed My signs among them—in order that you may know that I am the LORD.[23]

The biblical text explicitly connects the hardening of Pharaoh's heart and the other miracles in Egypt with the Israelites' recognition of God's omnipotence.[24]

To summarize what we have discovered thus far, Gersonides' interpretation of Genesis 15 hinges on Abraham's concern that his descendants will not have the requisite level of intellectual perfection to merit individual providence and inherit the land of Canaan. God's response is read by Gersonides as an attempt to assure Abraham that his worries are unfounded. God informs Abraham that by witnessing the miracles in Egypt his descendants will acquire the perfection necessary for claiming their inheritance.

While we have managed to explicate the important points in Gersonides' interpretation of Genesis 15, there is much here that still requires explanation. For one, it is not at all clear how God's assurances have answered Abraham's initial concerns about the conditional nature of individual providence. If the miracles in Egypt are designed to bring the Israelites to intellectual perfection, what then ensures that the miracles themselves will occur? Will these events not also be conditional upon the worthiness of Abraham's offspring? In other words, Gersonides appears to have merely displaced the problem. If Abraham is concerned that his descendants will not be worthy of inheriting the land of Canaan, God's promise regarding the miracles in Egypt does not seem to help very much. Presumably, these miracles are also an act of providence that will occur only if Abraham's offspring have sufficient merit.

Another problem closely connected to this one is that Gersonides is extremely vague about the meaning of the covenant ceremony solidifying God's promise to Abraham. To appreciate what is missing in Gersonides' exposition of this ceremony, we must first review the same philosophical assumptions that helped us understand Gersonides' reading of God's dialogue with Noah. According to Gersonides' philosophical premises, the content of prophetic visions is shaped to one degree or another by the prophet's imagination, which embodies the general communications from the Active Intellect in concrete images. Gersonides would therefore view the conversation between God and Abraham in Genesis 15 along with the covenant ceremony that accompanies that dialogue as products of Abraham's imagination.[25]

We must also be reminded that according to Gersonides the imaginative content of prophetic visions is by no means meaningless. Such imagery, if properly decoded, may reveal important philosophical truths. Therefore, if we are to understand Gersonides' interpretation of the covenant ceremony, he must inform us what this imagery symbolizes in philosophical terms.

As we saw in our examination of the flood story, Gersonides was quite explicit in explaining the philosophical symbolism of the covenant with Noah. In his commentary on Genesis 15, however, Gersonides is much less generous to his reader. Some of the covenant imagery is decoded by Gersonides: The birds of prey that descend on the carcasses of the sacrifice represent the Egyptians who will try to destroy the covenant. The fire passing between the pieces is representative of God, who often appears in fire.[26] But with regard to the covenant ceremony as a whole, Gersonides is much more vague:

ON THE DAY THAT THE LORD MADE A COVENANT WITH ABRAHAM:[27] to give his offspring the entire land of the Canaanite clans; that is to say, He informed him that He will with certainty cause [Abraham's] descendants to be worthy of His protecting them with this type of providence.[28]

It would seem that the covenant in some way symbolizes God's assurance that the Israelites will be worthy of providence as a result of the miracles they will witness in Egypt; however, this still does not tell us very much.

Let us look at the first problem. How, according to Gersonides, does God's promise to Abraham address his concerns about the conditional nature of individual providence? In particular, how does God's prediction regarding the miracles in Egypt get around this difficulty?

Gersonides' interpretation of the divine promise can be understood only with the help of an important clue provided in the *Wars*. One will recall that in his brief discussion of inherited providence in the *Wars*, which we analyzed in the last chapter, Gersonides refers to the covenant with Abraham:

> In this manner, you will find that God made a promise to Abraham regarding divine providence over his offspring when He said, "but I will execute judgment on the nation they shall serve";[29] God thus told him about the miracles that He would bring to punish the Egyptians, that were due to divine providence resulting from conjunction of the chosen forefather [i.e., Abraham] with Him.[30]

Here a key point is provided by Gersonides which is missing in his commentary on Genesis 15. The miracles in Egypt that rescue the Israelites from slavery occur as a result of providence inherited from Abraham.

If we combine this information with Gersonides' exposition of Genesis 15, it becomes clear that there are actually two forms of providence working in tandem to ensure the inheritance of the land of Canaan to Abraham's offspring. Providence inherited from Abraham is responsible for the miracles in Egypt that inspire the Israelites to achieve intellectual perfection. Once the Israelites attain this perfection, they are then in a position to earn providence on their own, and it is this latter form of providence that enables them to inherit the land of Canaan.

In a helpful passage in his commentary on Deuteronomy, Gersonides brings the whole picture into focus:

> ... because of God's providence over the Patriarchs, their offspring after them are always protected so that they will not be destroyed. On account of this providence, God watched over Israel while they were in Egypt and took them out of there with extraordinary wonders and miracles in order to bring them closer to worshipping Him so that they would be worthy of inheriting the land [of Canaan]. For this same reason, He gave them the perfect Torah. It was given to them in an extraordinary manner at Mount

Sinai to bring them without doubt to an adherence to the perfect Torah so that they would merit being given the land which God had sworn to our forefathers He would give to their offspring.[31]

Here the coordination of providence inherited from Abraham and providence earned by the Israelites themselves is clearly delineated. Inherited providence allows the Israelites to achieve perfection so that they may then merit their own providence and conquer the land of Canaan.[32]

We can now make much better sense of Gersonides' interpretation of God's promise to Abraham. Inherited providence is undoubtedly the key factor that in Gersonides' mind provides the assurance that God's promise to Abraham will be fulfilled. It soon becomes apparent why this form of providence serves this function. What is important to realize is that inherited providence offers protection to one's descendants regardless of their state of perfection. Its very purpose, after all, is to safeguard a person's loved ones simply by virtue of their blood relationship with him. Thus, if Abraham's descendants are protected by inherited providence, he need not worry about whether they will merit reward. When the proper time arrives for the Israelites to conquer the land of Canaan, Abraham's providence will function for their benefit, whether or not they have achieved perfection. In fact, its role will be to provide that very perfection that they may be lacking.

Put another way, God can promise unconditionally that Abraham's offspring will merit reward because they will be subject to a form of providence that will have already been earned by Abraham. Even if Abraham's descendants are not worthy of their own providence, inherited providence will make sure that they achieve the perfection necessary for claiming their inheritance.

These observations also help clarify the meaning of the covenant ceremony in Genesis 15. This ceremony, it would seem, is a metaphor for inherited providence. That is, when the covenant imagery in Abraham's vision is properly deciphered, it is nothing but an imaginative representation of this philosophical conception.

The identification of the covenant with inherited providence is clearly confirmed in a number of passages in Gersonides' commentary on Exodus. One such passage is Gersonides' interpretation of God's decision to redeem the Israelites from slavery in the second chapter of Exodus:

. . . divine providence over righteous men can extend to their offspring after them. That is why [the biblical text] says that God remembered His covenant with the Patriarchs,[33] and for that reason He was aroused to see the Children of Israel[34] and to exert providence over them even though the appointed time [of the redemption] had not come.[35]

Here Gersonides explicitly equates inherited providence with the Patriar-chal covenant. God's 'remembering' the covenant, when translated into philosophical terms, means simply that providence inherited from the Pa-triarchs has become activated to redeem the Israelites from slavery.

What is important to notice here is that Gersonides has once again managed to interpret the covenant concept so as to avoid any suggestion that God is personally involved in human affairs. The sealing of the covenant is not an objectively real event, but rather a metaphor produced in Abraham's prophetic vision. When properly interpreted, the covenant refers to inherited providence, which like all other forms of providence functions according to impersonal laws.

One more series of observations is in order. Our understanding of Gersonides' commentary on Genesis 15 can be further enriched by exam-ining the rabbinic and medieval sources he uses as a basis for his philo-sophical interpretation of the biblical text. As is often the case in his biblical commentaries, Gersonides does not cite these sources; nonetheless, their influence is not hard to trace.

Gersonides follows the lead of a number of traditional commentators who are troubled by the apparent insolence of Abraham's question that seems to demand proof from God that his offspring will inherit the land of Canaan. Some rabbinic sources are unforgiving. Not only is Abraham guilty of impropriety in asking the question; according to one opinion, the slavery in Egypt forecast in response to this query is meant as punishment for this misdemeanor.[36]

There are other sources that try to construe Abraham's request as re-flecting legitimate concerns. For instance, in *Bereshit Rabbah*, Abraham's question is seen not as a challenge to God, but as an enquiry about the wor-thiness of his offspring for receiving divine favor. God's response accord-ing to this source is that the sacrifices the Israelites will perform in the Temple service will provide merit for the fulfillment of the divine promise:

> R. Hama b. Hanina said: [Abraham spoke] not as one making a complaint, but he asked Him: "Through what merit [will I inherit the land]?" God replied: "Through the merits of the atoning sac-rifices which I will institute for thy sons."[37]

Ibn Ezra, Naḥmanides, and Gersonides all follow this second ap-proach. These exegetes elaborate on the midrashic view by arguing that Abraham's worries about the fulfillment of God's promises are justified because prophecies regarding future benefit are always conditional upon the worthiness of the recipient. God therefore provides a covenant guar-anteeing that his descendants will acquire their reward unconditionally.[38]

It should also be noted how Gersonides deviates from ibn Ezra and Naḥmanides in his understanding of God's promise. For the latter two exegetes, God's promise is simply that the Israelites will inherit the land; for Gersonides the promise is of a more indirect nature. God is guaranteeing only that the Israelites will become *worthy* of divine providence which will, in turn, enable them to inherit the land. They will acquire this merit only when they witness the miracles in Egypt and achieve intellectual perfection. Gersonides therefore injects a philosophical element here that is absent from the commentary of the other two exegetes.

Gersonides' interpretation of God's promise to Abraham also appears to draw from a disagreement in aggadic sources regarding the reason for the redemption of the Israelites from Egypt. In a number of sources, opinion is sharply divided over whether the Israelites are rescued from slavery by virtue of their own merit or the merit of the Patriarchs. *Mekhilta de-R. Ishmael* contains perhaps the oldest record of this dispute. There we find an argument between Shemaiah and Avtalyon about the splitting of the Red Sea. The former claims that the faith of Abraham is responsible for that miracle, while the latter claims that it is the faith of the Israelites themselves that causes the Sea to split:

> Shema'yah says: "The faith with which their father Abraham believed in Me is deserving that I should divide the sea for them." For it is said: "And he believed in the Lord."[39] Abtalyon says: "The faith with which they believed in Me is deserving that I should divide the sea for them." For it is said: "And the people believed."[40]

A similar dispute between R. Joshua and R. Eleazar of Modi'in is reported over the miracle of manna and the salvation of the Israelites from the Amalekites.[41]

This specific tension is part of a wider conflict in rabbinic sources.[42] Shemaiah's position can be grouped with other opinions that see the Israelites as somehow needing outside merit to bring salvation from the Egyptian slavery. For some like Shemaiah, it is the Patriarchs who provide such merit, either by their righteousness or through God's covenant with them. For others, the Israelites are saved by virtue of the merits of the unborn in coming generations.[43]

There is an equally strong voice in the sources, exemplified in Avtalyon's view, which claims that the Israelites are redeemed by virtue of their own merits. This view is expressed in several ways. There are those who attribute the redemption to some individual or group of individuals among the Israelites who, by their righteousness, bring redemption for the rest of the nation. Thus, in one source, it is the righteousness of Moses and

Aaron that is responsible for the redemption of the rest of the Israelite nation.[44] In another source, the Israelites are redeemed because of the righteous deeds of the Israelite women.[45] There are also those who see the
redemption as consequent upon the merits earned by the entire Jewish
people. Thus, Matiah ben Heresh expresses the opinion in a passage in
Mekhilta that the Israelites are commanded by God to perform circumcision and offer the paschal lamb in order that they have the merit needed
for redemption.[46]

What is most interesting about Gersonides' interpretation of the
covenant is that it appears to reconcile the major opposing viewpoints into
one formulation. In Gersonides' view, providence inherited from the Patriarchs expresses itself precisely by attempting to bestow upon the Israelites the initiative to earn providence by themselves. It is therefore a
combination of Patriarchal merit and the merit earned by the Israelites
themselves that makes it possible for them to claim the land of Canaan as
their inheritance.[47]

Our first step into Gersonides' biblical commentaries has yielded
fruitful results. We now have a philosophical framework for understanding the covenantal relationship between God and the Jewish people in the
earliest phase of their history. Gersonides' commentary on Genesis 15 provides valuable information regarding the covenant with Abraham and
how it guides events from the time of Abraham up to the conquest of
Canaan. This constitutes a significant advance beyond the *Wars* where, as
we observed earlier, Gersonides does not really grapple with the covenant
concept.

Our most important discovery is that the covenant in Abraham's
prophetic vision is symbolic of inherited providence. Providence inherited
from Abraham functions as a 'covenant' in the sense that it is the key factor guaranteeing that Abraham's descendants will take possession of the
land of Canaan, a location especially receptive to divine providential emanations. Inherited providence accomplishes this end by bringing the miracles in Egypt which ensure that the Israelites achieve intellectual
perfection and earn the providence necessary for conquering the land of
Canaan.

With this interpretation, Gersonides manages to address the philosophical difficulties inherent in the covenant concept, which were raised
at the beginning of our discussion. One problem was that the covenant
concept in general implies a personal agreement between God and human
beings, an idea that if taken literally conflicts with Gersonides' metaphysics. In his reading of Genesis 15, Gersonides has managed to circumvent this difficulty. According to Gersonides' interpretation, the covenant

between God and Abraham is a metaphorical image produced in Abraham's vision that, when properly understood, refers to inherited providence. Inherited providence, like all other forms of providence, functions according to impersonal laws. The covenant with Abraham, therefore, does not mean that God interacts with human beings in any personal way. It is nothing more than a symbol for a special type of providential law.

Another problem was the unconditional nature of the covenant with Abraham, which implied that the implementation of the agreement between God and Abraham would be from God's end alone, a notion that again would assume a more active role on God's part than Gersonides' philosophy could allow. Gersonides' interpretation of Genesis 15 circumvents this difficulty as well. The unconditional guarantee that Abraham's descendants will receive reward is due to the peculiar character of inherited providence. Normally, individual providence is operative only on condition that the recipient is worthy of reward. Inherited providence, by contrast, is not at all dependent on the merit of the recipient, since it is conferred because of one's association with a righteous ancestor. Thus the Israelites are sure to inherit the land of Canaan, regardless of their state of perfection, simply because they are Abraham's descendants.

Our analysis of Gersonides' explication of Genesis 15 has also highlighted a number of important features in his exegetical writing. For one, what is evident in Gersonides' exposition of Genesis 15 is the complete interdependence between his biblical commentary and the *Wars*. There was practically no point in Gersonides' interpretation of Genesis 15 that could be fully understood without the help of philosophical material in the *Wars*. Conversely, there were also passages in the *Wars* that could be clarified only with the help of insights from the biblical commentaries.

The interdependence between the two was especially evident in our analysis of the covenant ceremony. Neither the *Wars* nor the *Commentary on the Torah* was sufficient to provide a full philosophical account of this event. At the end of the fourth book of the *Wars*, Gersonides discusses the role of the miracles in the redemption of the Israelites but makes no mention of inherited providence as the factor responsible for those miracles. The passage at the end of book six of the *Wars* deals briefly with inherited providence but does not clearly explain its importance for the fulfillment of the covenant. The *Commentary on the Torah* offers a line-by-line exegesis of Genesis 15 but does not really clarify the identification of the covenant with inherited providence. It was only when we assembled these disparate sources that the elements of Gersonides' interpretation of the covenant with Abraham fell neatly into place.

What is also noteworthy in Gersonides' commentary on Genesis 15 is the high level of philosophical expertise that he seems to assume in his audience. We saw on a number of occasions that in the course of his commentary Gersonides did not always indicate when he was drawing on material from the *Wars*. It was entirely up to the reader to make those connections. Thus, for instance, in our analysis of Gersonides' interpretation of the prophetic communications received by Noah and Abraham, we had to supply a number of philosophical premises from the *Wars* regarding prophetic visions in order to make sense of Gersonides' reading. Even when Gersonides explicitly cited material from the *Wars*, his explanations were often too brief to be fully understood without a thorough acquaintance with that work. All of this would indicate that Gersonides takes for granted a comprehensive knowledge of the *Wars* on the part of his reader.

Finally, we saw that Gersonides' explication of Genesis 15 was to be understood not only with help of the philosophical material in the *Wars*; it also had to be read as an outgrowth of the exegetical tradition that preceded him. Gersonides' commentary on Genesis 15 betrays the influence of a variety of rabbinic and medieval sources that he creatively adapts to his philosophical interpretation of the biblical text. Here, too, the sources of Gersonides' views are left for the reader to discover.

What we have gleaned from Gersonides' commentary on one short chapter in the Bible will be of importance for the rest of our study. With regard to content, we will see that Gersonides' interpretation of the covenant with Abraham is only the beginning of a much broader theory that will be developed as the biblical narrative progresses. With regard to method, our analysis has made us aware that Gersonides' biblical commentaries are highly complex, and that a proper examination of these works requires a sensitivity to a host of factors—exegetical, rabbinic, and philosophical—which all play a role in Gersonides' explication of the biblical text.

FOUR

From the Slavery in Egypt to the Conquest of Canaan

This chapter will build upon our previous discussion by attempting to glean more information from the rest of Gersonides' *Commentary on the Torah* regarding the covenant with Abraham and its function up to the time of the conquest of Canaan. While Gersonides' commentary on Genesis 15 provides the basis for a philosophical understanding of the covenant with Abraham, his speculations on the subject are by no means exhausted in his interpretation of this chapter. The progress of events in the rest of the Pentateuch is dictated by the terms of the covenant—even though the closing chapters of Deuteronomy stop just short of its complete fulfillment—and it is in his explication of these events in his *Commentary on the Torah* that Gersonides often provides new insights into the nature of the covenant and its role in the early history of the Israelites.

We will be focusing primarily on Gersonides' commentary on Exodus. It is in Exodus that the process leading to the fulfillment of the covenant with Abraham is initiated with the slavery of the Israelites in Egypt and their subsequent redemption. These events provide Gersonides with the opportunity to offer some of his most important speculations regarding the issues that concern us—in particular, the role of inherited providence in the fulfillment of the covenant.

We should first make a brief observation about terminology. In his commentary on Exodus, Gersonides begins to describe the divine promise to Abraham with the biblical phrase, *berit 'avot*, or "covenant with the Patriarchs." At one point, Gersonides notes that the plural *'avot* seems inap-

55

propriate, given that the covenant was made exclusively with Abraham; but the problem is quickly dismissed with the claim that even though the covenant originates with Abraham, it is reaffirmed in prophetic visions with the other two Patriarchs.[1] From now on, we will therefore refer to the covenant with Abraham and the covenant with the Patriarchs as one and the same thing.

In order to appreciate the philosophical insights that Gersonides' commentary on Exodus offers regarding the Patriarchal covenant, we must begin with Gersonides' explanation for the slavery in Egypt. The slavery presents a formidable problem for traditional and scholarly commentators alike: why it is that the Israelites endure such suffering? The biblical narrative itself offers no explicit explanation for what appears to be an extended punishment.

For Gersonides, there can be only two possible explanations for suffering. Evil can befall an individual or group, either because of the normal effects of the constellations or because of providential suffering. In the first instance, calamities are an unavoidable product of the beneficial effects of general providence. In the second, a harmful event can occur to an individual or group protected by individual providence to preempt some greater disaster.[2]

In an important passage in his commentary on Exodus, Gersonides clarifies that the slavery in Egypt is due to the first cause; the Israelites are the victims of harmful effects programmed into the natural order. Gersonides further explains that the slavery could have been avoided altogether if the Israelites had been at the proper level of perfection necessary for experiencing individual providence. The problem was that their perfection was far from adequate to merit such protection. Evidence for their deficient condition is the behavior of the two Israelites in the second chapter of Exodus who quarrel with each other before Moses attempts to intercede.[3] Not only do these men respond insolently to Moses' attempted intervention; they are in Gersonides' mind ultimately responsible for informing Pharaoh of the death of the Egyptian guard at the hands of Moses.[4] Gersonides sees these actions as representative of the low level of moral perfection of the entire Israelite nation at the time.[5]

In the same passage, Gersonides makes another interesting claim. Up to the passing of Joseph's generation, the righteous behavior of the Israelites had temporarily allowed them to circumvent the deleterious effects of the constellations:

> . . . the harsh exile which they [i.e., the Israelites] experienced was
> due to their wicked deeds. If they had improved their actions and
> had drawn closer to God to the best of their ability, they would

not have experienced this harsh exile. For this reason, you find that the exile did not begin until the death of Joseph, all his brothers and that whole generation—even though it had already been decreed that they [i.e., the Egyptians] would enslave them and oppress them four hundred years. . . . [6]

Thus, Gersonides contends, the Israelites were initially able to stave off the slavery until their moral condition deteriorated.

Everything Gersonides is saying here is, of course, perfectly consistent with his positions in the *Wars*. There Gersonides makes it clear that human beings are able to circumvent the harmful events programmed into the natural order by virtue of their free will. This point is alluded to in the conclusion of the above passage: ". . . [the exercise of the] right choice [of action] can contravene this [natural] order as we have explained in the second [book] of *The Wars of the Lord* and in our *Commentary on Job*."[7]

What is most important about Gersonides' remarks here is that they shed new light on the role of inherited providence in the fulfillment of the covenant. Gersonides is effectively telling us that inherited providence might not have been required at all for the redemption of the Israelites from Egypt if the Israelites had been at the proper level of perfection. The Israelites could very well have avoided the slavery and the need for redemption altogether, had they simply been worthy of providence on their own. In fact, the thrust of Gersonides' remarks is that this alternative scenario would have been far preferable to one that actually came about.

The implication here is that inherited providence is, in fact, an optional factor in the redemption of the Israelites. It functions as a providential "back-up mechanism" that comes into play when other forms of providence are not available. It redeems the Israelites only because they are not worthy of individual providence and because general providence is not working in their favor.

Gersonides explicitly depicts inherited providence as an alternative mechanism for rescuing the Israelites in his remarks on the well-known verses at the beginning of the sixth chapter of Exodus. In this biblical passage, God speaks to Moses and informs him that He appeared to the Patriarchs as 'El Shaddai before revealing the Tetragrammaton. Included in Gersonides' explication of this cryptic statement are speculations about inherited providence:

> . . . AS 'EL SHADDAI: That is to say, the God in whose existence is that which is sufficient to emanate what is required for the existents in the most perfect manner.[8] It is as if He is stating that He appeared to the Patriarchs with this name so that if what He promised them [i.e., the redemption] is not possible by virtue of

the order determined by the heavenly bodies, He will bring this good from the order determined by the divine providence which is conjoined to the holy Patriarchs. If it is not possible by virtue of general providence,[9] it will be possible by the providence which is conjoined to those who are conjoined to Him. We explained this completely in book six of *The Wars of the Lord*.[10]

Here Gersonides clearly describes inherited providence, represented by the name *'El Shaddai*, as an alternative force which will redeem the Israelites only if general providence fails to come to their rescue.

When inherited providence does become operative, what effect does it have? In one passage, Gersonides seems to indicate that at least initially it softens the worst impact of the slavery. Gersonides notes that despite the best efforts of the Egyptians to enslave and oppress the Israelites, the biblical narrative is quite emphatic in pointing out that the Israelites continue to be "fertile and prolific."[11] In an interesting passage, Gersonides attributes the resilience of the Israelites to a promise made by God to Jacob. In Genesis 46:3–4, God informed Jacob that He would make his descendants "a great nation" while they were in Egypt, and that He would personally "go down" there with them. Gersonides gives the following philosophical interpretation of this promise and its fulfillment:

> The first *to'elet* is with regard to theoretical issues. We are informed of the fulfillment of that which God[12] promised to Jacob: that in Egypt He would make him into a great nation and that He would go down there with them. That is, His providence would be conjoined there with his offspring. It is for this reason that [the biblical narrative] reports that the Children of Israel "were fertile and prolific and multiplied"[13] more than was normal for them. God caused good [things to happen] to them there, i.e., that they would find food and all that they needed due to their proliferation. . . . Thus, despite the great effort which Pharaoh exerted to prevent their proliferation and the intensity of his oppression of them, God's extraordinary providence over them increased their proliferation and strength. . . . [14]

In this passage, Gersonides never specifically identifies the form of providence that helps the Israelites in the initial stages of the slavery; however, inherited providence is the only one to which he could be referring. As we have already shown, the Israelites at this point are certainly not worthy of providence of their own, nor is general providence working in their favor. What mitigates the harshness of the slavery must therefore be providence inherited from the Patriarchs.

Of course, the main function of inherited providence is to act as a re-demptive force. As we saw in our last chapter, inherited providence is sup-posed to rescue the Israelites from Egypt and in so doing provide them with the means to earn their own providence. The miracles in Egypt are meant to convince the Israelites of God's sovereignty so that they will achieve intellectual perfection and be worthy of the providence necessary for inheriting the land of Canaan.

All of this is reiterated in Gersonides' commentary on Exodus. How-ever, a new element appears here which is most important. In a number of passages, Gersonides suggests that inherited providence redeems the Is-raelites only at the point when they are threatened with complete destruc-tion. This idea is most clearly expressed in Gersonides' explication of the dialogue between God and Moses at the burning bush. In the biblical text, God begins His address to Moses by acknowledging the suffering the Is-raelites are experiencing:

> I have marked well the plight of My people in Egypt and have heeded their outcry because of their taskmasters: yes, I am mind-ful of their sufferings. I have come down to rescue them from the Egyptians and to bring them out of that land to a good and spa-cious land, a land flowing with milk and honey. . . . [15]

In Gersonides' interpretation of this statement, God's decision to redeem the Israelites is equated in philosophical terms with the activation of prov-idence inherited from Abraham.[16]

Thus far what Gersonides is saying is consistent with what we saw in his commentary on Genesis 15. But Gersonides now adds an unexpected twist in his interpretation of the redemption process. At this point in the biblical narrative, he explains, the proper time for the redemption has not actually arrived. That is, the four hundred year period originally predicted for the slavery has not elapsed, a conclusion supported elsewhere by elab-orate numerical calculations.[17] Yet the oppression which the Israelites are experiencing is so severe—as is evident from their outcries to God—that their very survival is being threatened and the covenant is in danger of not being fulfilled. For this reason, inherited providence is activated a number of years earlier than the predicted time in order to rescue the Israelites from their suffering.[18]

Gersonides' interpretation is conveniently summarized in one of his *to'aliyyot:*

> . . . divine providence extends from the righteous to their off-spring after them. Thus, the Israelites were not [in a state of per-fection] such that it was possible for them to receive providence,

since the name, *YHVH*, was not known to them.[19] Despite all this, God exercised providence over them, roused Himself to attempt to give them the land of Canaan as had been promised to the Patriarchs, and heard their groans when they cried out to Him, due to His covenant with the Patriarchs. Were it not for this, the covenant would not have been fulfilled since the Israelites would have perished because of the intensity of their suffering.[20]

What is most significant here is that Gersonides depicts inherited providence as a force that redeems the Israelites only at a moment of crisis. It brings an end to the slavery only at the point of desperation, when the very survival of the Israelites is being threatened and God's promise to the Patriarchs is in danger of never being fulfilled.[21]

At this point of our discussion, a much clearer picture has begun to emerge regarding the role of inherited providence in the redemption of the Israelites and the fulfillment of the covenant with Abraham. It would appear that in Gersonides' thinking inherited providence is meant to serve in a highly defined and restricted role. In particular, inherited providence is depicted as a force that functions on behalf of the Israelites not as a primary defense against harm, but only when it is absolutely needed. It is an emergency measure, a last resort to save the Israelites when no other option is available. Thus, inherited providence comes into play to assist the Israelites and soften the impact of the slavery only when they have recourse to no other form of providence. When inherited providence finally redeems the Israelites, it does so only when it is clear that they are threatened with complete physical destruction.

That inherited providence is an emergency measure is also implied by the fact that its role is very much a temporary one. It brings an end to the slavery in Egypt, but only in such a way as to prepare the Israelites to experience providence on their own once again. It is there to tide the Israelites over in a time of crisis, not to be a permanent form of protection.

These conclusions find strong support in another portion of Gersonides' commentary on Exodus. Inherited providence comes in as an important factor in Gersonides' reading of the dialogue that takes place between God and Moses in the aftermath of the golden calf incident. Here again, inherited providence is depicted as a temporary, emergency measure that becomes operative when other forms of providence are not available and when the Israelites are threatened with annihilation.

Gersonides' interpretation of this dialogue is somewhat complex, a problem that is partly due to the difficulties inherent in this portion of the biblical text. It will therefore require some effort on our part to explicate the role of inherited providence in this section of Gersonides' commentary.

As a preliminary note, we should first point out that one problem with Gersonides' interpretation is that he never offers an explicit philosophical explanation for God's threat to destroy the Israelites and make Moses the father of a new nation.[22] My best guess is that Gersonides would see this threat as a case of providential suffering. Support for this speculation can be found in his interpretation of the flood story. There we saw that Gersonides utilized the notion of providential suffering to account for a similar scenario: God's decision to destroy the world by flood while sparing Noah. The destruction was interpreted as an instance of providential suffering for the sake of mankind as a whole in that the long-term good of mankind was best served by getting rid of an incurably sinful race while saving Noah. The hope was that Noah's progeny would generate a world better suited for achieving moral and intellectual perfection.[23] Here a similar reasoning can be used. God threatens to destroy the Israelites and preserve Moses for the sake of the long-term spiritual well-being of the Israelite nation. This intended course of action is based on the prospect that Moses and his progeny will more likely achieve perfection and experience providence than the Israelites who have worshiped the golden calf.[24]

Yet Gersonides' lack of clarity on this point does not really affect our immediate concerns. Let us go to the next portion of the dialogue between God and Moses. According to the biblical text, Moses successfully convinces God not to destroy the Israelites.[25] Gersonides suggests that God does not carry out his threat because such a course of action would deeply upset Moses. Gersonides specifically alludes to the capacity of providential laws to extend to a righteous man's relatives and friends, even when they themselves are not worthy of providence. The Israelites are therefore spared because of providence over Moses.[26]

It is in Gersonides' remarks on the next exchange between God and Moses that inherited providence comes into the picture. In the biblical text, Moses ascends the mountain once again to pray for forgiveness on behalf of the Israelites.[27] For Gersonides, the reason for Moses' return is that up to this point God has only promised Moses that He would spare the Israelites from total destruction but not from lesser forms of suffering. The Israelites have still not regained the protection of individual providence which they had previously. Moses must therefore plead on behalf of the Israelites once again in order that this form of providence be reinstated.

The important passage for our purposes is Gersonides' interpretation of God's response to this second prayer offered by Moses. In the biblical narrative, God responds to Moses' concerns by promising that He will punish only those who have sinned against Him. God then adds the following cryptic comment: "Go now, lead the people where I told you. See,

My angel shall go before you. But when I make an accounting, I will bring them to account for their sins."[28]

This passage is particularly troublesome for Gersonides. When an angel appears in a prophetic vision, it is almost always interpreted by Gersonides as a symbolic representation of the Active Intellect, a common association in medieval philosophy. The problem here is that God is making reference to an angel that will clearly be involved in concrete future events outside the prophetic vision Moses is presently experiencing. To what then could the angel refer?

Two possibilities are suggested by Gersonides. The angel may refer in metaphorical terms to the operations of general providence. God is informing Moses that because of the sin of the golden calf, the Israelites are not deserving of protection afforded by individual providence. From this point on, they will be protected only by general providence that will provide a lesser form of protection. When God adds that He will make the Israelites "account for their sins," He is referring to the possibility that the Israelites will be subject to chance events against which general providence offers no defense. The second and preferred explanation for Gersonides is that the angel is a metaphor for inherited providence. It is this form of providence that will give the Israelites protection against harm, seeing as they are not deserving of individual providence in their own right.[29]

The next series of exchanges between God and Moses in the biblical text are not at all clear. Apparently Moses is not satisfied with God's response and appears to convince Him to give the Israelites a second chance. Moses then receives the second set of tablets.[30] According to Gersonides' interpretation, what Moses objects to is God's plan to provide the Israelites with protection from inherited providence alone. Moses pleads with God to give the Israelites the opportunity to have their own individual providence restored. Moses' wish is granted with the giving of the second set of tablets, which gives the Israelites the opportunity to commit themselves once again to observing the commandments, an action that brings with it the reinstatement of individual providence.[31]

The key point to notice here is that the role of inherited providence is completely consistent with the function ascribed to it in the redemption of the Israelites from Egypt. Inherited providence once again functions as an emergency measure. It comes into play at a moment of crisis, when the Israelites are threatened with annihilation and are not deserving of providence in their own right. Moreover, it is once again conceived of as a temporary remedy that should not replace providence that the Israelites earn on their own. It is for this reason that Moses eventually pleads with God for individual providence to be restored.

Another way in which Gersonides' commentary on the exodus story enlightens us is by providing important details about how inherited providence inspires the Israelites towards intellectual perfection in the process of rescuing them from slavery. In Gersonides' interpretation of Genesis 15, we saw that inherited providence was to accomplish this goal by bringing the miracles in Egypt in order to convince the Israelites to believe in God and devote themselves to His service. It becomes clear in the Exodus commentary that these miracles constitute only one of several factors that help the Israelites achieve perfection. Chief among these is the Torah. The giving of the Torah, like the miracles, occurs as a result of providence inherited from Abraham. Its specific function is to inspire the Israelites toward perfection by offering them instruction in moral and intellectual truths.

The importance of the Torah is first emphasized in Gersonides' remarks on the dialogue between God and Moses at the burning bush. This issue comes up in Gersonides' interpretation of the exchange, in which Moses seeks reassurance from God about his worthiness for rescuing the Israelites from slavery:

> Moses said to God, "Who am I that I should go to Pharaoh and free the Israelites from Egypt?" And He said, "I will be with you; that shall be your sign that it was I who sent you. And when you have freed the people from Egypt, you shall worship God at this mountain."[32]

Following earlier commentators, Gersonides interprets Moses' question as reflecting a twofold concern. First, in asking "who am I to go to Pharaoh," Moses expresses doubts about his worthiness to confront Pharaoh. His fear is that he lacks the oratorical ability to perform the function asked of him. Second, by questioning whether he can "free the Israelites from Egypt," Moses voices an additional uncertainty about whether the Israelites are even deserving of redemption. They are so lacking in perfection, Moses argues, they may not be worthy of divine providence. The redemption would therefore serve no purpose, since the Israelites would be unable to conquer the land of Canaan after leaving Egypt.[33]

Gersonides reads God's response to Moses as an attempt to allay these two fears. God's promise, "I will be with you," first assures Moses that he will carry out his mission to Pharaoh successfully because of providence that Moses will receive from God. As far as the worthiness of the Israelites goes, God promises Moses that they will merit the land of Canaan with the help of providence inherited from the Patriarchs. With the assistance of inherited providence, the Israelites will be guided to worship God "at this mountain."[34] There, they will receive the Torah, and through the observance of its commandments will attain the perfection needed to inherit the land of Canaan:

> YOU SHALL WORSHIP ME ON THIS MOUNTAIN: [God said:] "that shall be your sign"[35] that Israel will have the requisite perfection upon leaving Egypt to be worthy of the conjunction of My providence with them so that I can bequeath the land of Canaan to them before the end [of the period of slavery] has been reached. That is, they will agree on this mountain to worship Me and to keep My commandments immediately after their leaving Egypt. . . . Given that this is the case, it is fitting that My providence be conjoined with them to bring them to the land of Canaan as I have promised you.[36]

The Torah thus plays a crucial role, in the same way that the miracles do, in ensuring that the Israelites are worthy of providence.

In a slightly different formulation, Gersonides suggests that the witnessing of the miracles in Egypt is a necessary precursor to the acceptance of the Torah by the Israelites:

> The first *to'elet* is to make known the abundance of miracles which God generated for Israel in order that they would believe in Him and so that they would be prepared to receive this perfect Torah[37] which guides [one] towards all perfections. . . . [38]

The giving of the Torah and the miracles in Egypt are not the only factors that help the Israelites achieve perfection. Gersonides also sees the Passover sacrifice as aiding in this process. This ritual is designed to rid the Israelites of the false beliefs they have learned from the Egyptians during their slavery. Gersonides explains that Egyptian idolatry consisted of worshiping the constellation Aries, the sign of which was the ram, and that the Egyptians therefore refrained from sacrificing or eating sheep. The Israelites are commanded by God to sacrifice a lamb so that they see the futility of these beliefs:

> The benefit from this commandment [i.e., the Passover sacrifice] along with the commandments accompanying it[39] was to draw the Israelites away from the deficient beliefs of the Egyptians. For they [i.e., the Egyptians] thought it abominable to sacrifice sheep and eat them, since they thought that their God was the constellation Aries.[40]

Gersonides goes on to explain that this ritual makes its point not only by demonstrating to the Israelites that there is no harm in sacrificing a lamb, but by showing them that such an action even results in their salvation.[41]

One other factor that helps the Israelites achieve intellectual perfection is a number of philosophical teachings that Moses imparts to them prior to the exodus. According to Gersonides, these teachings were originally received by Moses in his dialogue with God at the burning bush, in which Moses asks for God's name and receives the enigmatic response "'*Ehyeh 'Asher 'Ehyeh*," often rendered, "I am that I am."[42] In Gersonides' reading, the substance of Moses' question is philosophical. Moses wants to acquire a philosophical understanding of God's nature, which he believes the Israelites will undoubtedly want to know. Gersonides interprets God's response as an attempt to answer this question with a concentrated lesson about the uniqueness of God's being and unity.[43]

According to Gersonides, the benefits these philosophical teachings provide for the Israelites are alluded to at the beginning of the sixth chapter of Exodus, the passage in which God explains to Moses that He revealed the name '*El Shaddai* to the Patriarchs but did not make Himself known through the Tetragrammaton:

> BUT I DID NOT MAKE MYSELF KNOWN TO THEM BY MY NAME, *YHVH*: I.e., to Israel. The meaning of this [statement] is that there was a time that My name—which is *YHVH*—was not made known to Israel, as it has now been made known by you through your teaching[44] it to the Elders of Israel. Despite this [lack of knowledge], I attempted to fulfill My covenant with them that was [sealed] with the Patriarchs to give them the land of Canaan. . . . Even more remarkable than this is that I also heard the groans of the Children of Israel before My name was made known to them. . . . Given that this was the case [i.e., that I responded to them without their knowledge of My name], it is evident that they are now more worthy that My providence be conjoined with them, since My name has now been made known among them.[45]

God explains to Moses that the Israelites, having learned from him the exalted philosophical teachings represented by the divine name, are now in a much better position to merit redemption. If God was previously willing to save the Israelites by virtue of inherited providence alone, how much more should He be willing to redeem them, now that they are in a greater state of intellectual perfection.[46]

Thus, in addition to the witnessing of the miracles in Egypt, the Israelites achieve perfection with the help of a number of other factors. The teachings contained in the Torah, the Passover sacrifice, and the philosophical teachings regarding God's nature which Moses receives at the burning bush—all assist the Israelites in meriting individual providence.

At this point in our discussion, the analysis of Gersonides' interpretation of the Patriarchal covenant and its function up to the time of the conquest of Canaan is, for the most part, complete. There are, however, a couple of loose ends that still need to be tied up. While Gersonides' interpretation of the Patriarchal covenant is highly original and creative, the biblical narrative presents several obvious problems for Gersonides' theory that must be addressed. For one, the biblical text makes clear that the Egyptians are no less witnesses of God's miracles than the Israelites. Why then do the Egyptians not achieve intellectual perfection and divine providence along with the Israelites? Why is it that only the Israelites benefit from the miracles? A more difficult problem is the consistently rebellious behavior of the Israelites, from the exodus onward. If the whole purpose of the miracles in Egypt is to convince the Israelites to believe in God's existence and to devote themselves to His service, what explains this behavior? Have the miracles somehow failed to accomplish their purpose?

While Gersonides never explicitly poses these questions, there are passages in his commentary on Exodus that clearly indicate he is well aware of them. With regard to the first difficulty, there are passages in the biblical text explicitly emphasizing that it is very much part of the divine plan for the Egyptians to witness the miracles and acknowledge God's omnipotence. For instance, just before the splitting of the Red Sea, God tells Moses that He will cause Pharaoh to pursue the Israelites so that "I may gain glory through Pharaoh and all his host" and that "the Egyptians shall know that I am the LORD."[47]

If the Egyptians see the same miracles as the Israelites and come to believe in God's power, why is it that the Egyptians do not achieve intellectual perfection as well? Gersonides addresses this problem in his comments on the verses just cited:

> ... AND THE EGYPTIANS SHALL KNOW THAT I AM THE LORD: that is, Israel will not have to fear that the Egyptians will pursue them any longer because it will be clear to them [i.e., the Egyptians] that "I am the LORD" due to the great plague which I will bring upon them. On account of this, they will be afraid to continue pursuing the Children of Israel. This is the benefit which the Israelites will receive when the Egyptians will know God's extraordinary might, because He will wage war on behalf of Israel. *For it was not the intention here to bring the Egyptians to belief in God; this is plainly obvious* [italics added].[48]

Gersonides argues that when the biblical text refers to the acknowledgment of God by the Egyptians, it means that the Egyptians have learned only to fear God so as not to pursue the Israelites. What Gersonides is implying is that their recognition of God's sovereignty is by no means one of proper philosophical understanding and that they therefore do not qualify for any providential reward.

Another point in the narrative in which the Egyptians appear to recognize God's power is with the plague of lice. The Egyptian magicians are able to reproduce Moses' actions for the first three plagues, but when the plague of lice occurs, they are unsuccessful. In astonishment, the magicians proclaim: "This is the finger of God."[49]

Gersonides' handling of this passage is equivocal. Two interpretations of the magicians' proclamation are offered. According to the first, the Egyptians plainly acknowledge God's power. The magicians admit that Moses' miracles are genuine and that their imitation of the miracles has been nothing more than mere trickery. However, in the second explanation, Gersonides quotes ibn Ezra's interpretation, according to which the magicians do not acknowledge God at all:

> It is possible that they [i.e., the magicians] said that it is a plague of God by virtue of the pattern [of the stars] and was not done by Moses and Aaron, as ibn Ezra has written. They said this as if to point out that Moses and Aaron had no advantage over them.[50]

Here the statement of the magicians is interpreted to mean that they attribute the miracle to the normal influences of the constellations. The magicians refuse to acknowledge that Moses and Aaron have produced the miracle by virtue of any special connection with God.

Gersonides does not express preference for one of these explanations. However, it is evident that the second one addresses our original question. According to this interpretation, the Egyptians remain as stubborn as ever in refusing to acknowledge God's sovereignty and are therefore unable to gain any providential benefit from witnessing the plagues.

Perhaps the most serious problem for Gersonides' understanding of the covenant and its role in the events following the exodus is that the Israelites themselves appear to be unconvinced of God's sovereignty after witnessing the miracles in Egypt. Throughout the story of the exodus and the account of the wandering of the Israelites in the desert, there are several occasions when the Israelites reject Moses' leadership and rebel against the God who has liberated them from Egypt.

What explains the apparent failure of the miracles to convince the Israelites to be obedient to God? Gersonides addresses this problem in one passage by arguing that the unruly behavior of the Israelites is due to the duration of the slavery. They have been "immersed in the opinions of the Egyptians and their customs" for such an extended period of time that they have great difficulty accepting "correct belief." Here, Gersonides places the blame for the Israelites' conduct squarely on the shoulders of the Egyptians.[51]

In other passages, Gersonides elaborates on this explanation by informing us that the corrupting influence of the Egyptians is quite specifically their belief in dualism. As a result of living among the Egyptians, the Israelites are inclined to believe that there are two gods: one good and one evil. It is this dualist thinking that, besides obscuring the truth, inspires the Israelites towards active insurrection. The Israelites consistently suspect that it is, in fact, the evil deity who has rescued them from Egypt, a hypothesis that appears to gain support from the pain and suffering this deity inflicts upon the Egyptians. The Israelites rebel on a number of occasions, because they fear that the evil deity will inflict upon them the same kind of suffering experienced by their enemies.

Gersonides shows great ingenuity in reading a number of passages in light of this novel interpretation. It is actually Pharaoh who, according to Gersonides, first plants the idea that an evil deity is responsible for the miracles in Egypt. In one of the many false starts in which Pharaoh appears ready to free the Israelites, he bids the Israelites farewell, but adds: "*u-re'u ki ra'ah neged penekhem.*"[52] This statement, which is somewhat ambiguous, is taken by Gersonides to mean: "Behold, there is evil [that lies] before you."[53] According to an anonymous interpretation which Gersonides quotes, Pharaoh's words reflect his belief in dualism. Pharaoh is warning Moses that it is an evil deity who is acting on behalf of the Israelites, and that the Israelites are imperiling themselves by entrusting themselves to such a god:

> I saw written in a treatise that a wise man had told Pharaoh, the king of Egypt, that there are two gods; one, who is the agent of evil, and another, who is the agent of good. . . . It is my opinion that for this reason Pharaoh said, "*u-re'u ki ra'ah neged penekhem.*" He thought that the God of Israel was the agent of evil, since he had seen His miracles which He had performed in his midst. For this reason, he [i.e., Pharaoh] said to them [i.e., Moses and Aaron] that they are inviting evil [to befall them] by following their God, because He will only cause them evil.[54]

In the same passage, Gersonides explicates two other biblical passages with the help of this interpretation. When Moses pleads on behalf of the Israelites after the sin of the golden calf, he argues that God should not destroy the Israelites because the Egyptians will then say, "It was with evil intent (*be-ra'ah*) that He delivered them. . . ."[55] According to Gersonides, Moses is alluding here to the dualistic beliefs of the Egyptians and arguing that God's destruction of the Israelites will only confirm Pharaoh's view that an evil deity rescued them from Egypt. Gersonides again bases his interpretation on Moses' use of the key term, *ra`ah*, the same one which Pharaoh used in referring to the evil god.

With the help of these speculations, Gersonides also accounts for the rebellion of the Israelites at Marah in Exodus 15. This rebellion is due to the fear on the part of the Israelites that an evil deity has rescued them from Egypt, a fear that is heightened after their just having witnessed the destruction of Pharaoh's army at the Red Sea. Gersonides suggests that Moses performs the miracle of sweetening the bitter water in order to convince the Israelites that these fears are unfounded. This miracle demonstrates that the same God who killed so many Egyptians is also capable of purely benevolent action. In order to underscore the point, Moses deliberately uses the staff that split the Red Sea to sweeten the waters.[56]

There are at least two other places where Gersonides attributes the rebellious behavior of the Israelites to dualistic beliefs. Their complaints to Moses as they are being pursued by the Egyptians are explained in this manner,[57] as is the rebellion at Massah and Meribah in Exodus 17.[58]

The important point for our concerns is that Gersonides provides a rationale for explaining why the miracles in Egypt prove to be ineffective in bringing the Israelites closer to God. Ironically, the miracles produce the opposite of their intended effect. They serve only to distance the Israelites from God by reinforcing their fears that it is an evil deity who has rescued them from Egypt.

The advantage of this approach is not just that Gersonides is able to account for the unruly conduct of the Israelites; it also manages to interpret their behavior in terms far more respectable than the plain meaning of the biblical text would suggest. According to the biblical account, the Israelites consistently complain to Moses about what appear to be purely material concerns—whether it is their fear of annihilation when confronted with the onslaught of Pharaoh's army, or their concerns about having inadequate food and water in the desert. Gersonides cleverly interprets these complaints in a way that elevates them to legitimate philosophical concerns. In his reading, the Israelites are actually being motivated by a philosophically sophisticated—though incorrect—interpretation of events, based on the dualistic beliefs they have adopted from the Egyptians.

In his commentary on the golden calf story, Gersonides takes an approach that is less complicated than the one we have seen thus far. Gersonides attempts simply to minimize the seriousness of this rebellion with the claim that only a small number of Israelites actually participate in worshiping the calf, an approach previously adopted by Judah Halevi in the *Kuzari*.[59] Evidence for this interpretation is that, according to the biblical account, only three thousand of the six hundred thousand Israelites are killed in the aftermath of the incident. Gersonides argues that the numbers of those punished would certainly have been greater had more participated. Gersonides credits Aaron's subtle maneuvering for reducing the number of participants.[60]

Gersonides also appears to soften the rebellion by suggesting that at first the golden calf is meant to be a "talisman" (*talisma*). The Israelites build the calf with the hope that it will have the power to predict future events and lead them through the desert as Moses had done. Thus, the idol is actually meant to replace Moses, not God.[61]

Yet with all his exegetical ingenuity, Gersonides cannot entirely whitewash the sinful conduct of the Israelites. At a certain point, Gersonides bows to the force of the biblical narrative and concedes that the Israelites have simply failed to be convinced of God's sovereignty. The turning point for Gersonides is the rebellion in Numbers 13-4, which follows upon the report of the spies sent to survey the land of Canaan. In this episode, according to Gersonides' reading, it becomes clear that the recalcitrance of the Israelite nation has prevented them from learning the philosophical lessons that the redemption from Egypt was designed to teach. In one of his *to'aliyyot*, Gersonides sums up his assessment of the behavior of the Israelites:

> The fourth *to'elet* is to make known the wickedness of that generation. Despite the causes which God provided in order to prevent them from feeling regret upon encountering war and returning to Egypt[62]—despite all this, they said, "Let us head back for Egypt."[63]

Yet what is important to note is that despite the failure of the Israelites, Gersonides in no way imagines that God has given up His providential care for them. This point is expressed in Gersonides' commentary on Deuteronomy where the story of the spies is retold:

> The seventh *to'elet* is to inform [us] of the profundity of God's thinking. Despite the fact that the Israelites remained in the desert for forty years as a result of punishment, [God] used this [punishment] for [their] benefit—i.e., to test them whether they would or would not observe God's commandments so that the time could be determined when they would be ready to inherit the land. For this reason, also, [God] chastised them there immediately [after] their rebellion; this [i.e., quick punishment] is not customary for God, since He is long-suffering. Yet, for [the sake of] providential care over all Israel He did this in order to stop them from sinning toward God. For this reason, He also afflicted

them and deprived them of food for forty years in the desert in order to show Israel the miracles of God[64] so that they would be strengthened to keep His laws.[65]

The forty year sojourn in the desert with which God punishes the Israelites is interpreted by Gersonides to be an instance of providential suffering. By having the Israelites wander for forty years, God is allowing them an extended period to achieve perfection so that they will be able to inherit the land of Canaan.[66]

In his explication of events up to the end of the Pentateuch, Gersonides provides valuable new information about the dynamics of the Patriarchal covenant. Of particular importance is Gersonides' commentary on Exodus, where the redemption of the Israelites from Egypt furnishes him with the opportunity to offer significant insights regarding this issue.

First of all, we now have a much better conception of how Gersonides understands Abraham's original prophecy in Genesis 15. It is clear that the events predicted in Abraham's vision constitute only a probable scenario. The slavery in Egypt was a 'chance' event programmed into the natural order, and, therefore, the Israelites could have avoided it if they had been at the requisite level of intellectual perfection. In fact, as it turned out, the onset of the slavery was delayed for a period of time, because the Israelites temporarily achieved perfection. Moreover, the slavery that the Israelites eventually experienced ended sooner than originally predicted by Abraham. The suffering inflicted by the Egyptians was so great that inherited providence had to rescue the Israelites before the appointed time lest they be completely annihilated.

All of this is very much in line with Gersonides' philosophical views about prophecy. We must keep in mind that prophecies only predict what *should* happen, not necessarily what *will* happen. Due to the unpredictable nature of human initiative, what actually occurs may be different from what the prophet sees in his vision.

We should pause here to take note of the audacity of Gersonides' interpretation. It need not be emphasized how important the account of events in the Book of Exodus is for Jewish consciousness and identity, from biblical times onward. The slavery and redemption from Egypt constitute a focal point for some of the most central beliefs and practices in Judaism. It is therefore remarkable that Gersonides should suggest that these events were in fact entirely contingent. According to Gersonides' reading, there was no inherent meaning to the slavery of the Israelites in Egypt. It was simply the product of harmful effects produced by the constellations. If the Israelites had been at the proper level of perfection, there would have been no slavery, and, by implication, no need for redemption.

The most important insights which emerge from Gersonides' interpretation of the redemption concern the role of inherited providence in the fulfillment of Abraham's original prophecy. It becomes clear in Gersonides' commentary on the exodus story that inherited providence performs its function in a highly specific manner. Inherited providence is not a front line of defense against harm; rather, it is an emergency measure that comes into play when it is absolutely needed. It exerts its influence over the Israelites when they become enslaved and no other form of providence is available to assist them. It eventually redeems the Israelites only when they face complete destruction at the hands of the Egyptians. Furthermore, as an emergency measure, its influence is meant to be temporary. The plan is that by rescuing the Israelites through miracles, inherited providence will allow the Israelites to regain their capacity for experiencing providence on their own so that they will then be able to take possession of the land of Canaan.

Our analysis in this chapter has also provided insight into the means by which inherited providence brings the Israelites to intellectual perfection, so that they become worthy of individual providence. The miracles in Egypt are only one factor in an elaborate program designed to help the Israelites achieve this goal. Moses is commanded by God to elevate the intellectual level of the Israelites by teaching them a number of important philosophical truths about God's nature. The Israelites are also instructed to perform the Passover sacrifice, which serves the purpose of negating the false beliefs of the Egyptians that the Israelites have adopted during their stay in Egypt. Most important is that the Israelites receive the Torah, the central revelation that guides the Israelites toward moral and intellectual perfection.

FIVE

The Covenant at Sinai

THE TORAH AS PHILOSOPHICAL GUIDEBOOK

W e will now pause in our narrative through early Israelite history and devote a separate discussion, in this chapter and the next, to the role of the Torah in Gersonides' thought. As we saw in our last chapter, the Torah is the most important factor provided by inherited providence for ensuring that the Israelites are worthy of inheriting the land of Israel. It functions as a guidebook for bringing the Israelites to moral and intellectual perfection so that they can experience individual providence. Of course, its role does not cease with the settlement of the Israelites in their new homeland. It is assumed by Gersonides that the Torah also serves as a philosophical guidebook for the Jewish people throughout history so that they can continue to experience providence.[1] In order to gain a comprehensive understanding of Gersonides' conception of Jewish chosenness, we must therefore carefully examine his views on the Torah.

This topic is also important for our analysis of the covenant concept that has been our focus thus far. In the biblical text, the Torah itself is characterized as a covenant between God and the Israelites. Thus, if we are to construct a comprehensive picture of Gersonides' views on covenant, an examination of his conception of the Torah is imperative.[2]

THE PROPHECY OF MOSES

We will begin by looking at Gersonides' position on the prophecy of Moses. The Torah is, after all, the written record of Moses' prophetic revelation, and, therefore, its value for guiding the Israelites to perfection will be largely determined by the nature and quality of Moses' prophetic capabilities.

In an earlier discussion, we saw that for Gersonides the purpose of prophecy is defined almost exclusively in practical terms. It is one of the mechanisms of providence which allows the prophet to experience material well-being. By predicting the future, the prophet is able to avoid harm and achieve maximum benefit.[3]

A key question that must now be asked is whether prophecy also gives one access to philosophical knowledge not available to the ordinary philosopher. In his introduction to the *Wars*, Gersonides answers this question in the negative. The prophet does not acquire privileged philosophical information; he differs from the philosopher only in being able to predict the future:

> A prophet is necessarily a wise man. Thus, some of the things that are known by him are peculiar to him as a prophet, e.g., most of the things he predicts that will occur at a particular time; other things he knows simply because he is wise, i.e., the things that are known by him about the secrets of the world.[4]

Furthermore, Gersonides explains, the prophet must use the same philosophical methods the philosopher uses in order to arrive at truth. If the prophet were to receive his knowledge without the standard philosophical tools, he would not really have knowledge, but some inferior form of cognition.[5]

Gersonides admits that the prophet does tend to have a better grasp of theoretical truth than the ordinary philosopher; but this advantage has nothing to do with prophetic capability per se. The prophet is often a superior philosopher because prophecy is only conferred upon someone who has an excellent grasp of philosophical truth in the first place:

> The difference between a prophet and a wise man . . . lies merely in the [relative] ease with which the prophet obtains [his knowledge]. For the knowledge of the prophet is generally greater than the knowledge of a wise man who is not a prophet. . . . It is possible that there are things that a wise man who is not a prophet cannot apprehend, but which can be known by a wise man who is a prophet *insofar as he is wise*.[6]

Thus, prophecy is not a prerequisite for superior philosophical ability but is rather a consequence of it.[7]

If this were all that Gersonides had to say about prophecy as a source of philosophical knowledge, prophetic revelation and the scriptural record produced by it would offer no moral or theoretical guidance whatsoever. Prophecy would inform us only about future events. Gersonides, however, qualifies his position in several important ways. In the fourth chapter of the second book of the *Wars*, Gersonides devotes a separate discussion to the question of whether the prophet is capable of receiving knowledge of theoretical matters in a prophetic vision. After a series of deliberations, Gersonides concludes that theoretical knowledge can, in fact, be transmitted during prophecy, but only on rare occasions.

Now Gersonides initially poses the question without specific reference to Scripture. Yet it is clear as his discussion proceeds that the biblical text is a central concern here. In the course of his deliberations, Gersonides consistently refers to biblical sources, such as the celebrated first chapter in Ezekiel that according to the Maimonidean school contains important theoretical information; and it is primarily on the basis of this evidence that Gersonides concludes that prophecy can provide access to philosophical truths.

Gersonides goes on to pose another question: can the prophet receive theoretical knowledge without its causes, i.e., the demonstrations accompanying normal philosophical discourse? Gersonides reiterates his earlier position that without proper demonstration, the knowledge the prophet receives is not true knowledge. Gersonides therefore concludes that the prophet must receive the causes of such knowledge in his prophetic vision.

What about those passages in the Bible where there is no evidence that the theoretical knowledge was received with its causes? Visions concerning theoretical truths, such as the one experienced by Ezekiel, appear in the biblical text without any apparent philosophical proofs. Gersonides responds to this question by arguing that in such instances the causes must have occurred to the prophet while awake, presumably before the prophecy. Alternatively, the causes may be "obvious, too profound, or so numerous that their citation would be too lengthy."[8]

We should emphasize that what Gersonides is saying in this discussion does not contradict his position in the introduction to the *Wars* referred to earlier, but rather supplements it. The prophet still does not have access to philosophical truths that are unavailable to the ordinary philosopher. Prophecy merely provides him with a more convenient way of receiving those truths. At any rate, the important point for us is that Gersonides' observations here imply that the scriptural record produced by the prophets can serve as a valuable source for philosophical guidance—even if it is not an exclusive source.

There is one other crucial element in Gersonides' position regarding the role of the prophet as a purveyor of philosophical truth. In several passages in the *Wars* and in his biblical commentaries, he lists a number of features that distinguish the prophecy of Moses from that of all other prophets. The most important difference—and the one most relevant to our concerns—is that the focus of Moses' prophecy was not the prediction of the future but the acquisition of moral and theoretical knowledge. That is, while any prophet may occasionally receive philosophical knowledge in a prophetic vision, Moses' prophecy was unique in being *exclusively* occupied with this concern. It is for this reason that the Torah, as the record of Moses' prophetic communication, functions as the central source for guiding the Israelites to perfection in moral and intellectual matters.[9]

To sum up thus far, the entire Bible is a potential source for instruction on moral and theoretical truth. Since the prophet is capable of receiving philosophical knowledge as part of a prophetic vision, the biblical text will certainly contain this type of information. The Torah is distinguished from the rest of Scripture in having moral and theoretical truth as its sole focus because of the unique quality of Moses' prophecy.

There is a good deal more that needs to be said about Gersonides' views on Mosaic prophecy. Menachem Kellner is the only scholar, to my knowledge, who has appreciated the difficulties in Gersonides' handling of this question.[10] Kellner argues that Gersonides' position on Mosaic prophecy as presented in the *Wars* is significantly different from that which is found in his biblical commentaries. In the *Wars*, Gersonides depicts Mosaic prophecy as an entirely natural phenomenon that differed from that of other prophets only in degree. Thus far, Gersonides' position is in sharp contrast to that of Maimonides who saw Mosaic prophecy as qualitatively different from that of all other prophets.[11] Kellner then goes on to show that in his *Commentary on the Torah*, Gersonides contradicts his position in the *Wars* by emphatically asserting that no prophet of Moses' stature will ever arise again. In a crucial passage, Gersonides describes the prophecy of Moses as a miraculous phenomenon that cannot be duplicated. Thus, in the biblical commentaries Gersonides' position is very much in line with that of Maimonides. In evaluating these differing positions, Kellner concludes that Gersonides was inconsistent without being aware of it.

Kellner aptly draws out the implications of this whole question—implications that are highly relevant for our project. If Moses' prophetic capabilities were natural, there is no reason to rule out the possibility that another prophet of the same stature could arise. Furthermore, it is also theoretically possible that the new Moses could give a new Torah to guide and instruct another chosen people. As Kellner puts it, "to the extent that the election of Israel is grounded in the covenant at Sinai . . . it would seem that with the new Moses there could be a new chosen people."[12] With this position, the absolute uniqueness of the relationship between God and the Jewish people would therefore be threatened, at least from a theoretical standpoint. If Gersonides adopts the contrary view which sees Mosaic prophecy as a miraculous, non-repeatable phenomenon, the unique status of the Jewish people is assured for all time. It may be unlikely that Gersonides could have ever conceived of a new Moses who would lead another chosen people; still, the ambiguity of his position is troubling if we want a clear understanding of his views on the election of the Jewish people.

While Kellner's analysis is a valuable beginning, it can be shown that the problem is even more complex than he indicates. A reexamination of the sources to which Kellner refers and an analysis of some he does not consider, will demonstrate that the conflict is not just between positions taken in the *Wars* and those in the biblical commentaries; there are also important inconsistencies among passages within the commentaries themselves. In fact, three or four different approaches to Mosaic prophecy can be detected in Gersonides' writings.

We can begin by looking more closely at the position in the *Wars* to which Kellner refers. Gersonides discusses Mosaic prophecy in two brief passages in book two of that work. In his first reference to this issue, Gersonides identifies three features that distinguish Moses' prophecy from that of other prophets. First, Moses experienced prophecy awake while other prophets experienced prophecy asleep. Second, Moses felt no fear during his prophetic communications, a sensation normally accompanying prophecy. Finally, while other prophets experienced prophecy sporadically, Moses experienced it whenever he wished. These unique elements in Moses' prophetic experience are attributable to two causes. First, his intellectual faculty was completely perfect; and second, he was able to detach his intellect easily from the other cognitive faculties that normally interfere with prophetic communication.[13]

The important passage for us and the one to which Kellner pays special attention appears a little later in book two. There Gersonides reiterates that Moses was distinguished by a perfect intellect and by his ability to isolate this faculty from other cognitive functions. He then takes note of another feature which made Moses' prophetic capabilities unusual: his total preoccupation with human perfection. It was due to this characteristic that Moses' prophetic communications were exclusively concerned with perfection:

> Someone who is concerned only with human perfection will give information that concerns this perfection and the things that are conducive to its attainment insofar as they lead to this end. It would seem that in Moses (may he rest in peace) all these elements were conjoined: he was perfect in intellect, he could easily isolate [this faculty], and he devoted all his attention to human perfection only. Therefore, among all the prophets, his prophetic illumination was uniquely concerned with this perfection. In-

deed, the combined presence in one man of all three factors in the highest degree possible is extremely difficult; therefore, the Torah says: "Never again did there arise in Israel a prophet like Moses."[14]

Several important inferences can be drawn from this passage. First, implied here is a rationale for Moses' uniqueness among prophets as an instructor of intellectual perfection and giver of the Torah. Since Moses' mental energies were perpetually focused on human perfection, any prophetic communication he received was inevitably concerned with this issue. This conclusion is apparently based on Gersonides' principle that the prophet will tend to prophesy about those matters that preoccupy him at the moment of prophecy.[15]

The second point is Kellner's astute observation noted above that Gersonides leaves room for the possibility that another Moses may yet arise. Gersonides describes Mosaic prophecy as an entirely natural phenomenon consequent upon certain psychological prerequisites. There is therefore no reason that another Moses could not arise. Gersonides explicitly characterizes these psychological characteristics as "extremely difficult" to achieve—"difficult," as Kellner notes, but not impossible.[16]

In Gersonides' commentary on Numbers, we also find a passage that appears to view Moses' prophetic ability as a natural phenomenon. In this source, Gersonides for the most part reproduces his observations in the *Wars* with a number of variations that are not consequential. There is, however, one important difference that concerns Moses as giver of the Torah:

The second difference [between Moses and other prophets] is that I [i.e., God] speak to him "mouth to mouth"[17] without an intermediary, as it says[18] at the end of *ve-Zot ha-Berakhah* "[Never again did there arise in Israel a prophet like Moses] whom the LORD singled out face to face."[19] That is, there was no intermediary between them. He [i.e., God] said this because all prophets experience the influence of the imagination in the reception of prophecy; their cognitions are of particular matters, since there is no faculty for producing thoughts without the imagination, as we have explained in the second [book] of *The Wars of the Lord*.[20] However, the prophetic cognitions of Moses were universal cognitions and universal laws, as is the case with the commandments of the Torah and that which was reported in the account of creation. Thus, there was no prophet [who produced] a Torah [*navi' torah*][21] other than Moses.[22]

Here Gersonides gives a slightly different explanation for the emphasis on theoretical and moral guidance in Moses' prophecy. This time it is attributed to the absence of the influence of Moses' imaginative faculty in prophetic communication. Prophecy is achieved when the human intellect receives communications from the Active Intellect, which are then concretized in particular images provided by the imagination. It is for this reason that the prophet will tend to receive prophecies about events that concern himself or his loved ones; the general communications from the Active Intellect are embodied in those images that normally occupy the prophet's mind. What Gersonides appears to be arguing—albeit not very clearly—is that since Moses' prophecy was entirely unaffected by particular concerns of the imagination, he was the only prophet who experienced revelation with non-particular, universal meaning. He was therefore privileged to legislate universal norms for both theoretical and moral guidance.

This explanation appears to be in subtle contradiction to Gersonides' account in the *Wars*. In the *Wars*, what allowed Moses to provide guidance on moral and theoretical matters was that his mind was perpetually preoccupied with human perfection. According to the second explanation, it is the very *lack* of content in Moses' mind that enabled him to perform that function.

But despite the difference with the position in the *Wars*, this second account still sees Mosaic prophecy and the giving of the Torah as natural phenomena that can be explained entirely in psychological terms. Thus far the threat of a new Moses and a new Torah is still very much alive.

A cluster of passages in Gersonides' commentary on Deuteronomy takes an entirely different approach in an apparent attempt to respond to this threat. One such passage appears in Gersonides' commentary on Deuteronomy, where he explains why God rebuffs Moses' request to enter the Holy Land:

> . . . Moses did not achieve this exalted level of prophecy because of his greater natural disposition [*hakhanato ha-tiv'it*] to receive prophetic emanation. For if this were the case, God should not have responded to his request, "Enough! [Never speak to Me of this matter again],"[23] since he would certainly have added greater perfection to his prophetic capability according to this assumption[24] if he had entered the land of Israel, due to its special disposition for [helping one to achieve] prophecy. Thus, it is clear that Moses, our teacher, did not achieve this extraordinary level of prophecy because of his greater [natural] disposition [for prophecy] as compared to all other men. For this kind of disposition can be found in others, since this [disposition] is possible for this species [i.e., man], as explained in natural science. Furthermore, it will be explained in what follows, from the words of the holy Torah, that there is no prophet [who could produce] a Torah

[*navi' torah*] other than Moses, may he rest in peace. Therefore, it is clear that the remarkable level of Moses' prophecy, [which allowed] the divine Torah to be given by him, was [granted] from God by virtue of a miracle, in the same way that the event at Mount Sinai [occurred] by virtue of miracles.[25]

The first point to notice here is that Gersonides shows full awareness of the problem inherent in the naturalistic approach to Mosaic prophecy that is expressed in the *Wars* and in his commentary on Numbers. He says quite explicitly that if "natural disposition" alone were the issue, Moses would have no qualitative advantage over other prophets. What then distinguishes Moses' prophecy? Gersonides takes a new direction by claiming that the crucial distinction lies in the miraculous nature of Moses' prophetic capability, a divine gift that is not the product of Moses' own perfection. This miraculous quality also explains why God denied Moses' request to enter the land of Canaan. Since Moses had already achieved the highest possible level of prophecy through a miracle, there was nothing to be gained by allowing him to dwell in the land of Canaan.[26]

A key point that can easily be lost here is that Gersonides appears to equate the miraculous element of Mosaic prophecy quite specifically with the giving of the Torah. In summing up his thoughts in the passage just quoted, Gersonides explicitly says that "the remarkable level of Moses' prophecy, [*which allowed*] *the divine Torah to be given by him*, was [granted] from God by virtue of a miracle."

In the continuation of the passage, this point comes through even more forcefully:

> For this reason you should know that what we have said in the portion of Balak[27]—that there will arise a prophet in Israel and among the rest of the nations like Moses, i.e. the Messiah for whose arrival we hope—was not intended to mean that he would be a prophet [who could produce] a Torah [*navi' torah*]. This is not possible. Prophecy qua prophecy cannot produce a divine Law [*nimus toriyi*] unless by miracle, as was the case with Moses' prophecy. Rather, what this means is that he [i.e., the Messiah] will be like him [i.e., Moses] or greater than him with regard to all the things reported there; that is, miracles, signs and the other things that are connected to [the verse that] said: "Never again did there arise *in Israel* a prophet like Moses [italics added]"[28].

Gersonides claims that not only *can* another prophet with Moses' abilities arise; he certainly *will* arise in the person of the Messiah. The Messiah will have all the powers that Moses had and perhaps more. But Gersonides is emphatic to point out that the one thing the Messiah will not be able to do is produce another Torah. The promulgation of divine legislation can come about only by a miracle that Moses alone experienced. It is therefore clear that, for Gersonides, it is only the legislative function in Moses' prophecy that is miraculous and thus not reproducible.[29]

Another passage from the biblical commentaries upon which Kellner dwells extensively also focuses on the miraculous nature of Moses' legislative function:

> ... someone might ask: "Why is it not possible that there be another prophet, a prophet [who could produce] a Torah [navi' torah] of the likes of Moses? How could the Torah decree that no changes would ever be allowed in it, and that nothing would be added to it nor taken away from it? If this would be the case [i.e., if the Torah were mutable] his capability [i.e., that of Moses] to be a prophet [who could produce] a Torah would be for naught!" Here is the answer: There is no other who is equal to Moses in this matter. For this legislative prophecy of his [nevu'ato zot ha-toriyyit] functions like [all] miracles. No other prophet qua prophet has this ability, except by miracle. For God has made it clear that it is not His will either to produce another Torah, nor ever to add or detract permanently [from this present Torah]. ... [30]

Note that Gersonides reiterates that Moses' prophecy is miraculous and non-repeatable, and that he again equates its miraculous quality quite specifically with Moses' legislative function.

In these passages, Gersonides adopts an interpretation of Mosaic prophecy which clearly contrasts with the more naturalistic approach expressed in the first passages we examined. Gersonides now maintains that there is one factor in Moses' prophecy that cannot be accounted for by a natural explanation alone: Moses' legislative capabilities. With this alternative approach, the threat of a new Moses is nullified. While a new Moses may arise—and in fact one will when the Messiah arrives—he may be able to perform all the wondrous deeds that Moses performed, but he will never be able to produce a new Torah.

The major problem with this new position is that Gersonides says very little about the nature of the miracle that produces the Torah. Our earlier discussions of the Patriarchal covenant may provide important insight here. We should be reminded that what brings about the revelation of the Torah, according to Gersonides, is inherited providence, the force that furnishes the conditions for the Israelites to achieve intellectual perfection. Therefore it would appear that inherited providence is the source ultimately responsible for the miraculous quality of Moses' legislative capabilities. Viewed in this way, Moses acts as a sort of conduit for a miracle designed to benefit the entire Israelite nation. However, Gersonides never explicitly makes these connections.

What is most difficult to explain are Gersonides' repeated statements that the miraculous nature of Mosaic revelation precludes the possibility of another Torah being given. We have seen that miracles, like all providential events, occur when the proper conditions are met—that is, when an individual or group of individuals has achieved the requisite level of perfection.[31] Why then would the miraculous nature of Mosaic revelation rule out the possibility of another Torah being given? What would stop another nation worthy of providence from experiencing a similar miracle? While the likelihood of such an occurrence might be slim, it is hard to make sense of Gersonides' categorical denial that an event of this sort could ever be repeated.

There is still one other approach that can be detected in Gersonides' biblical commentaries regarding Mosaic prophecy. It is to be noted that in the passages offering a miraculous explanation for the uniqueness of Moses' prophetic capabilities, Gersonides also makes vague assertions that support for his position can be found in the biblical text. What we find is that in two other passages in his biblical commentaries, Gersonides relies exclusively on this approach by attempting to prove the uniqueness of Mosaic prophecy entirely on the basis of exegetical considerations. Let us refer, for example, to the following passage in Gersonides' commentary on Deuteronomy:

> . . . the Torah was not given to that generation [which received it at Mount Sinai] alone, but to all generations that are descended from them. For this reason, it said "It was not with our fathers that the LORD made this covenant" etc.;[32] it also said, "May they always be of such mind, to revere Me and follow all My commandments, that it may go well with them and their children forever";[33] it also said "so that you, your children and your children's children [may revere the LORD your God] and follow as long as you live, all His laws and commandments that I enjoin upon you. . . . "[34] All of this teaches that the Torah was given to the generations descended [from the Israelites] for all time. This is one of the fundamental principles of the Torah [pinnah mipinnot ha-torah]. It is also necessary by virtue of theoretical speculation ['iyyun], since it is not possible that a change of will be attributed to God as has already been explained. Moreover, the prophet has also stated, "For I am the LORD—I have not changed. . . . "[35]

Gersonides offers two reasons for his belief in the immutability of the Torah. One argument is philosophical: Gersonides claims that the Torah cannot change because divine will cannot change. Most of the passage, however, is occupied with exegetical evidence. Gersonides characterizes the Torah's immutability as one of the *pinnot ha-torah*, a fundamental principle of the Torah.

This terminology is highly significant. Elsewhere, I have argued that the *pinnot ha-torah* are principles central to Gersonides' thought. In brief, they are doctrines so basic to the world view of the Bible that they cannot be subverted by philosophical speculation under any circumstances. Doctrines such as prophecy, miracles, and providence are regarded as *pinnot ha-torah* by Gersonides, for without these conceptions the biblical text would be largely unintelligible.[36]

The immutability of the Torah appears to qualify as one of these principles on account of the assumption throughout the biblical text that the Torah and its laws are viable for all generations to come. In the above passage, Gersonides cites some of the biblical passages that clearly make this assumption.

In another passage, the identification of the immutability of the Torah as one of the *pinnot ha-torah* is justified on the basis of the contents of Deuteronomy 30. In this portion of the biblical text, Moses predicts God's punishment of the Israelites if they disobey Him and the reconciliation which will follow when they again follow His commandments. Gersonides interprets this future reconciliation as a reference to the messianic period and therefore concludes that the Torah's directives must be applicable for all time.[37]

Let us pause to review the variety of approaches Gersonides adopts towards Mosaic prophecy. Gersonides sometimes treats the prophecy of Moses as an entirely natural phenomenon. Implied in this approach is the possibility that another Moses will arise who could legislate another Torah. At other times, Gersonides singles out Moses' legislative capacity as the one aspect of his prophetic experience that cannot be reproduced. Gersonides argues this position in a number of ways. According to some passages, Moses' legislative capacity is distinguished from all his other talents by its miraculous quality—although Gersonides never clarifies why this renders Mosaic prophecy a non-repeatable phenomenon. In other places, he justifies the uniqueness of Moses' legislative capacity by hermeneutic means in designating the principle of the Torah's immutability as one of the *pinnot ha-torah*. Finally, in one passage, Gersonides suggests that an abrogation of the Torah is impossible because it would imply a change of divine will.

What explains this remarkable variation in Gersonides' views on Mosaic prophecy? The best answer to this question is probably the one that is the most obvious. What appears to be at the root of the problem is the central challenge of Gersonides' system of thought: the attempt to combine Aristotelian philosophical principles with the central doctrines of Judaism. Gersonides seems to realize full well that the uniqueness of Judaism and the Jewish people is highly dependent on the uniqueness of Mosaic prophecy. But since his philosophical principles lead him to view prophecy as a natural phenomenon, it is not easy for him to find justification for Moses' special status. What we therefore see in the sources we have examined is a good deal of uncertainty as Gersonides struggles to formulate a position on this matter.

We should also note that all of the sources arguing that Mosaic legislation is a non-repeatable phenomenon are contained in Gersonides' commentary on Deuteronomy. That commentary is the latest of all the sources we examined. It is therefore possible that Gersonides' views on Mosaic prophecy evolved in the course of his writings. The passages in the *Wars* and in his commentary on Numbers that treat Mosaic prophecy as a natural phenomenon may represent an earlier view that was later superseded in the commentary on Deuteronomy. This change was perhaps due a growing awareness on Gersonides' part that the uniqueness of Judaism could not be safeguarded without a stronger position on the special nature of Mosaic prophecy.

To sum up our discussion thus far, Gersonides holds the position that the sole function of the prophet is to predict the future. However, there are important qualifications to this position that give the prophet—and, consequently, the scriptural record he produces—a significant role in providing guidance on philosophical matters as well. For one, the prophet can on rare occasions receive prophecies pertaining to philosophical truths. Second, the prophecy of Moses is unique in being exclusively concerned with moral and theoretical truths. The Torah is therefore ideally suited to offer guidance for the achievement of human perfection.

A major point of ambiguity is the exact nature of the Torah's uniqueness. Granted that no Torah has ever been reproduced since Moses, is it possible that another prophet of Moses' capabilities will ever be able to legislate a new Torah? While in some sources Gersonides leaves open this possibility, in others he is determined to prove that Mosaic legislation is a non-repeatable phenomenon.

THE PHILOSOPHICAL CONTENT OF THE TORAH

Now that we have an understanding of Gersonides' views on how the Torah came into being, we are ready to examine in greater detail the role that the Torah serves. What kind of philosophical guidance does the Torah offer? How does it impart such guidance?

Let us first get a clearer picture of the purpose of the Torah's instruction. So far we have focused on the material rewards consequent upon observing the Torah's directives. The Torah is the most important in a series of factors—produced by providence inherited from Abraham—which enables the Israelites to experience divine providence of their own and inherit the land of Canaan. Once the Israelites settle in the land of Canaan, the Torah continues to confer material providential reward through its philosophical instruction.

Yet Gersonides makes it clear in a number of passages in his biblical commentaries that material reward is only one benefit that the Torah provides for the Israelites—and not necessarily the most important one. The Torah, by guiding the Israelites to intellectual perfection, also allows them to experience the highest manifestation of individual providence: immortality. This second function is alluded to in Gersonides' opening remarks to his *Commentary on the Torah* in which he describes the Torah as a set of directives that "thoroughly guides those who observe it to true felicity [*hazlahah 'amitit*]."38

Perhaps the most comprehensive statement linking the observance of the Torah to immortality is Gersonides' explication of a celebrated passage in Deuteronomy in which Moses challenges the Israelites to choose the path of obedience to God:

> See, I set before you this day life and prosperity, death and adversity. . . . Choose life—if you and your offspring would live—by loving the LORD your God, heeding His commands and holding fast to Him.39

For Gersonides, the opposition between "life" and "death" in this passage refers to spiritual reward and punishment—that is, immortality and the loss thereof; the contrast between "prosperity" and "adversity" refers to material reward and punishment:

> "Life" refers to the spiritual life [*hayyey ha-nefesh*], for this is true life; "prosperity" refers to material happiness because it also results from the observance of the Torah, as [explained] earlier.40

Furthermore, by instructing the Israelites to "choose life," Moses is emphasizing that the spiritual reward consequent upon observing the Torah's directives is "the essential telos" (*ha-takhlit ha-'azmi*) of the commandments. The Israelites are to perform the commandments for the purpose of achieving the spiritual reward of immortality, not for the sake of material gain.41

In the same passage, Gersonides explains that the two types of rewards are ultimately linked. By experiencing material prosperity, one is
more readily able to devote one's energies to achieving immortality:

These [material] rewards which also result from the observance
of the Torah guide [one] to achieving that life [i.e., immortality];
for it is not possible for one who lacks bread and clothing [to
achieve] complete concentration on speculative matters.[42]

The key discussion regarding the nature of the philosophical material
contained in the Torah is found in Gersonides' introduction to the *Commentary on the Torah*. There Gersonides divides the material of the Torah
into three categories. In the first category are the commandments which,
according to the Maimonidean model adopted by Gersonides, are intended to train us in moral and intellectual perfection. The second and
third categories apply to the narrative material in the Torah and follow a
division similar to that of the commandments. In the second category are
the teachings of "political science" (*ḥokhmah medinit*), including all matters
pertaining to ethical and political philosophy, which emerge from the stories of the Patriarchs and the history of the Israelites. In the third category
is instruction about the "science of existents" (*ḥokhmat ha-nimẓa'ot*)—i.e.,
natural science and metaphysics—which is also inferred from the narrative material in the Torah.[43]

This tripartite classification is rigorously applied throughout the *Commentary on the Torah*. The *to'aliyyot* at the end of each section of the commentary report in great detail what Gersonides has gleaned from the
biblical text in each of the three categories. This division of material is also
applied in most of Gersonides' commentaries on other books of the Bible.[44]

It should be emphasized that, for Gersonides' view, nothing less than
the entire content of the Torah is relevant for philosophical guidance. Even
a cursory analysis of his *Commentary on the Torah* will show the extent to
which Gersonides is intent on reading the Torah as a philosophical work.
No passage in the Torah escapes Gersonides' determined effort to wring
out as many philosophical lessons as he can. The *to'aliyyot* are often daunt-
ing to the reader, as Gersonides searches every corner of the biblical narrative for some philosophical lesson.[45]

Gersonides' determination to find philosophical meaning in every
passage of the Torah is particularly striking in his interpretation of the historical portions of the biblical text. The actions of the Patriarchs, Moses and
the Children of Israel are consistently reduced to a series of *to'aliyyot*. Gersonides will often glean philosophical lessons even from those passages in
which historical data appear to serve no obvious pedagogical end. Thus,
for example, Gersonides finds philosophical meaning in the genealogies of

generations between Adam and Noah and the list of Ishmael's descendants reported in Genesis. According to Gersonides, these lists are designed to resolve suspicions in the mind of the reader regarding the validity of the account of creation at the beginning of Genesis. One might doubt the truth of the creation story by reasoning that mankind could not have possibly experienced such great technological progress in the short span of time since creation. The Torah therefore gives a deliberately detailed account of how human culture developed in order to preempt this type of challenge.[46]

One should not conclude that Gersonides was uninterested in the Torah as history. In fact, one of the most frequent comments made by Gersonides about the narrative portions of the Torah is that the biblical text deliberately reports events in painstaking detail in order to add credence to their historicity.[47] However, it would appear that Gersonides consistently wants to prove the authenticity of the historical material in the Torah in order that the reader more readily adopt the philosophical lessons embodied in it. In the example cited above, for instance, the events in Genesis are historically accurate, but are reported in a specific manner in order to authenticate the creation story and the philosophical doctrines it contains. Thus, for Gersonides the Torah is history; but the historical record achieves its true meaning as *prophetic revelation* only through the teachings in the three categories which provide philosophical guidance.

Let us now take a closer look at each of these categories. We will begin with the divine commandments which make up the first category. As noted already, Gersonides follows Maimonides in dividing the commandments into those which provide moral instruction and those which are concerned with correct intellectual belief.[48] Gersonides' analysis of the commandments, however, is not a mere imitation of that provided by Maimonides. First, Gersonides' explanations of the commandments are often more detailed and are frequently based on a wider range of scientific data than that which Maimonides uses. Thus, for example, in his explanation of laws regarding animals forbidden for consumption, Gersonides applies principles in Aristotelian natural science and zoology in a manner far more thorough than Maimonides.[49] Gersonides also draws frequently from his expert knowledge of astronomy and astrology to explain the commandments. In his discussion of the Sabbath, for instance, one reason Gersonides offers to explain why the Sabbath is a day of rest is that the seventh day is under the influence of Saturn, which is potentially harmful. It is therefore advisable to refrain from work on that day.[50]

Gersonides also tries to answer the criticisms Maimonides and his followers received in response to the attempt to rationalize the commandments. A central point of conflict was Maimonides' effort to explain some of the commandments as reactions to idolatrous practices in the period in which the Torah was given. Many of the so-called *hukkim* were explained this way. Thus, the injunction against wearing wool and linen in the same garment, for example, was seen by Maimonides as negating the practices of idolatrous priests who wore these materials as part of their ritual.[51] Critics charged that such explanations relegated the commandments to the status of historical relics with no contemporary value.

Gersonides responds to this problem by consistently supplementing Maimonides' historical explanations with other philosophical reasons that are of more contemporary significance. In the case of the prohibition against wearing wool and linen together, for example, Gersonides reiterates Maimonides' historical explanation but then adds that the separation of wool and linen teaches another important philosophical lesson. By refraining from mixing vegetable and animal products in the same garment, we are taught to differentiate between the vegetative form and the animal form.[52]

This type of allegorical explanation is common in Gersonides' commentaries. Frequently he will interpret the commandments as directives that instruct one in the distinction between the various types of forms and their hierarchical arrangement. There are, according to Gersonides, seven basic levels of forms. Furthermore, Gersonides often emphasizes that since the highest of the forms is God, an appreciation of the hierarchy of forms is important for ensuring our belief in His existence.[53] Gersonides considers the Tabernacle to be of particular significance with regard to these matters. In a lengthy exposition in his commentary on Exodus 25-7, Gersonides interprets the details in the structure of the Tabernacle as a comprehensive and highly organized series of allegories for the various types of forms.[54]

Yet, for Gersonides even this type of explanation for the commandments emerges from a specific historical context. According to Gersonides, idolatry is not the only corrupting influence that the Torah had to combat in the time of Moses. Gersonides claims that the Torah also had to contend with the teachings of pre-Socratic materialism described in the opening chapters of book A of Aristotle's *Metaphysics*. This school, according to a curious anachronism on Gersonides' part, was the reigning philosophical school at the time of the giving of the Torah, and its major doctrine was that all existence and change could be accounted for by the material cause. The philosophical lessons relayed by the commandments in allegorical form were meant quite specifically to overcome this incorrect view and to teach the Israelites that existence and change could be explained only by acknowledging efficient, final, and formal causation—in addition to the material cause.[55]

Gersonides will often make sense of the commandments with the help of this theory. The Tabernacle in particular is seen by Gersonides as playing a vital role in combating materialist thinking. The structural details of the Tabernacle provide comprehensive instruction by means of allegory that is meant to teach the Israelites about the three causes that the materialists did not recognize.[56]

Frequently Gersonides will also explain the philosophical instruction provided by the narrative portions in the biblical text against the background of his theory. For instance, one of the reasons Gersonides offers for the appearance of the creation story at the beginning of the Torah is that the Israelites were in a state of deep ignorance regarding efficient and formal causation because of materialist influences. The creation story was therefore presented in the opening chapters of the biblical text in order to remedy these problems with a concentrated course in natural science and metaphysics.[57]

But it is important to note that despite his use of historical context as an explanation for the commandments, Gersonides still manages to avoid the problems inherent in Maimonides' approach. Maimonides undercut the contemporary significance of the commandments by explaining them in relation to the idolatrous practices in the time of Moses. Gersonides' supplementary theory does not invite the same criticism. For sure, the Torah's instruction is designed to combat specific philosophical schools in the time of Moses and must therefore be understood in historical context. However, in the course of battling an outdated materialism, the Torah nonetheless offers guidance on all the basic philosophical issues in natural science and metaphysics that Gersonides saw as highly relevant in his own time. Thus, Gersonides succeeds in providing a historical explanation for the Torah's directives without canceling out their contemporary value.

Gersonides also attempts to provide a corrective to Maimonides' controversial views on the sacrifices and the Temple cult. For Maimonides, the sacrifices were originally idolatrous practices that were sublimated for the purposes of divine worship, a position that invited particular scorn and criticism from the anti-Maimonidean camp.[58] Gersonides supports Maimonides' interpretation but does not see in his approach a sufficient explanation for the sacrifices. In a passage in his commentary on Genesis, Gersonides argues that Maimonides' explanation does not account for the fact that biblical figures, such as Noah and the Patriarchs, performed sacrifices well before the advent of the Israelites.[59]

Gersonides therefore concludes that sacrifices, both before and after the establishment of the Temple cult, had another purpose: they helped one achieve prophecy. The sacrificial ritual accomplished this purpose by strengthening the intellect of the person performing the ritual while at the same time weakening the other powers of his soul. The division of the animal in preparation for the sacrifice empowered the intellect by causing one to contemplate the order in the natural world. The sight of the animal being consumed by fire caused the powers of the sentient soul to be weakened by vividly illustrating the corruptibility of all matter. In this way, Gersonides tries to invest the sacrifices with a more positive function than Maimonides.[60]

In passages in his commentary on Leviticus, Gersonides supplements Maimonides' position on the sacrifices with a different approach. There he argues that Maimonides' explanation does not account for the remarkable detail of the sacrificial rituals. If God's purpose was simply to channel idolatrous practices towards divine worship, we would have received only general instruction to perform sacrifices in service to God. Gersonides reasons that the sacrifices in all their detail must therefore be designed to teach valuable philosophical lessons.[61] In a lengthy section, Gersonides argues that the sacrifices in Leviticus, like many of the commandments, teach us about the primacy of form over matter.[62] A similar approach is taken with regard to the Levitical laws of purity and impurity. These laws are also designed to instruct us about the importance of the formal cause.[63]

Gersonides is also sensitive to the overall problem of rationalization as a means for circumventing the commandments, another difficulty that dogged the Maimonidean camp. Gersonides appears to have this issue in mind in his introduction to the *Commentary on the Torah,* when he insists that the reasons for the commandments are never entirely known. Gersonides claims that we can come up with only probable, not certain, reasons for them.[64] The implication here is that one can never assume that by knowing the reason for a particular commandment one can then find another means to accomplish the same goal.

In a number of passages in the commentary on Deuteronomy, Gersonides makes this logic explicit. According to Gersonides, the danger of circumventing the commandments is the substance of God's cryptic statement in Deuteronomy 29:28, "Concealed acts concern the LORD; but with overt acts, it is for us and our children ever to apply all the provisions of this Teaching." Gersonides' interpretation of this verse is summarized in one of his *to'aliyyot:*

> The fifth *to'elet* which is one of the most important of the fundamental principles of the Torah [*pinnot ha-torah*] is that God did not command us to obey the words of the Torah just with regard to that which is overt in them. This we are commanded to do for all generations to come. For that which is concealed in the words of the Torah—that is, the underlying meanings towards which the

Torah intended the commandments to guide [us]—is something which cannot be known completely except by God alone. This [point] is what safeguards men from transgressing some of the commandments[65]—[i.e.,] by thinking that they have understood the reason that the Torah intended this [particular] commandment and that therefore one need not observe this particular commandment. [The Torah] therefore erected with this [principle] a fortified wall to protect the Torah so that one will not say that its words are [to be observed] according to that which is concealed and not according to that which is overt.[66]

Let us now move on to the second and third categories in Gersonides' scheme that concern the narrative portions of the biblical text. Gersonides sees this material as providing instruction in the same two areas that the commandments address. The narrative portions, however, do not offer a mere repetition of the philosophical lessons taught by the commandments. The teachings of the second category which concern ethical and political philosophy are seen by Gersonides as a "completion" (shelemut) of the moral commandments. The third category which concerns instruction in natural science and metaphysics is similarly a "completion" of the commandments that regulate our beliefs.[67]

What Gersonides means here is clarified in his commentary on Deuteronomy. While explicating the first lines of Moses' poem at the beginning of Deuteronomy 32, Gersonides explains that the commandments provide only general guidance in moral and theoretical truth, and that the narrative portions of the Torah are necessary for filling in the missing details in both areas. It is in this sense that the second and third categories are a "completion" for the commandments.[68]

The second and third categories are not only more comprehensive than the commandments, but as Gersonides also explains in his introduction to the Commentary on the Torah, the material in these categories relays its instruction in a pedagogical manner superior to that of the commandments. For one, the commandments do not require one to understand the lessons that they teach but only to perform prescribed actions. With the teachings contained in the narrative portions of the biblical text, one must actually comprehend the philosophical instruction for this material to be of any value. Furthermore, the lessons taught by the commandments are related "indirectly" (be-shenit) through "parable" and "imitation" (ḥikuy, mashal), while the biblical narrative is more "direct" in its teachings.[69]

Gersonides provides an additional reason to explain why the narrative portions of the Torah must provide instruction in ethical and political philosophy beyond that which is offered by the commandments. If the

Torah were to provide full legislation in this area, the laws would be so numerous and cumbersome that most people would not be able to observe them. Therefore, the Torah relays most of its ethical teachings through stories from which moral lessons can be inferred.[70]

The third category of material, which includes knowledge about natural science and metaphysics, is considered by Gersonides to be the most important one. The whole purpose of the Torah is to guide one towards intellectual perfection, a goal more directly addressed by this third category than the other two. Gersonides admits that knowledge in the areas of natural science and metaphysics can be attained through conventional philosophical speculation. However, since this knowledge can be achieved only with great difficulty, the Torah is often of great assistance to us in these areas.[71]

It is important to point out that this third category is the only one in which Gersonides envisions an interaction between the biblical text and pure philosophical speculation. The first two categories do not lend themselves to philosophical demonstration. As noted above, Gersonides believes that philosophical enquiry can never provide adequate explanation for the commandments and the purpose they serve; one can find only probable reasons for them.[72] Gersonides takes a similar position with regard to ethics and political philosophy. These are disciplines in which there can be no demonstrative certainty, a view that has its roots in Aristotle and Maimonides.[73] The Torah is therefore the sole and sufficient source for providing norms in these areas.[74]

These observations help explain why Gersonides does not discuss the commandments or ethics in the *Wars*. They have no place in a treatise explicitly concerned with philosophical demonstration.[75] Gersonides therefore reserves his discussion of the commandments and ethics for the biblical commentaries, since it is only through revelation that one acquires certainty in these areas.[76]

It is important that we say something about the manner in which the Torah provides assistance for philosophical speculation in the areas of natural science and metaphysics. Since this issue touches on large areas of Gersonides' thought, we must be content with mapping out only general principles. The central programmatic statement on the relationship between philosophy and Scripture is contained in Gersonides' introduction to the *Wars*. Gersonides adopts the approach of Maimonides, according to which the biblical text must be interpreted to conform to truths discovered independently by reason:

> ... if reason causes us to affirm doctrines that are incompatible with the literal sense of Scripture, we are not prohibited by the Torah to pronounce the truth on these matters, for reason is not incompatible with the true understanding of the Torah.[77]

Like Maimonides, Gersonides declares his willingness to interpret the Torah to affirm the eternity of the universe, if reason were to require us to believe in that doctrine.[78]

With each of the issues discussed in the *Wars*, Gersonides therefore adopts the method of first conducting a thorough philosophical investigation and then showing how his conclusions are confirmed in the Torah.[79] Yet Gersonides emphasizes in a number of passages that the Torah does not serve an exclusively passive role in philosophical enquiry. With respect to some philosophical problems—especially the difficult ones—the Torah itself directs the philosopher towards the truth. The Torah becomes part of the philosophical investigation by furnishing valuable clues to solve philosophy's most difficult problems.[80] In his discussion of creation in book six of the *Wars*, for example, Gersonides includes a lengthy exegesis of the biblical account of creation, which he claims was instrumental in guiding him towards his theory.[81] Even more noteworthy is his analysis of miracles at the very end of the treatise, which is based entirely on data provided in biblical sources.[82]

This function is not the only active role that Scripture plays. As we have already seen, Gersonides throughout his philosophical and exegetical writings also alludes to *pinnot ha-torah*, or "fundamental principles of the Torah," which are doctrines derived from Scripture that play an important role in philosophical discourse. These principles define the direction and the limits of philosophical enquiry by specifying those concepts basic to the intelligibility of Scripture.[83]

The relationship between philosophical enquiry in natural science and metaphysics, on the one hand, and Scripture, on the other, is therefore one of interdependence. The biblical text must be interpreted to conform to demonstrative truth. However, Scripture is itself an important factor at all stages of philosophical enquiry. It provides crucial hints and clues that serve as data in the initial stages of the enquiry. It also guides the whole direction of the enquiry by specifying a series of irrefutable principles derived from biblical sources.[84]

To summarize, we now have a comprehensive picture of Gersonides' conception of the Torah as philosophical guidebook. The Torah provides guidance in all areas of moral and theoretical knowledge in order to help the Israelites achieve perfection. The most immediate result of this perfection is individual providence that allows for material reward. But this is not the only reward the observance of the Torah brings; by assisting in the perfection of the intellect, the Torah also facilitates the achievement of immortality.

There are three categories of material in the Torah that help in the quest for perfection: the commandments, the narrative material dealing with political and ethical philosophy, and the narrative material concerned with natural science and metaphysics. The two categories of narrative material provide instruction similar to that offered by the commandments, but in greater detail and in more direct fashion. The knowledge provided by the Torah in the third category is unique in that it can be discovered by independent philosophical speculation. Still, the Torah provides valuable assistance to the philosopher even in this area by furnishing valuable data as a basis for philosophical reasoning and for conveying fundamental biblical principles that guide the direction of philosophical enquiry.

In many respects the Torah's philosophical lessons are best understood in historical context. Gersonides endorses Maimonides' theory that the Torah's teachings can often be explained against the backdrop of the idolatrous practices of the period in which the Torah was given. However, Gersonides is aware of the problems inherent in this approach and therefore proposes another historical theory to supplement that of Maimonides. Many of the Torah's directives, Gersonides argues, have to be understood as a response to the philosophy of materialism prevalent at the time of the giving of the Torah. In order to combat this school of thought, the Torah provided instruction on all issues in natural science and metaphysics. With this theory, Gersonides accounts for the content of the Torah in historical terms while at the same time investing it with greater philosophical sophistication and contemporary significance than Maimonides does.

THE TORAH AS COVENANT

We are now in a position to evaluate Gersonides' conception of the Torah as covenant. It should first be noted that Gersonides is almost entirely reticent on this issue throughout his biblical commentaries. Even in his remarks on the revelation at Mount Sinai in his commentary on Exodus 19, Gersonides does not say much about this covenant from a philosophical standpoint.

Gersonides' reticence may seem surprising given that he provides important philosophical information on the covenant with Abraham when the biblical text affords him the opportunity. Yet, it does not require much reflection to surmise why the Sinai covenant is not the subject of much discussion. This covenant fits much more neatly into Gersonides' philosophical system than the covenant with Abraham, and, therefore, Gersonides seems to have assumed that the philosophical meaning of this covenant would be transparent to his reader.

Our point here can best be understood by referring back to an earlier discussion where we took note of two major problems that the Patriarchal covenant raised for Gersonides. One difficulty was that Gersonides' impersonal God could not participate in such an agreement—at least not in any literal sense. Even more problematic was the unconditional nature of the covenant with Abraham. Not only was God involved in what appeared to be a personal agreement with Abraham, but this agreement was also depicted as a unilateral arrangement in which God seemed to be the only active member.

We need not review Gersonides' response to these problems. The important point is that the Sinai covenant presents far less of a challenge to Gersonides, because with this covenant the second problem does not arise. Unlike the covenant with Abraham, the covenant at Sinai is clearly conditional, in that God promises reward to the Israelites provided that they observe His commandments. A covenant of this kind can be easily translated into philosophical terms, given the conditional nature of providential reward. In Gersonides' philosophical system, individual providence is dependent upon moral and intellectual perfection. The Sinai covenant can therefore be understood as follows: If the Israelites are obedient to the Torah's directives, they will achieve perfection and experience providential reward; if they are disobedient, they will not experience providence and will be subject to the punishment of harmful chance events.

The fact that the biblical text depicts this covenant as a personal agreement between God and the Israelites presents no great difficulty. We have demonstrated in earlier chapters that for Gersonides all divine actions appearing to come from a personal God are really the product of impersonal laws. Thus, at Mount Sinai the Israelites essentially forge a covenant with impersonal providential laws, not with a personal God.

This interpretation underlies all of Gersonides' references to the Sinai covenant in his biblical commentaries. For instance, let us look at Gersonides' explication of Exodus 19:5, the verse in which God introduces the Sinai covenant just before Moses receives the first set of tablets: "Now then, if you obey Me faithfully and keep My covenant, you shall be My treasured possession among all peoples. Indeed, all the earth is Mine." In Gersonides' reading, this statement is rendered as follows:

NOW THEN, IF YOU OBEY ME FAITHFULLY in that you observe My commandments and KEEP MY COVENANT which I am sealing with you to be My people and to observe all the words of the Torah . . . YOU SHALL BE MY TREASURED POSSESSION AMONG ALL THE PEOPLES in that [I will] protect you and exercise providence over you. For INDEED ALL THE EARTH IS MINE to do as I please with it, and for this reason, I will be able to preserve you by virtue of your having the advantage of My providence.[85]

Here Gersonides clearly equates the covenant at Sinai with the stipulation that if the Israelites observe the commandments, they will experience providential reward.

It is here that we might mention the covenant of circumcision in Genesis 17. Like the Sinai covenant, circumcision is also cast by the biblical text in conditional terms; if Abraham's descendants observe the circumcision ritual, they will be rewarded by God.[86] It is therefore no surprise that Gersonides interprets this covenant in much the same way that he does the Sinai covenant. In fact, Gersonides simply treats circumcision as he does all other commandments; it helps one achieve perfection, which in turn makes one worthy of divine providence. According to Gersonides, this particular ritual is designed to help bring perfection in the moral realm by weakening the male sexual organ and quelling sexual desire.[87]

The one peculiarity that Gersonides must explain is that the commandment of circumcision antedates the other directives given at Mount Sinai. Gersonides accounts for this anomaly by arguing that this commandment had to be given early because of the sexual promiscuity of the Canaanites around whom Abraham and the other Patriarchs lived. Circumcision was meant to protect Abraham and his offspring from being influenced by this culture by weakening the male sexual impulse.[88]

In order to tie our entire discussion together, let us conclude with some observations about the relationship between the covenant at Sinai and the Patriarchal covenant. It is important not to lose sight of the fact that Gersonides sees the Sinai covenant as a secondary expression of the Patriarchal covenant. What this means in philosophical terms is that providence inherited from Abraham is responsible for the revelation of the Torah, which in turn provides the Israelites with the means to earn providential reward and inherit the land of Canaan.

Our discussion in this chapter adds significant complications to his picture. For one, because of Gersonides' uncertainties about Mosaic prophecy, the exact connection between the two covenants is not entirely clear. If the source of the Sinai covenant is in fact the Patriarchal covenant, it would follow that Moses is a channel through which inherited providence expresses itself in providing the Israelites with the Torah. But given that Gersonides adopts a variety of approaches towards Mosaic prophecy, it is difficult to come up with precise determinations about the relationship of Moses' revelation to providence inherited from Abraham.

What has also emerged from our discussion is that while the initial purpose of the Torah is the fulfillment of the terms of the covenant with Abraham, it would seem that the Torah in some respects transcends that purpose. The Torah provides the Israelites with the opportunity to earn material and spiritual reward quite independent of their concern for inheriting the land of Canaan. Certainly, there is no question in Gersonides' mind that the Israelites will continue to observe the Torah's directives even after they enter the land of Canaan.

Our conclusions here set the stage for a discussion of Gersonides' views on the concept of covenant once the Israelites are settled in their new homeland. But before we look at the post-conquest phase of Jewish history, we must turn our attention in the next chapter to one more important issue regarding the Torah as philosophical guidebook.

SIX

The Torah and Esoteric Discourse

One question we did not raise in the preceding discussion and which we will now take up is Gersonides' attitude toward esoteric discourse. As is well known, Maimonides' view was that Scripture deliberately conceals its most important philosophical teachings from the uneducated masses and that it is only the philosophically trained elite who can properly discern these teachings. Does Gersonides in any way adopt this esoteric approach toward the reading of Scripture? Does he also believe that the Bible addresses different audiences at their respective levels of philosophical understanding?

While this issue in some respects leads us away from the central concerns of our project, a discussion of Gersonides' attitude towards esotericism is valuable to us for two reasons. First, it will complete our discussion in the last chapter by sharpening our understanding of Gersonides' views on the Torah as a philosophical guidebook. We saw that for Gersonides the Torah is a versatile resource, in that it provides philosophical instruction for the Israelites in the time of Moses while also meeting the pedagogical needs of subsequent generations. The question now is whether the Torah also has the versatility to speak at the same time to audiences with varying levels of philosophical training.

Even more important, an investigation of Gersonides' attitude towards esoteric discourse in Scripture inevitably leads us to a larger question regarding Gersonides himself. For Maimonides, the need to hide philosophical truth was by no means limited to the Bible. Maimonides' own major work, *The Guide of the Perplexed*, was deliberately composed in the same esoteric style that he imputed to the biblical text. Thus, our analysis has implications for understanding Gersonides' own writings. If there is any evidence that Gersonides favors esotericism in his interpretation of Scripture, we must ask what impact this factor has on our interpretation of his own work.

This question is especially important for our study, given our emphasis on Gersonides' biblical commentaries. There is an understandable temptation to see these writings as nothing more than popular, exoteric works that do not represent Gersonides' true philosophical views. Indeed, as we mentioned in our introduction, Julius Guttmann adheres to this position, although he offers no evidence to support his claim.[1]

We certainly have not taken this approach in our study thus far. Yet, if there is merit to be found in Guttmann's suggestion, our analysis of Gersonides' biblical commentaries would be seriously affected. The issue of esotericism, therefore, deserves careful study if we are to have an accurate understanding of the role the biblical commentaries play in the development of his philosophical thinking.

No scholar has fully engaged the question of esotericism in Gersonides' thought. The prevailing assumption seems to have been—with the exception of Guttmann's position—that Gersonides was opposed to esoteric discourse, and, therefore, not much more need be said about this issue.[2] Indeed, observations from our last chapter appear to confirm this conclusion. It is highly significant that, according to Gersonides' interpretation, Moses taught the uneducated Israelites the entire range of philosophical doctrines in natural science and metaphysics after their exodus from Egypt. We saw that for Gersonides the creation story and the construction of the Tabernacle were central components in Moses' pedagogical program for providing the Israelites with comprehensive instruction on all the major issues in these areas of knowledge.[3]

This depiction is in striking contrast to that of Maimonides. As a staunch exponent of esotericism, Maimonides did not believe the Israelites in Moses' time to be capable of the philosophical sophistication that Gersonides attributes to them. Maimonides' attitude is best reflected in his interpretation of the sacrifices that we looked at in the last chapter. Since the Israelites could not comprehend sophisticated philosophical speculation, they had to be brought to an awareness of God through the transformation of idolatrous practices to which they had been accustomed. Certainly, Maimonides would never have conceived of Moses explaining the entire doctrine of creation to the Israelites. Maimonides consistently underscores the esoteric nature of this doctrine that must be revealed to the elite only by way of hints and riddles.[4]

Yet, a careful examination of Gersonides' writings will reveal that his position on esotericism is more complex than has been appreciated. Any assumption that Gersonides rejects esotericism out of hand is immediately dispelled by an important passage in the introduction to his *Commentary on the Song of Songs*. There Gersonides clearly incorporates Maimonides' esoteric approach towards Scripture by claiming that the Torah addresses the elite and the masses in accordance with their respective levels of philosophical training.

Gersonides' remarks are part of a discussion in which he emphasizes the need for prophetic revelation to assist man in his discovery of philosophical truth and pursuit of perfection. He claims that the Torah is the portion of Scripture most suited for this function because of its capacity to address a diverse audience. It communicates philosophical truth to the masses and to the philosophically trained elite according to their respective capacities and thus assists all people in achieving perfection.[5]

Gersonides does not elaborate in any great detail on how the Torah communicates on these two levels. A full exposition of this subject, he claims, would carry him far afield. He therefore provides a single example to illustrate his point. Gersonides argues that the Torah, for instance, gives different messages to different audiences regarding the purpose of the commandments. For the elite, the Torah makes known that the true aim of the commandments is to prepare one for conjunction with God. The masses, however, cannot appreciate this benefit due to their lack of philosophical training. Therefore, in many places, the Torah also promises material reward for the observance of the commandments. Even if this is not the true aim of the commandments, it is one to which the masses can more easily relate. Gersonides concludes that if the Torah trains the masses to follow the commandments for material gain, there is the hope that they will eventually come to learn that the true reward for adhering to the commandments is conjunction with God.

Gersonides' thoughts are summarized in the following passage:

It [i.e., the Torah] hinted at this end and commanded it—it being cleaving to God—and referred to many of the wonderful speculative matters in some of the narratives and commandments, and in describing the sanctuary and its implements, as if guiding the elite to [the realization that] the rest of the commandments are for this end. However, it said for the multitudes, concerning many of the commandments, that they who observe them will thereby achieve length of days and many [other] fanciful felicities, and the opposite concerning those who do not observe them, even though the Torah commandments are not for this purpose. This is so since the multitudes cannot picture the purpose of the Torah commandments, since a man will not desire to perform some action if he cannot picture some advantage for himself; thus, the Torah guided [the multitudes] to fulfill these commandments first for this purpose, and through performing this worship first not for its own sake they will be guided to doing it afterwards for its own sake.[6]

Gersonides concludes this passage with remarks about other books of the Bible. Some books in the biblical text address either the masses or the elite, while others, such as the Torah and the Book of Proverbs, speak on both levels simultaneously. The Song of Songs is unique in that it addresses only the elite with philosophical truths not beneficial to the masses.[7]

One would have expected that this issue would crop up frequently in Gersonides' exegetical writings in the course of his exposition of the biblical text. In fact, there are only a few instances in which Gersonides explicitly makes reference to a dual message provided by Scripture. One example is his interpretation of the celebrated passage in Deuteronomy 6:4, "Hear, O Israel! The LORD is our God, the LORD is one." Gersonides sees in this imperative a double meaning. To the elite, Moses is commanding that one comprehend God's existence and oneness by means of philosophical verification. For the masses, who cannot achieve this kind of philosophical understanding, the commandment is an imperative to believe in those same concepts but without rational justification.[8]

Another place in which the dual meaning of Scripture comes into play—this time rather extensively—is in Gersonides' interpretation of the sacrificial rites in Leviticus that are connected with repentance. A theme consistently running through Gersonides' discussion of these sacrifices is that they were instituted for the sake of the masses, who require concrete rituals in order to be convinced that their sins have been forgiven:

> God wanted that a sacrifice accompany repentance in order that the sinner be more convinced that his sin has been atoned for. For the masses [hamon ha-ʾanashim] cannot imagine that a man is wicked and that afterwards his wickedness is wiped away through inward repentance which involves no action whatsoever. Therefore, God commanded that they perform these sacrifices in the revered House in which there resides the Divine Presence, and [that the sacrifices be performed] by the revered person [i.e., the priest] who was chosen for the service of God in order to complete the atonement for the sinner through repentance. He also commanded for this reason that he place his hands upon the head of his sacrifice and confess his sins over it in order to convince him that it is as if those sins have been removed from him and have been transferred to the head of the animal. . . . [9]

We should also point out that the Torah's dual message regarding the reward for the following commandments which Gersonides discusses in his introduction to the *Commentary on the Song of Songs* is also alluded to in his *Commentary on the Torah*. In the preceding chapter, we saw that Gersonides interprets a number of passages in the Torah as referring simultaneously to the material and spiritual rewards that follow upon the observance of its commandments. Gersonides is also explicit in emphasizing that the Torah favors the latter reward as the true goal of the Torah's teachings. Yet, in none of these references does Gersonides explicitly point out that the Torah is addressing different audiences.[10]

Gersonides is not entirely clear about why the Torah conceals philosophical truths from the masses. The implication in the introduction to the *Commentary on the Song of Songs* is that they are simply incapable of comprehending sophisticated philosophical concepts. In a couple of passages in his *Commentary on Proverbs*, Gersonides goes a step further by suggesting that philosophical truths can even cause harm to those untrained in philosophy. This point comes through in Gersonides' explication of Proverbs 10:14, which states that "the wise store up knowledge." Gersonides interprets this statement to mean that philosophers must withhold their views because they may "harm some of the masses" due to the latter's "incapacity to understand their true intent."

A lengthier statement of a similar type appears in Gersonides' interpretation of Proverbs 11:13:

> A TALE-BEARER[11] REVEALS SECRETS, BUT A TRUSTWORTHY SOUL KEEPS A CONFIDENCE: . . . he who gives away the secrets of wisdom in divine and very obscure matters is as repugnant as a tale-bearer because by this [action] he causes great harm to people. However, he who is a trustworthy soul and on this account restrains himself from doing that which will cause people to err conceals wisdom from him who is not worthy of it.[12]

Gersonides, however, never specifies what harm the knowledge of philosophical truths will bring.

Our observations here raise troubling questions. First, if Gersonides believes that philosophical teachings should not be revealed to the masses, why then did Moses provide the uneducated Israelites with a full range of philosophical truths after the exodus from Egypt? Even more important, how are we to read Gersonides' *own* writings? Does Gersonides' support for esoteric discourse mean that we must look for hidden doctrines in his works as well?

These questions can be addressed by taking note of what I believe to be a key component in Gersonides' attitude towards esoteric discourse, one that significantly softens the impact of esotericism on his thinking. There are strong indications that Gersonides has confidence that the gap separating the elite from the masses is one that can be overcome. Gersonides seems to feel that the masses can be brought to a level of philosophical sophistication, provided that there is proper and skillful guidance. His fear that harm might come about by revealing philosophical truths to the masses appears to be limited to those cases in which philosophical truth is revealed indiscriminately and without proper instruction. It is only in these instances that the imparting of philosophical truth can be detrimental to the uneducated masses.[13]

There are a number of sources that provide evidence to support this interpretation. Even in the central passage in Gersonides' *Commentary on the Song of Songs*, where he expresses his most explicit support for esotericism, we detect optimism that the masses can be brought to a much higher level of philosophical awareness. In his remarks about the purpose of the commandments, we saw Gersonides argue that the masses are promised material reward by the Torah because they are unable to appreciate the more exalted spiritual reward that is the true aim of the commandments. Yet, it is important to note that Gersonides also hastens to add that "through performing this worship first not for its own sake, they [i.e., the masses] will be guided to doing it afterwards for its own sake."[14] Thus, Gersonides expresses hope that the masses will, in fact, come to understand the deeper philosophical significance of the commandments.

Our point comes through more clearly in a passage in Gersonides' commentary on Numbers, in which he explains why the Tetragrammaton was pronounced only within the confines of the Temple:

> ... it is not proper to reveal this exalted name except in a place designated for worshipping Him, because on this account [i.e., it being a place of worship] one will always find in that place those who comprehend the secret of this name as much as it is possible.[15] This will protect those who hear [the name] from harm through misunderstanding its meaning, because in that place [there] will be someone who will protect them from such misunderstanding.[16]

Normally, the masses should not have been exposed to the divine name because they might have misconstrued its philosophical meaning. However, the presence of philosophically trained priests safeguarded the uninitiated from any harm. Here we see quite clearly Gersonides' conviction that the masses can be taught philosophical truths, so long as there is proper philosophical guidance available.[17]

Most important, our interpretation helps explain why Gersonides is untroubled by Moses imparting a wide range of sophisticated philosophical truths to the uneducated Israelites. In this case, Gersonides seems to feel that there was no concern about the Israelites learning these truths, since there was obviously proper philosophical guidance. Given that Moses was the greatest prophet and philosopher of all time, the quality of philosophical instruction the Israelites received was undoubtedly of the highest order.[18]

Our interpretation of Gersonides' attitude towards esotericism gets its strongest support from a series of remarks made in his own major philosophical work, *The Wars of the Lord*. In his introduction to the *Wars*, Gersonides states quite clearly that in his treatise he will not adopt an esoteric style, since "it is not proper for someone to withhold what he has learned in philosophy from someone else." Gersonides explains that the imparting of wisdom is the highest expression of the *imitatio Dei* principle. Just as God created the universe without benefit to Himself, so should the philosopher be selfless in imparting his wisdom to others.[19]

An even stronger statement about esotericism is made in another passage in the introduction to the *Wars*. Gersonides raises the issue of esoteric discourse in a larger discussion regarding the order of topics in his treatise. For Gersonides, the mark of a well-written philosophical work is not just the quality of its argumentation, but its clear organization as well. Gersonides therefore lays out seven principles that account for the sequence of topics in the *Wars*.[20]

It is Gersonides' discussion of the third of these principles that is of greatest interest to us. According to this principle, the author must arrange his material so that the easier material is presented first. In this way, the reader will be prepared to absorb the more difficult material as he proceeds. Gersonides then goes on to explain why it is that some treatises are difficult to understand. Such obscurity, he claims, is sometimes nothing more than a ploy to conceal the author's flaws and weaknesses. At other times, Gersonides adds, obscurity is used for the specific purpose of esoteric discourse by which the author attempts to conceal views that might be harmful to the masses.

Gersonides emphatically rejects any such obfuscation in his own work:

. . . we wish that the amplitude of our language, as well as its explanation and proper order, will make our intentions, together with their profundity, explicit to the reader.[21]

It is important to note that Gersonides does not denounce esotericism in principle here. He affirms only that his own treatise will not adopt this type of discourse.

Does Gersonides then have no fear of openly revealing philosophical truths? A close examination of the introductory remarks to the *Wars* will show that Gersonides is more than mildly concerned about this problem. What appears to worry him in particular are those people in his audience who adhere to traditional beliefs that are at odds with the philosophical views he is about to demonstrate. Gersonides addresses this problem in his discussion of the seventh of his principles, which determine the order of topics in the *Wars*:

> Seventh, when an author realizes that some of his discussions explain things that are strange to the reader because of the opinions with which the latter is familiar and habituated from youth, so that the reader is upset by them even if he finds no logical inconsistencies in them, and for this reason would be prevented from obtaining knowledge from the rest of the book—then the author should arrange his material in a way that is appropriate to what he wants to convey to his reader. [That is,] he should present first the material that is not so strange to the reader; in this way, the author will wean him away gradually from his [intellectual] heritage, so that his former opinions will not prevent him from obtaining the truth on that question.[22]

Gersonides expresses optimism that those in his audience who hold traditional beliefs in conflict with philosophical truth can be gradually drawn away from their incorrect views. To accomplish this end, Gersonides intends to place the more controversial material at the end of his treatise. Gersonides reasons that by the time his reader comes to this material, he will have unwittingly loosened his attachment to his inaccurate views.

Gersonides compares this procedure to what doctors do in the healing of patients. A doctor who is attempting to cure someone who does not realize he is ill must introduce his therapy in a gradual manner so as not to overwhelm his patient. Similarly, in a written philosophical treatise, the author must disabuse his reader of his traditional beliefs in incremental fashion in order to be an effective pedagogue.

What is important to notice here is that these remarks fall neatly in line with our understanding of Gersonides' position on esotericism. While Gersonides is sensitive to the problem of openly revealing philosophical truths to a traditional audience, he does not see the concealment of his views as the preferred solution. Gersonides attempts to address this difficulty by bringing the traditional reader to a more sophisticated philosophical awareness through a carefully executed pedagogical program that is predicated on the proper organization of material in his treatise. Thus, we see once again that proper and skillful philosophical guidance obviates the need for esoteric discourse. This rule apparently applies equally to a written philosophical work, such as the *Wars*, as it does to the kind of oral teaching used by Moses for instructing the Israelites.[23]

Gersonides also anticipates the possibility that, despite his best efforts, some readers in his audience will be unable to relinquish their philosophically incorrect views due to their attachment to traditional beliefs. At the end of the first book of the *Wars*, Gersonides appears to address this precise problem:

> If anyone thinks that religious faith [*'emunah*][24] requires a conception of human perfection different from the one we have mentioned because of the literal meaning of certain passages about the Garden of Eden and Gehenna in various Midrashim, Aggadot, and statements of the prophets, let him surely know that we have not assented to the view that our reason has suggested without determining its compatibility with our Torah. For adherence to reason is not permitted if it contradicts religious faith; indeed, if there is such [a contradiction], it is necessary to attribute this lack of agreement to our own inadequacy. Hence, it is clear that someone who believes this [i.e., the view of the Torah] should follow his religious faith. This is incumbent upon all the faithful; for if the door were open to any philosophical doubt with respect to religious faith, religious faith would disappear and its benefits for its adherents would vanish. Moreover, [all kinds] of controversies and confusion would arise among the believers unless there is religious faith, and as a result of this, definite harm will come about. This fact should not be overlooked. The point we have made here should be understood as applying to every other part of our book; so that if there appears to be a problem concerning which our view differs from the accepted view of religious faith, philosophy should be abandoned and religious faith followed. The incompatibility is to be attributed to our shortcomings.[25]

A full explication of this passage will require substantial discussion. Let us begin by noting that some scholars have interpreted Gersonides' remarks here as a statement about his own philosophical method. Touati, for instance, claims that this passage is intended to qualify Gersonides' earlier assertion that the biblical text must always be interpreted according to the teachings of philosophy. Here, Touati argues, Gersonides affirms that in certain instances Scripture takes precedence over philosophical demonstration. More precisely, Gersonides is alluding to the *pinnot ha-torah,* the fundamental biblical doctrines that cannot be subverted by philosophical speculation.[26]

It is unlikely that this is the intent of the passage. First, reference to the *pinnot ha-torah* is noticeably absent here. Instead, Gersonides repeatedly refers to "religious faith" as the factor that takes precedence over philosophy. More impòrtant, the focus of this passage is quite clearly on political, not philosophical concerns. Gersonides begins his statement by addressing the reader who adheres to a religious faith that is philosophically inaccurate because of his reliance on a "literal reading" of biblical and rabbinic sources. In other words, he is someone who has not responded to the program of gradual philosophical education mapped out in the introduction to the *Wars* because of a stubborn attachment to traditional beliefs. Gersonides' position is that, for political reasons, it is better that such a person remain committed to his religious faith and ignore the doctrines set forth in the *Wars*. Gersonides expresses concern that the well-being of the community is in danger of serious disruption if the religious faith of this type of person is threatened.

Support for our interpretation can be found in a clearer understanding of the key term in this passage which characterizes the outlook of the reader he is addressing: *''emunah,'* or religious faith. This is a problematic word. To my knowledge, there is no other place where Gersonides refers repeatedly to the concept of *'emunah* in the way that he does here. Furthermore, this term takes on a wide range of definitions in medieval Jewish philosophy, a factor that only complicates our attempt to arrive at Gersonides' understanding of the term in the passage before us.[27]

Still, there are indications that in this passage at least, *'emunah* is used in a pejorative sense to refer to a simplistic and dogmatic religious faith. For one, *'emunah* is consistently contrasted with *'iyyun,* or knowledge attained through philosophical speculation. Moreover, in his introduction to the *Wars* Gersonides clearly uses the verbal root of the term *'emunah* in reference to a simplistic form of belief:

> . . . without a doubt many people will reject our ideas because they find in them something unfamiliar to them by virtue of the opinions they hold, which do not derive from philosophical or fundamental principles of the Torah [*pinnot ha-toriyyot*] but which they inherited. However, we are not concerned with these people; *for it is sufficient for them to believe* [*ya'aminu*], *not to know* [*yede 'u*] [italics added]. We are concerned with those who are deeply perplexed by these questions and who are not satisfied

with what is merely said about the secrets of existence but with what can be conceived [about them].[28]

Here Gersonides contrasts those who merely "believe" (*ya'aminu*) what they are told with those who rationally understand (*yede'u*).[29] It is this very same reader whom Gersonides appears to be addressing at the end of book one of the *Wars*.[30]

Further insight into Gersonides' statement at the end of book one can be gained by noting the timing of his remarks. In the two chapters immediately preceding this passage, Gersonides introduces for the very first time in his treatise philosophical interpretations of biblical and rabbinic sources. These texts are used by Gersonides to support his views on immortality, the subject of the first book.[31]

Upon reflection, it is no surprise that at this point in his treatise Gersonides shows concern about the views of the stubborn traditionalist. Gersonides is obviously anticipating that it is here that such a reader will voice his first objections to the views expressed in the *Wars* on account of the unorthodox treatment of the classical sources in the preceding section. Our point finds support in the opening line of the passage at the end of book one, in which Gersonides addresses anyone who disagrees with him "because of the literal meaning of certain passages about *the Garden of Eden and Gehenna* in various Midrashim, Aggadot, and statements of the prophets [italics added]."[32] Here Gersonides clearly expresses concern about reactions to his reading of the classical sources pertaining to the afterlife.

We can take our analysis one step further by also noting the historical context from which Gersonides is speaking. The conflict between philosophical and traditional interpretations of immortality and the world to come had been one of the central features in the first phase of the Maimonidean controversy in the period shortly before Gersonides' lifetime. Though it was by no means the only issue, Maimonides' position on immortality and the world to come figured prominently in a protracted debate that centered on the question of resurrection.[33]

In light of this controversy that was still smoldering in Gersonides' lifetime, it is understandable that Gersonides chose the end of book one in the *Wars* to address the traditional reader. Gersonides' position on immortality and the world to come which is delineated in the first book was similar enough to that of Maimonides to warrant concern. Gersonides must have perceived the danger in espousing a position that had created so much strife a short time earlier. Gersonides therefore attempts to preempt conflict by placating the stubborn traditionalist and encouraging him to stay with his religious convictions in the event of any disagreement with his own positions. Gersonides' emphasis on avoiding the "harm" that the community would experience as a result of "controversies and confusion" over matters of religious faith could very well be allusions to the strife that had been brought about by the Maimonidean controversy.[34]

Our theory that Gersonides had the dispute over Maimonides' writings in mind is strengthened by striking similarities between Gersonides and Maimonides on the nature of the problem and its solution. Gersonides' concern that the literal reading of biblical and rabbinic sources provides the masses with erroneous views on such subjects as immortality is found in Maimonides' *Treatise on Resurrection*—the work in which Maimonides attempts to answer criticisms regarding his eschatological beliefs.[35]

Gersonides' tolerance for these incorrect views also has roots in Maimonides. In his *Treatise on Resurrection*, Maimonides allows his readers to adhere to their incorrect views if they are incapable of more sophisticated philosophical conceptions. The same view is also expressed on a number of occasions in the *Guide* with reference to inaccurate conceptions of God. Those uneducated in philosophy can hold onto these views as long they do not adopt a corporeal conception of God.[36]

But let us not lose sight of our original concern. What is most important to notice is that even when Gersonides is confronting the recalcitrant traditionalist who refuses to accept correct philosophical belief, he in no way suggests that he will deal with the problem by systematically concealing his true opinions. Gersonides' recommendation is that this type of reader voluntarily disengage from the philosophical ideas that disturb him. Thus, once again, esoteric discourse is not the preferred solution.

What may be confusing is that in the passage at the end of book one of the *Wars*, Gersonides explicitly makes *himself* subservient to the advice that he gives to this reader. Gersonides declares that "we have not assented to the view that our reason has suggested without determining its compatibility with our Torah."[37] With this statement, Gersonides seems to be placing himself in the same camp as the traditionalist who must desist from philosophical speculation when it disturbs his faith. Yet, it is likely that this is nothing more than a ploy to appease those to whom the passage is directed. His central concern, after all, is the welfare of the community of believers, a cause that could only benefit by a statement on his part in support of religious faith.

Gersonides' position on esotericism can best be summed up by comparing it with that of Maimonides. For Maimonides, Scripture carefully conceals its true philosophical teachings from the masses on account of the harm that might be caused to those uninitiated in this type of speculation. But it is not just Scripture that must relay philosophical truth in this manner. Maimonides also believes that it is imperative for all subsequent treatises imparting philosophical knowledge to adopt esoteric discourse in order to safeguard the masses from harm. It is for this reason that Maimonides uses this form of discourse in the *Guide*.[38]

Gersonides has certain points in common with Maimonides. He agrees that philosophical truths in Scripture are communicated in esoteric fashion. He also voices fear about the harm philosophical truths can cause to the untrained reader. However, in contrast to his predecessor, Gersonides sees the discrepancy between the elite and the masses as one that can be overcome. With proper guidance, no one has to be excluded from the esoteric teachings of the Torah or from sophisticated philosophical speculation. Thus, there was nothing wrong with Moses teaching the Israelites a wide range of philosophical truths; his expert guidance no doubt ensured the proper transmission of these concepts. Nor is there need to worry about the philosophical truths openly discussed in the *Wars*. Gersonides carefully arranges his material in order to soften the impact of his unorthodox positions on those in his audience of a more traditional stripe.

Gersonides also accepts the fact that there are some who will be unable to abandon their traditional beliefs. This sector of his audience is quietly encouraged to keep its religious faith, desist from reading further, and attribute any difficulty to Gersonides' own shortcomings. According to Gersonides, it is better for the sake of the community's well-being that this type of reader have inaccurate philosophical views rather than lose his religious faith. But even here, Gersonides does not resort to the elaborate scheme of concealment that Maimonides adopts.

The general impression one gets is that while Gersonides is wary of the harm that philosophical truth can cause, he does not have the same degree of fear that we see in Maimonides. There seems to be a trust on Gersonides' part that if philosophical knowledge is packaged properly, anyone can learn from it.

The contrast between Maimonides and Gersonides on this point is vividly illustrated in their respective interpretations of Moses' revelation at the burning bush. In the *Guide*, Maimonides praises Moses for hiding his face at the sight of the bush, and sees in this gesture a metaphor for the care and caution one must exercise in approaching the study of philosophy.[39] In Gersonides' reading, the story teaches precisely the opposite lesson. Gersonides interprets Moses' initial attempt to catch a glimpse of the bush as a reflection of his eagerness to understand the meaning of the vision.[40] For Gersonides, Moses' action teaches us that one should always pursue philosophical speculation ambitiously and energetically.[41] Thus, where Maimonides advocates care and caution towards philosophical learning, Gersonides encourages adventuresome curiosity.[42]

One final question needs to be considered. Is there any evidence that Gersonides adopts an esoteric form of discourse in his biblical commentaries? The answer to this question appears to be firmly in the negative. There is no major philosophical position in the *Wars* that is not discussed in his exegetical writings, including his most controversial positions: creation from a preexistent primordial matter, or the notion that God cannot have certain knowledge of future events involving human action.[43]

Most telling is the fact that a doctrine Gersonides explicitly identifies as an esoteric teaching is one that is discussed in a number of places in the biblical commentaries. We saw earlier that Gersonides views the notion that the commandments are primarily for gaining spiritual reward as an esoteric truth, and that in his exegetical writings Gersonides often refers to this doctrine.[44]

Nor do we find in the biblical commentaries the kind of sensitivity to the traditional reader that Gersonides expresses in the *Wars*. There is no suggestion on Gersonides' part that he will adopt a strategy to soften the impact of his views for those unaccustomed to philosophical thinking. His philosophical positions are stated without any apparent concern about the reaction they might elicit.

Why is Gersonides so unconcerned about revealing philosophical truths in his biblical commentaries? The answer to this question might lie in Gersonides' expectation that the audience for his commentaries would have a thorough familiarity with the *Wars*. A number of observations support this conjecture. For one, in his introduction to the *Commentary on the Torah*, Gersonides explicitly states that this work is directed to those who have already had training in philosophy.[45] Moreover, throughout his commentaries Gersonides will often refer to philosophical concepts in the *Wars* by doing nothing more than citing their location in that work. In these cases, he seems to expect the reader to be fully acquainted with the *Wars*, or at least to have the capacity to find the relevant passage and make sense of it. Even in those instances in which Gersonides summarizes his views in the *Wars*, his remarks are often too succinct to be fully appreciated without a prior familiarity with this work. In our own discussion, we have seen any number of instances in which Gersonides assumes not only knowledge of the doctrines in the *Wars*, but also the ability to apply those doctrines to the biblical text.

With all this in mind, it is apparent why Gersonides shows no great concern about openly discussing his philosophical positions in the biblical commentaries. The manner in which he presents his positions in these works is designed to select for those readers who are already acquainted with the *Wars*. Gersonides can therefore be sure that his reader has already been properly initiated in the study of philosophy.

Our discussion of Gersonides' position on esoteric discourse gives us a more complete picture of how the Torah serves as a philosophical guidebook. The Torah not only addresses all generations, it also offers guidance to audiences with different levels of philosophical training. For this reason, it is the most perfect of the revealed Scriptures.

But our interests here go well beyond Gersonides' position regarding the Torah. We now have a much better understanding of the style of philosophical discourse that Gersonides adopts in his own writings. While Gersonides imputes esoteric discourse to the biblical text, he appears to have rejected it in his own writing. It is not that he is insensitive to the problems that might arise in openly revealing philosophical truths. Rather, he chooses to deal with this problem with a strategy other than concealment in the belief that the proper presentation of philosophical truths circumvents the need for esoteric discourse.

We will conclude on a historical note. In retrospect, Gersonides' approach toward esotericism proved to be somewhat naive. He paid a high price for the openness with which he expressed his philosophical views. Not long after his death, his works would be the target of an anti-philosophical backlash.[46] It would seem that, despite his best efforts, Gersonides did not wean his readers away from their traditional beliefs quite as successfully as he might have hoped.

SEVEN

From the Conquest of Canaan to the Present Exile

At this point of our discussion, we have a comprehensive picture of how providence operates on behalf of the Israelites up to the conquest of Canaan. We are now ready to move on and examine Gersonides' understanding of Jewish history after the Israelites settle in their new homeland. In this chapter we will concern ourselves with events up to and including the second exile. A separate discussion will be devoted to the messianic era in the next chapter.

Gersonides provides philosophical information about the post-conquest phase of Jewish history in a number of places—though not as extensively as he does for the period before the conquest. Central in this regard, of course, are Gersonides' commentaries on the historical books of the Bible in the Prophets and Writings. Gersonides wrote commentaries on all these works—Joshua, Judges, I and II Samuel, I and II Kings, Ezra, Nehemiah, Esther, and I and II Chronicles.

The *Commentary on the Torah* is also surprisingly rich in material on the period beyond the conquest. Of particular importance are Gersonides' interpretations of passages, such as Leviticus 26 and Deuteronomy 32, which contain prophecies about the future of the Israelites once they settle in their new homeland. In the course of explaining these predictions, Gersonides often provides valuable information regarding divine providence and how it influences events throughout Jewish history.

We should also make special mention of Gersonides' *Commentary on Daniel*. Gersonides treats the prophetic predictions in this book as prescriptive for the entirety of Jewish history up to and including the messianic period. Here again Gersonides supplies important philosophical information for our purposes while explicating the biblical text.

It is important to note that Gersonides' commentaries on the later historical books of the Prophets and Writings are not as philosophical as his other exegetical works. This is perhaps due in part to Gersonides' desire to avoid repetition. Philosophical issues relevant to the biblical history are dealt with extensively in the *Commentary on the Torah*, and, therefore, in his commentaries on the later books of the Bible, he will frequently make reference to philosophical ideas by simply alluding to discussions in his *Commentary on the Torah*.[1] Nonetheless, we will discover that these commentaries contain an abundance of information that is of great value for our project.

THE ORIGINAL COVENANT WITH ABRAHAM

Let us begin by consolidating our understanding of how Gersonides views the post-conquest period according to the plan of the Patriarchal covenant. The picture that has emerged up to this point is as follows: The substance of the covenant is that individual providence inherited from Abraham furnishes the necessary conditions for the Israelites to earn individual providence on their own and to inherit the land of Canaan. The most important of these conditions is the Torah, which instructs the Israelites to achieve moral and intellectual perfection. Once the Israelites are in the land of Canaan, they will have the opportunity to continue receiving providential protection through the observance of the Torah's directives. Moreover, experiencing providence will be facilitated by the fact that the land of Canaan is especially suited for the reception of providential emanations.

There are a number of details that need to be added to this scenario. First, a few more observations are in order regarding the special status of the land of Israel. In a number of passages, Gersonides points out that while the entire land is receptive to providential emanations, there are locations within the land of Israel that are particularly susceptible to these emanations. The site of the Temple in Jerusalem is the most important of these locations.[2] Antecedents for these ideas are not hard to find. The influence of Judah Halevi is most evident here. Touati also points to ibn Ezra and Averroes as possible sources for Gersonides' views.[3]

In several places, Gersonides mentions another advantage in having the Israelites settle in the land of Canaan. In addition to the land's receptivity to providential emanations, "the gathering of perfected individuals [in one location] greatly assists in the achievement of perfection."[4] That is, it is not just the special quality of the land per se that is important; there is a social dimension here as well. The concentration of an entire people in *any* land devoted to divine worship will certainly enhance the prospects of perfection for all individuals in the collective.

It is also important to emphasize that the ultimate value in settling in the land of Canaan and experiencing providence is not just that the Israelites will acquire material reward, but that they will achieve immortality as well. The twofold nature of providential reward is underscored in a number of passages in Gersonides' biblical commentaries. For example, Gersonides makes this point in his interpretation of Deuteronomy 30:15-20, the passage in which Moses challenges the Israelites to "choose life" through obedience to God as they prepare to enter the land of Canaan. As we noted in a previous discussion, Moses' challenge is interpreted as a reference to immortality, which the Israelites can achieve upon proper observance of the commandments.[5] But what is significant for us here is Gersonides' rendering of the final verse of this passage which mentions the land of Israel:

> AND THE LENGTH OF YOUR DAYS TO DWELL UPON THE LAND:[6] for this good [i.e., material reward][7] will be consequent upon it as well [i.e., dwelling in the land]; in addition, it [i.e., dwelling in the land] also guides the Israelites in a most perfect manner to the acquisition of that life [i.e., eternal life],[8] since that land has a disposition [allowing] for man to experience providential emanation, as we have noted many times.[9]

Gersonides informs us that as a location specially suited to providential emanations, the land of Israel allows the Israelites to gain both material and spiritual reward.

What also needs to be emphasized is the central role Gersonides envisions for the Tabernacle after the Israelites have settled in their homeland. We have already dealt with the importance of the Tabernacle and the rituals associated with it in imparting philosophical truths to the ignorant Israelites as they wander through the desert. The centrality of the Tabernacle is in no way diminished once the Israelites conquer Canaan. A theme that runs throughout Gersonides' commentaries is the continuing importance of the Tabernacle and its heir, the Temple built by Solomon, as focal points for philosophical instruction in the national life of the Israelites. The pilgrimages mandated three times a year by the biblical text are precisely for the purpose of bringing the Israelites into the Temple precincts so that they can absorb the philosophical truths that the Temple and its rituals embody. Thus, if having the Israelites settle in the land of Canaan provides the proper social setting for achieving perfection as we noted above, the Temple is the focus of that social setting.[10]

Concomitant with Gersonides' emphasis on the Temple is the importance accorded to the priesthood. Gersonides offers reasons for having priests in addition to their tending to the maintenance of the Temple and the performance of sacrificial rituals. For one, the priests serve as teachers of philosophical wisdom for the rest of the Israelites. Since the structure of the Temple and the ritual performed therein reinforce the most important philosophical truths, the priests are ideally suited for this role. It is for this reason, Gersonides argues, that the Torah mandates that the material needs of the priests are to be supported by a system of tithes. This system is specifically designed to ensure that the priests are not occupied with material concerns and are thus able to pursue philosophical studies without distraction. The priests are also expected to cultivate the capacity for prophecy, a highly valuable talent that benefits the entire Israelite nation. It is anticipated that many of the priests will experience prophecy because of their intense devotion to intellectual perfection.

Gersonides also offers a reason to explain why a single family—that of Aaron—was chosen for the priesthood to the exclusion of all others. The selection of one family devoted to divine worship symbolically reinforces an important philosophical truth: the oneness of God. A similar reason accounts for the fact that the worship of God takes place in one central location. The singular location also reinforces the conception of God's unity.[11]

Gersonides also attempts to explain why the Levite tribe to which Aaron's family belonged was designated for service in the Temple. This he attributes to their genetic superiority, an assertion that is never clearly explained. Gersonides, however, does offer an argument, also genetically based, to explain why Aaron's line was chosen for the priesthood from among the Levites while that of Moses was not. Gersonides points out that since Moses had a Midianite wife, his lineage was not as suited to assuming the sacred functions of the priesthood as that of Aaron, who married an Israelite woman:

> God chose the tribe of Levi from the other tribes because it was the most select of them "from birth, from the womb, from conception."[12] From it [i.e., the tribe of Levi], He chose Aaron and his offspring, since he was from the most select family in the tribe of Levi and the most predisposed towards perfection. [God's] intention was not [to choose] the children of Moses, since their lineage was not perfect on the side of their mother in that she was a Midianite. The opposite [was true] for the offspring of Aaron, since their mother was from a highly select [Israelite] family.[13]

In another passage, Gersonides justifies the consideration of genetic factors in choosing Aaron's line with the claim that a person's offspring will inevitably inherit his natural qualities. As Gersonides succinctly puts it, "perfection was [to be found] in Aaron's offspring, since the nature of the source is to be found in that which is hewn from it."[14]

THE EXTENSION OF THE COVENANT

We must now move on to discuss an intriguing twist in Gersonides' interpretation of the covenant with Abraham, one that will have a significant impact on the direction of our study. The assumption all along has been that the covenant with Abraham is fulfilled with the entry of the Israelites into the land of Canaan, in that God's original promise to Abraham in Genesis 15 has come true. What this means in philosophical terms is that the providence inherited from Abraham has accomplished its intended purpose and is no longer needed because it has ensured that the Israelites are at the proper level of intellectual perfection to earn their own providence and conquer the land of Canaan.

But Gersonides makes a remarkable claim that will force us to reevaluate this picture. In references scattered throughout his commentaries, Gersonides maintains that the Patriarchal covenant is not actually fulfilled with the conquest of Canaan. In fact, it is still unfulfilled in Gersonides' own day and will remain so until the messianic era. In philosophical terms, this means that the providence inherited from Abraham still protects the Israelites after the conquest of Canaan and will continue to protect them until the coming of the Messiah.

An understanding of the extension of the covenant is very important for our project, since it is key to Gersonides' understanding of the relationship between God and the Israelites, from the conquest onward. Much of the remainder of this chapter will therefore be occupied with the explication of this phenomenon. Let us first attempt to delineate the theoretical underpinnings of this idea. Perhaps the most important passage for this purpose is one that appears in Gersonides' commentary on Deuteronomy, where he formulates the theory of an extended covenant on the basis of the following biblical source in Deuteronomy 7:7-13:

> It is not because you are the most numerous of peoples that the LORD set His heart on you and chose you . . . but it was because the LORD favored you and kept the oath He made to your fathers that the LORD freed you with a mighty hand and rescued you from the house of bondage, from the power of Pharaoh, king of Egypt. Know, therefore, that only the LORD your God is God, the steadfast God who preserves the covenant and the good[15] to the thousandth generation of those who love Him and keep His com-

mandments, but who instantly requites with destruction those who reject Him. .·.. And if you obey these rules and observe them carefully, the LORD your God will preserve the covenant and the good[16] for you that He made on oath with your fathers. He will favor you, bless you and multiply you . . . in the land that He swore to your fathers to assign to you.

This passage begins with what appears to be a reference to the Patriarchal covenant. Moses reminds the Israelites that it was the "oath" that God made with their "fathers" that was responsible for their rescue from Egypt. But what is most important for our concerns is that the passage goes on to describe how that same covenant will continue to benefit the Israelites once they enter their new homeland. The biblical text twice specifies that God will "preserve the covenant and the good" for the Israelites so that they will experience blessing even in the land of Canaan.

In the following statement Gersonides attempts to explain this promise:

The nineteenth *to'elet* informs [us] that God delays [the implementation of] good things which He has promised to the righteous until a time when they will be of greatest good. For this reason, it is possible that He will delay them [i.e., these good things] "to the thousandth generation" in order to implement those good things in such a way that they will not be negated and in such a manner that they will be of utmost possible perfection. . . . [The biblical text] said this [i.e., that God preserves the good to the thousandth generation] to explain that in order to bring good things upon Israel, God delayed for a long time the implementation of the good which He had promised to Abraham with the result that it has not yet reached its fulfillment. It would seem as if this was the reason that Israel would not be annihilated by the evil that they deserved as a consequence of their worshipping idols, i.e., that His covenant with the Patriarchs would not be nullified. God reserved the complete implementation of that good until a time that there would be no possibility for evil to occur to them afterwards, as the prophet said, "For then I will make the peoples pure of speech, so that they all invoke the LORD by name and serve Him with one accord."[17]

It has already been made clear that this good has not been completely implemented. For God swore to Abraham that He would give his offspring a land of ten nations;[18] yet, the Torah reports that Israel conquered only seven nations.[19] Moreover, it says in the Torah that when God extends our borders, we will add three cities to the six cities of refuge.[20] This is something which has not yet occurred according to what has come down to us in the events [reported] in the words of the prophets. This shows that the extension of the border will be in the days of the King Messiah which we hope will come hastily in our day, may it be [God's] will. . . . [21]

There are a number of important claims in this passage that need to be elucidated. Gersonides begins with a general principle that God delays the implementation of the good until a time that it can be of greatest benefit. Gersonides then applies this principle to the covenant with Abraham by arguing that God delayed the fulfillment of the covenant until the messianic period in order that the covenant continue to exert a protective influence over the Israelites even after they enter Canaan. The apparent reasoning here is that as long as the terms of the covenant do not come to fruition, the Israelites cannot be destroyed; after all, there obviously can be no fulfillment of the covenant without them. Gersonides further points out that this protection explains why the Israelites were not annihilated when they became involved in idolatrous practices later on in their history. It was the covenant that safeguarded them from destruction.

Why the messianic period is the best time for the fulfillment of the covenant is not adequately explained by Gersonides. In the passage above, he vaguely refers to the messianic era as a time in which "there would be no possibility for evil to occur to them [i.e., the Israelites] afterwards." What Gersonides appears to be saying is that the messianic period is an ideal time for the terms of the covenant to be implemented, because it will be an era of everlasting world peace. In such a period, the need for Israel to experience the providential protection provided by the covenant will be greatly diminished, since its enemies will no longer pose a threat.

But Gersonides may also be implying something more subtle here. The messianic period is the best point in history for the covenant to be fulfilled, perhaps because in that era all nations will worship the one true God—as is evident from the prooftext in Zephaniah 3:9—and therefore the Israelites will not be in danger of being seduced by the idolatrous practices of other nations. That is, the messianic period is one in which the Israelites will live in an environment that is not only physically secure, but spiritually secure as well. In such a world, the Israelites will no longer be in need of the protective influence accorded by the covenant because they are sure to earn their own providential reward in uninterrupted fashion.

What the incomplete fulfillment of the covenant means in practical terms, according to Gersonides, is that the Israelites never actually conquered the entire land promised to Abraham. Two proofs are adduced by

Gersonides to back this claim. First, in Abraham's original prophecy in Genesis 15, God refers to ten Canaanite nations that Abraham's descendants are expected to conquer;[22] yet, in a passage in Deuteronomy this list is inexplicably reduced to seven.[23] Evidently, Gersonides concludes, the Israelites never conquered three of the Canaanite nations.

The other argument for the incomplete fulfillment of the covenant is formulated with the help of a passage in Deuteronomy 19, in which Moses spells out various prescriptions regarding the cities of refuge. Gersonides focuses specifically on the following verses:

> And when the LORD your God enlarges your territory, as He swore to your fathers, and gives you all the land that He promised to give to your fathers . . . then you shall add three more towns to those three.[24]

Gersonides notes that the events referred to here—the enlargement of territory and the establishment of three more cities of refuge—are not reported in the later biblical history. Gersonides concludes that this passage must therefore be alluding to a portion of Canaan that was promised in the original covenant with Abraham but was never conquered.[25]

We are now ready to translate Gersonides' position into philosophical terms. The notion that God delays implementing the good until it is most beneficial is clearly a statement about providence. What Gersonides is saying is that providential laws will tend to function in a manner that maximizes their beneficial effect. It is this principle that causes the fulfillment of the covenant to be delayed.

Now the covenant, as we have demonstrated, is a metaphor for providence inherited from Abraham. Therefore, what Gersonides is really telling us is that to maximize its beneficial effect, inherited providence continues to exert its influence over the Israelites until the messianic period. In this way, it can protect them from harm throughout history. With the tendency of the Israelites to adopt idolatrous practices, this protection proves to be most beneficial, as Gersonides sees it. As a result of their sinful behavior in their later history, the Israelites are in constant danger of severing their contact with God and losing divine providence. During these times, inherited providence safeguards the Israelites from harmful chance events that might destroy them.

In the messianic era, matters will be different. Inherited providence will no longer be needed, because without the physical threat of their enemies, the Israelites will no longer require the same degree of protection. Moreover, since the Israelites will not be subject to the pernicious influence of idolatry among neighboring nations, there is no fear that the Israelites will sever their ties with God. Intellectual perfection and divine providence will be the norm for all nations.

While our explication of the extension of the covenant may be an accurate understanding of Gersonides' views, there are obvious problems here. What precisely does Gersonides mean when he says that God "delays" the implementation of the covenant for the most propitious time? Does this imply that the providential plan mapped out in Abraham's original prophecy has somehow changed? And if so, does this mean that Gersonides is violating his philosophical principles by suggesting that God has experienced a change of will? That a prophecy should not turn out exactly as predicted is, of course, acceptable to Gersonides. As we have mentioned on several occasions, human initiative can alter the course of events determined in the divine mind and can therefore invalidate a prophetic prediction.[26] The difficulty with the extension of the covenant is that the direction of events predicted in Abraham's prophecy seems to have changed even without the influence of human action.

One way to address this problem is to examine more carefully Gersonides' original interpretation of the covenant with Abraham in Genesis 15. That the Patriarchal covenant will be fulfilled only in the messianic era is an idea that is, in fact, alluded to in Gersonides' commentary on that chapter. There Gersonides takes note of the discrepancy between the number of Canaanite nations mentioned in Abraham's prophecy and those listed in the passage in Deuteronomy and concludes that the last three nations will be conquered only in the messianic era.[27] This is precisely the same argument for the extension of the covenant that Gersonides offers in the passage we just examined in his commentary on Deuteronomy. Therefore, one could argue that divine will has by no means experienced a change, since Gersonides believes that the extension of the covenant to the messianic era was the intent of Abraham's prophecy from the outset.

Of course, this interpretation still leaves us with the problem of clarifying what Gersonides means when he says that God "delays" the fulfillment of the covenant. This terminology seems inappropriate if the extension of the covenant to the messianic period was intended in Abraham's prophecy all along. Now it is possible that we are trying to read Gersonides in too literal a fashion. What Gersonides might be saying is that God "delays" the covenant only in the sense that the influence of inherited providence extends for an unusually long period of time after Abraham's death—to the end of history, in fact. As we will see in chapter nine, Gersonides often will use metaphorical language of this sort to describe divine activity. Understood in this sense, the delay of the covenant would not present a problem with regard to divine will.

However, there is another difficulty with interpreting Gersonides in this way. In the text of Genesis 15, God explicitly promises that Abraham's offspring will return to the land of Canaan "in the fourth generation,"[28] a statement that would suggest that the covenant is to be fulfilled once the Israelites leave Egypt and well before the messianic era. In his comments on this passage, Gersonides does not seem to question the plain meaning of the text.[29] Thus, the philosophical meaning of Gersonides' assertion that God delays the fulfillment of the covenant remains somewhat unclear.

Yet, even if the extension of the covenant is philosophically problematic, we can certainly get a better understanding of why Gersonides insists on this far-reaching claim by introducing another set of considerations. What convinces Gersonides that the covenant remains unfulfilled appears to have been more than the explicit proofs delineated above demonstrating that the entire land of Canaan was not conquered by the Israelites. There are also a number of important biblical passages clearly indicating that the influence of the Patriarchal covenant is still operative after the conquest.

We have already encountered a passage of this kind. Gersonides' programmatic statement on the extension of the covenant, with which we began our analysis in this section, was based on Deuteronomy 7:9-13, a passage in which Moses refers to the Patriarchal covenant as a source of blessing even after the Israelites settle in their new homeland. But this is by no means the only passage of this type. For instance, in II Kings we are told that when the Israelite king Jehoahaz was being threatened by King Hazael of Aram, God came to Jehoahaz's rescue because of the Patriarchal covenant:

> But the LORD was gracious and merciful to them, and He turned back to them for the sake of His covenant with Abraham, Isaac, and Jacob. He refrained from destroying them and He still did not cast them out from His presence.[30]

Here we have clear evidence that the Patriarchal covenant protects the Israelites well after the conquest.[31]

Most important are a number of instances in the Torah in which the Patriarchal covenant is depicted as the force that will rescue the Israelites from a predicted future exile. Again, these passages support Gersonides' contention that the Patriarchal covenant continues to exert influence even after the conquest of Canaan.

A passage of this type can be found in the fourth chapter of Deuteronomy. After specifying that the Israelites will be exiled from their land upon disobedience to God, the biblical text goes on to describe the reconciliation which will follow:

But if you search for the LORD your God, you will find Him, if only you seek Him with all your heart and soul—when you are in distress because all these things have befallen you and, in the end of days,[32] return to the your LORD your God and obey Him. For the LORD your God is a compassionate God: He will not fail you, nor will He let you perish; He will not forget the covenant which He made on oath with your fathers.[33]

The plain meaning of the biblical text would suggest that the influence of the Patriarchal covenant extends well past the conquest of Canaan in order to redeem the Israelites from future exile.

Another passage of this kind appears in Leviticus 26—traditionally known as the *tokheḥah*, or "chastisement"—where we find the same scenario as in Deuteronomy 4. In this chapter, the Israelites are also threatened with exile if they do not obey God's word; and once again, God promises reconciliation:

When I, in turn, have been hostile to them and have removed them into the land of their enemies, then at last shall their obdurate heart humble itself, and they shall atone for their iniquity. Then I will remember My covenant with Jacob; I will remember also My covenant with Isaac, and also My covenant with Abraham; and I will remember the land.[34]

Here the covenant with the Patriarchs again plays an important role in ending the future exile.

Passages of this sort must have also been a central inspiration for Gersonides' view that the terms of the covenant would be fulfilled specifically with the advent of the messianic era. Gersonides consistently identifies the future exile in these texts as the one which the Jews are experiencing in his own day. The redemption, which is always predicted to follow the exile, is nothing other than the inauguration of the messianic period.

This eschatological scenario is succinctly delineated in Gersonides' interpretation of the passage in Deuteronomy 4 to which we just referred:

WHEN YOU ARE IN DISTRESS BECAUSE ALL THESE THINGS HAVE BEFALLEN YOU . . . IN THE END OF DAYS: In this passage, [the Torah] hinted at this long exile which we are experiencing today scattered among the nations as a result of our sins and the sins of our fathers. Therefore, it said "in the end of days" that this [i.e., the redemption] will occur after a very long time. WHEN YOU RETURN TO THE LORD YOUR GOD AND OBEY HIM: That is to say, then you will return to God and keep His commandments. For God is a A COMPASSIONATE GOD

[and] His providence will not depart from you completely. NOR WILL HE LET YOU PERISH completely because of your sins. HE WILL NOT FORGET THE COVENANT WHICH HE MADE ON OATH TO YOUR FATHERS to give the land of Canaan to their offspring after them. Because of His covenant with the fore-fathers, it necessarily follows that He will not destroy you, be-cause in that case the covenant would be nullified.[35]

In Gersonides' reading, the exile in the "end of days" is the present exile, while the redemption that follows is the one which will herald the begin-ning of the messianic period. Furthermore, the notion that the covenant continues to function until the messianic era is implied here as well. Ger-sonides accepts at face value the biblical text that states that the covenant is a factor in the rescue of the Israelites from exile.[36]

In some instances, the biblical text makes reference to a covenant that is operative past the conquest, but without specifying whether it is allud-ing specifically to the Patriarchal covenant. In such cases, Gersonides sometimes assumes nonetheless that the text has this covenant in mind. For example, in Nehemiah 9:32 the Levites refer to God as one who "pre-serves the covenant and the good."[37] While there is no indication here which covenant the text is referring to, Gersonides interprets this passage as an allusion to the Patriarchal covenant—probably by analogy with Deuteronomy 7:9 and 7:12 in which the same phrase is used explicitly in connection with the Patriarchal covenant.[38]

The point of all this is to show that Gersonides' position on the exten-sion of the covenant appears to have been inspired, at least in part, by an impressive abundance of biblical evidence. While the account in Genesis 15 seems to assume that the covenant will be fulfilled with the entrance of the Israelites into Canaan, there are any number of biblical passages to in-dicate that this covenant continues to influence events well past the con-quest. At no point, however, does Gersonides explicitly draw all this evidence together in order to support his position.

What is being argued here is that Gersonides in effect treats the ex-tension of the covenant as one of the *pinnot ha-torah*. It is an idea supported by so much evidence in the biblical text that it is a fundamental biblical principle that must be accepted. Our conjecture is, in fact, confirmed by a passage in Gersonides' commentary on Deuteronomy in which he de-scribes one such principle that clearly implies the notion that the covenant is yet to be fulfilled:

The tenth *to'elet* is one of the *pinnot ha-torah*. That is, [the Torah] informed us that by virtue of observing all the Instruction [i.e., the Torah] that He commands us today—the goal of which is to love

God and follow His ways forever—God will complete the giving
of the land to us which He gave to the Patriarchs. . . . [39]

The biblical principle delineated here specifies that the observance of
God's commandments will ensure that the Israelites get full possession of
the land promised to the Patriarchs; but the important point for our purposes is that this principle is predicated on the notion that the terms of the
original covenant were never implemented.[40]

Finally, we should point out that Gersonides' position on the extension of the covenant is undoubtedly influenced by sources in rabbinic literature as well. The proofs Gersonides adduces to show that the covenant
was not fulfilled because the land was never fully conquered are not original to him. A number of rabbinic and medieval thinkers see the conquest
of the three remaining nations and the building of three more cities of
refuge as events reserved for the messianic period.[41]

That biblical sources suggest a role for the Patriarchal covenant
past the conquest also does not go unnoticed in rabbinic literature. In
a number of rabbinic passages, various views are offered regarding the
duration of Patriarchal merit. Most relevant for us is the opinion of a
R. Aḥa, who in two passages expresses the view that the merit of the Patriarchs will last forever. As proof of his position, R. Aḥa cites the passage in Deuteronomy 4, to which we referred earlier, that alludes to the
role of the Patriarchal covenant in rescuing the Israelites from future
exile. Apparently, R. Aḥa also believed that the exile and redemption described in such passages refer to the present exile and the coming messianic redemption.[42]

Taking the extension of the covenant into account, we can now offer
a more complete description of how providence operates on behalf of
the Israelites after the conquest. Once the Israelites settle in the land
of Canaan, they are in an ideal position to earn divine providence. Not
only will observance of the commandments bring intellectual perfection,
they are in a location which is particularly receptive to providential emanations. However, in times when the Israelites fall away from proper
observance and are not worthy of their own providence, providence
inherited from Abraham will continue to protect them from harm. The
major difficulty with all this is that Gersonides does not give an adequate
explanation for the notion that the covenant continues to exert an influence even after the conquest of Canaan. It is not clear whether Gersonides believes that this was predicted in Abraham's original prophecy,
or whether he settles on the philosophically problematic position that
the direction of events predicted in Abraham's prophecy has somehow
been altered.

THE FUNCTION OF INHERITED PROVIDENCE
AFTER THE CONQUEST

Let us now examine more carefully how inherited providence protects the Jewish people from the time of the conquest of Canaan to the present exile. We saw that in Gersonides' interpretation of the exodus story,
inherited providence had a clearly defined role. It functioned as a temporary emergency measure to rescue the Israelites when they were faced
with complete destruction and no other form of providence was available
to protect them. What happens after the conquest of Canaan? Does inherited providence continue to perform this specific function? The problem in
answering this question is that Gersonides' views on the role of inherited
providence are not as well developed with respect to the post-conquest period as they are for the period preceding the conquest. Nonetheless, there
is enough information scattered throughout Gersonides' commentaries to
construct a fairly coherent position on this matter.

What emerges in a number of passages in Gersonides' exegetical
works is that once the Israelites are settled in Canaan, inherited providence, in fact, continues to operate as a sort of providential back-up mechanism. To start with, there are strong indications that inherited providence
continues to protect the Jews against only the worst kind of disaster—that
is, complete destruction. Evidence for this observation is that Gersonides
consistently uses forms of the verb, *kilah*, "to annihilate," to describe the
state of affairs that inherited providence is meant to ward off. Thus, for example, in a passage cited earlier in which Gersonides discusses the extension of the covenant to the messianic period, he states that inherited
providence is the force that ensures that Israel "would not be annihilated"
(*lo' yikhalu*) if they worship other gods.[43]

Moreover, as with the redemption from Egypt, it would seem that inherited providence comes into play only when other forms of providence
are not available. This point emerges in Gersonides' commentary on
Leviticus 26, where he interprets a statement made by God regarding the
protective function of the covenant during the predicted exile:

> Despite all their [i.e., the Israelites'] excessive rebellious behavior,
> My providence will be with them to some degree while they are
> in the land of their enemies. I have not permitted their enemies to
> destroy them so that My covenant with them will be nullified, for
> I am the Lord their God. And if they are not worthy that My prov-
> idence be conjoined with them on their own account, some de-
> gree of providence will be conjoined with them on account of the
> covenant with the Patriarchs in such a manner that their offspring
> will not be destroyed and My covenant nullified. The conjunction

of His providence with us nowadays while we are in exile is clearly evident, for despite the fact that our enemies rule over us and want to harm us, we [continue to] survive among them.[44]

Note that the Patriarchal covenant is again depicted as a force that protects the Jews from complete destruction, and that, furthermore, it performs this function when they are "not worthy" of providence "on their own account."

Another passage reinforcing the notion that inherited providence continues to function as a last resort is found in Gersonides' commentary on Deuteronomy, where he interprets the celebrated verses describing the punishment traditionally known as *hester panim*, or the hiding of the divine countenance:

> The fifteenth *to'elet* is to inform [us] about a kind of punishment different from the other kinds [discussed] previously; i.e., God will take away His providence from those that rebel against Him, abandon Him and nullify His covenant. They will be abandoned to chance events as it says, "I will hide My countenance from them and they shall be ready prey. . . ."[45] One who is afflicted in this way will [still] experience some good fortune on account of general providence. However, "at the time that their foot falters,"[46] they will experience a tremendous fall. For this reason, you find that the kings of Israel had some good fortune, even though they did that which was evil in the eyes of God. But when their foot faltered, they were decimated. They would have been completely annihilated had it not been for God's providence over the Patriarchs.[47]

In this passage, Gersonides reiterates information about *hester panim*, which is contained in the fourth book of the *Wars*. As we noted in an earlier chapter, Gersonides understands *hester panim* as the state of affairs that is brought about when a righteous individual or nation is not worthy of individual providence. God "hides His countenance" in the sense that such an individual or nation is vulnerable to harmful chance events.[48]

But what is most significant here is the statement Gersonides adds at the end of the passage regarding the Patriarchal covenant. We are told that the Israelites, in fact, experienced the effects of *hester panim* during the period of the kings, when they lost their capacity for providence and suffered great losses inflicted upon them by their enemies. Had it not been for the covenant, Gersonides notes, the Jews would have been "completely annihilated." Thus, we see once again that inherited providence functions to protect the Jewish people from the worst type of catastrophe, and that it does so only when no other form of providence is there to assist them.

Another point that emerges from this passage is that when the Patriarchal covenant protects the Jews, it does so only in a limited way. According to Gersonides, the Israelites were "decimated" by their enemies during the period of the kings before inherited providence came to their rescue. Thus, while inherited providence plays a valuable protective role, it would appear that it is not as potent a form of protection as the providence one earns on one's own.[49]

This position is also consistent with observations made earlier regarding the role of inherited providence in the exodus story. We noted that inherited providence muted the worst effects of the slavery in Egypt in its initial phases but was not able to stop the suffering of the Israelites altogether until they were threatened with complete destruction. We also saw in Gersonides' interpretation of the golden calf episode that inherited providence was not able to offer a level of protection sufficient to satisfy Moses, and that it was for this reason that he demanded of God that the full protection accorded by individual providence be reinstated.[50]

By what mechanism does inherited providence protect the Israelites after the conquest? It is clear from some passages in Gersonides' commentaries on later books of the Bible that inherited providence performs its function by simply warding off an immediate physical threat. That is, it brings about a miraculous intervention of sorts. In one instance, Gersonides makes this suggestion by doing little more than accept the plain meaning of the biblical text. In an earlier discussion, we cited the following passage from II Kings, in which King Jehoahaz and the northern Israelite kingdom are rescued from the Arameans on account of the Patriarchal covenant:

> But the LORD was gracious and merciful to them, and He turned back to them for the sake of His covenant with Abraham, Isaac, and Jacob. He refrained from destroying them and He still did not cast them out from His presence.[51]

In this passage, the physical threat posed by King Hazael appears to be directly neutralized by the Patriarchal covenant.

In one of his to'aliyyot, Gersonides provides a philosophical interpretation of this passage:

> ... even though Israel is sinful towards God, providence is conjoined to them by virtue of the Patriarchs in such a way that they will not be destroyed. Thus, [the biblical text] told us that because God saw Hazael's oppression of Israel which was of a magnitude that he might have destroyed them were it not for God ... God took pity on them, was merciful to them and turned towards them by virtue of His covenant with Abraham, Isaac and Jacob, and saved them from the hand of Hazael.[52]

Here Gersonides makes the now familiar identification between the Patriarchal covenant and inherited providence. Most important, he tacitly accepts the notion that the Patriarchal covenant confers physical protection of the kind described in the biblical text.

In several passages, Gersonides assumes that the covenant confers protection on the Jews, even when there is no explicit reference to it in the biblical text. In II Kings 14, for example, the biblical text tells us that God grants victory to the Israelites during the reign of Joash son of Jeroboam despite their sinful behavior, because God has resolved "not to blot out the name of Israel from under heaven."[53] Now, there is no mention here of the Patriarchal covenant; nonetheless, Gersonides assumes that it is this very factor which protects the Israelites from danger.[54]

The same point is illustrated by a passage in Gersonides' *Commentary on Esther*, in which he comments on a statement made by Mordecai to Esther just after Haman has issued his decree regarding the Jews. In the biblical text, Mordecai warns Esther of the consequences that will follow if she is not willing to exert the effort necessary to rescue her people from the hands of Haman:

> Do not imagine that you of all the Jews, will escape with your life by being in the king's palace. On the contrary, if you keep silent in this crisis, relief and deliverance will come to the Jews from another quarter, while you and your father's house will perish.[55]

Gersonides attempts to make sense of Mordecai's cryptic reference to "relief and deliverance" which "will come to the Jews from another quarter" by interpreting it as an allusion to the Patriarchal covenant. As Gersonides puts it, what Mordecai means is that God "creates causes 'from another quarter' on account of His covenant with the Patriarchs." Mordecai's message to Esther, therefore, is that if she is not willing to offer assistance to her people, surely the covenant will protect them.[56] Thus, once again, Gersonides makes the assumption that the biblical text is referring to the Patriarchal covenant even when there is no explicit mention of it.

While all of these examples indicate that inherited providence can safeguard the Jews by simply warding off immediate physical danger, it would appear that this is not the only way it performs its function. A whole other dimension of the protective role of inherited providence is alluded to in Gersonides' interpretation of Leviticus 26 and Deuteronomy 28-30, the celebrated *tokhehah* portions.

These portions of the biblical text are characterized by detailed lists of blessings and curses. The Israelites are informed that their behavior in keeping God's laws will determine whether they will experience the blessings or the curses once they settle in the land of Canaan. What makes these sections of Gersonides' exegetical works particularly valuable is that he sees them as prescriptive for all the major events in Jewish history up to the messianic period. Gersonides correlates the blessings with periods of prosperity—such as those of Joshua, David and Solomon. The curses are correlated with all the hardships the Jews experience, including both exiles. These portions therefore provide a survey of Gersonides' views regarding the entirety of Jewish history.[57]

Most important for our purposes is that Gersonides provides philosophical information about how providence operates on behalf of the Jewish people throughout their later history. Gersonides' interpretation of the blessings does not require much explanation. Here Gersonides makes use of philosophical principles already familiar to us from earlier discussions. If the Israelites obey God's laws, they will achieve intellectual perfection, become worthy of divine providence, and then experience the material rewards promised in the biblical text.[58]

The curses described in the *tokhehah* portions are more ambiguous from a philosophical standpoint. The key question is whether these punishments are due to providential suffering or God's total abandonment of the Israelites to chance events. In fact, Gersonides tells us, the former alternative is correct. In his commentary on Deuteronomy, he provides the following reasoning for this position:

> [The biblical text] makes it clear that just as the blessings[59] are due to individual providence, so the curses[60] are due to individual providence for the purpose of chastising them. . . . It is not possible that the curses which extend to all things in "the city" and "the field"[61] are due to general providence. Indeed, whenever evil, loss, and destruction affect all of the actions which a man performs in an ongoing fashion,[62] it is not possible that it be due to general providence. Likewise, there could not be ongoing pestilence if it were not due to this [i.e., individual providence]. For it is rare and unusual that a plague should occur in this manner due to general providence.[63]

Gersonides argues that the punishments described in the *tokhehah* portions are too intense to be attributed to mere chance occurrence and must therefore serve a more directed purpose. They are surely the result of providential suffering which is designed to chastise the Israelites when they are no longer obedient to God.[64]

Gersonides provides a number of other significant details about the dynamics of these punishments in the course of his commentary on both *tokhehah* portions. For one, he emphasizes that the punishments occur only when the Israelites have sinned in the worst possible way by worshiping other gods. Moreover, the punishments do not come into effect until it is clear that the Israelites have refused to heed the warnings of God's prophets. Finally, one of the major themes running throughout Gersonides' interpretation of these punishments is that they come in "incremental fashion"—that is, with increasing severity. In his explication of the specific curses, Gersonides expends a good deal of energy demonstrating that each punishment is worse than the previous one. These points are clearly expressed in a passage in Gersonides' commentary on Leviticus 26:

> The Torah has informed us that the types of severe punishments reported in this portion will not afflict the entire nation except on account of those grave sins which destroy the Torah in its entirety. Take note that even in the times when Israel worshiped idols, God held off punishment and chastised them with the help of the prophets until it became clear that they refused to be disciplined, as it says, "Why do you seek further beatings / That you continue to offend?"[65] It is on account of the intensity of divine providence over Israel that He brings these punishments to chastise them in incremental fashion (be-hadragah).[66]

But there is one more ingredient Gersonides adds to his interpretation of these chastisements that is crucial for our concerns. According to a passage in Gersonides' commentary on Leviticus, the punishments described in the tokheḥah occur on account of inherited providence. This point is made in one of the toʿaliyyot at the end of Gersonides' explication of Leviticus 26:

> ... because of the intensity of providence over the righteous, it will continue in their offspring after them; thus, when they [i.e., the offspring] depart from the ways of the Torah—which is the reason for all perfection departing from them—God will chastise them with chastisement upon chastisement in order that they not become mired in those deficient opinions and will again acquire the perfection which they have abandoned.[67]

The one problem with this passage is that while Gersonides claims that the source of the providential punishments is inherited providence, he does not tell us who it is exactly that bequeaths this providence. Yet, the overwhelming likelihood is that Gersonides is referring to providence inherited from the Patriarchs. Support for this conjecture can be found in an interesting passage in Gersonides' *Commentary on II Kings* in which he provides a philosophical interpretation of events during the reign of Ahab, the wicked Israelite king:

The fifteenth [to'elet] clarifies the intensity of God's providence over Israel on account of His covenant with the Patriarchs. Thus, you find that even though the Israelites deserved to have God hide His face from them and abandon them because of the severity of their sins, [God] brought forth events which would discipline them, when it became apparent to God that many of Ahab's activities would cause Israel to depart completely from God. This [He brought about] in incremental fashion [be-hadragah]. First, He showed Ahab and Israel the truth of the prophets' words and curses, for they saw that the curse which Joshua placed on anyone who would build the city of Jericho was fulfilled.[68] This was a sign for them that the curses which are written in the Torah come to pass for those who do not obey its commandments. Since they did not learn their lesson from this [i.e., the incident at Jericho], God showed them that the curses of His prophet would come to pass immediately if they did not return to God. Therefore, it says that Elijah said to Ahab that "there will be no dew or rain in these years" except at God's bidding.[69] This would occur [i.e., God would reverse his decree] only if they returned to worshiping Him. When He saw that they did not learn their lesson here, even though they saw the implementation of the prophet's forecasts and curses, [God] caused Elijah to return to Ahab and do something which would clearly show that the Lord is God, [i.e., perform] an extraordinary miracle from which it would also be clear and evident that the Baal was of no worth.[70] The goal was that Israel would return to the worship of God and kill the prophets of the Baal. But when God saw that Ahab did not succumb to this [lesson], He showed him miracles which brought good things so that he would know that He is Lord; He promised these good things through His prophet. The result was that he was victorious with only a small number of men over the king of Aram and all the kings who were with him.[71] He [i.e., God] repeated this action so that the belief in God would strengthen in his heart.[72] Despite all this, he did not learn his lesson, and for this reason, the evil which occurred to him came to pass.[73]

In this passage, Gersonides is clearly making use of the concepts discussed in his exegesis of the tokhehah portions. The providential punishments during the days of Ahab have all the characteristics Gersonides ascribes to the curses appearing in Leviticus and Deuteronomy. Thus, the troubles the Israelites experience in the above passage occur when they have abandoned God and are no longer worthy of their own providence. Furthermore, they are meant to discipline the Israelites in order to convince them to return to God. Finally, they proceed in increments of severity (*be-hadragah*), as Gersonides painstakingly demonstrates. But what is most important for us is that Gersonides explicitly informs us that these punishments are the result of providence specifically inherited from the Patriarchs. At the very beginning of the passage, Gersonides states that the chastisements occur "on account of His covenant with the Patriarchs."[74]

It is not clear why Gersonides feels the need to posit inherited providence as the source of the providential punishments in the *tokhehah* in Leviticus. Normally, providential suffering is simply the result of one's *own* providence. There is also no obvious cue in the biblical text itself to suggest that inherited providence is the source of the punishments. While the Patriarchal covenant is mentioned in the *tokhehah* portions, it serves the purpose of rescuing the Jews from exile, not punishing them.

Yet with a little reflection, the logic of Gersonides' position becomes apparent. It is important to keep in mind that when the punishments in the *tokhehah* portions come into effect, the Israelites have completely abandoned God. In this case, therefore, the Israelites are not worthy of providence of *any* kind. Consequently, Gersonides is forced to conclude that the only form of providence that can produce the chastisements described in the biblical text is one that is not their own, i.e., providence inherited from the Patriarchs.

We now have another way of understanding Gersonides' original assertion that inherited providence protects the Jews from destruction throughout the rest of their history. Inherited providence can accomplish this end by bringing chastisements when the Israelites have completely forsaken God. These chastisements are designed to convince the Jews to repent so that they can once again experience their own providence and avoid the catastrophic effects of chance events. All of this may seem paradoxical in that God is inflicting harm in order for the Jews to avoid harm. However, one must keep in mind that with chance events, the Jews risk utter and complete annihilation. Therefore, as painful as providential suffering may be, the abandonment to chance events is potentially much worse.

What is somewhat perplexing is how little Gersonides says about this manifestation of inherited providence. While it is alluded to in his commentary on Leviticus 26, this reference, as we have seen, is extremely brief. In his commentary on the other *tokhehah* portion in Deuteronomy 28, Gersonides makes mention of providential suffering but not inherited providence as its underlying cause.[75] Furthermore, one might have expected that Gersonides would allude to this manifestation of inherited providence in his commentaries on the historical books of the Prophets and Writings. It is here, after all, that many of the providential chastisements predicted in the *tokhehah* portions begin to come true. However, with the exception of his remarks on events in the days of Ahab, Gersonides is almost entirely silent in this regard.

Nonetheless, I think it is safe to assume that Gersonides considered the providential punishments incurred by inherited providence as an important factor in Jewish history. Gersonides' comments on the *tokheḥah* in Leviticus make it clear enough that this expression of providence is the source of the curses which are, in turn, correlated with the suffering that characterizes much of later Jewish history. If he did not say more about the role of inherited providence in his commentaries on events reported in the later historical books of the Bible, it may be that he assumed his reader would be familiar with his remarks on this matter in his commentary on Leviticus. As we noted at the beginning of this chapter, Gersonides, in his commentaries on the Prophets and Writings, seems to have expected his reader to be thoroughly acquainted with the philosophical insights in his *Commentary on the Torah*.

To sum up our discussion thus far, inherited providence continues to be operative even past the conquest of Canaan. It protects the Israelites when they are not worthy of their own providence and are vulnerable to chance events that might completely destroy them. Inherited providence performs its protective function in one of two ways. It can safeguard the Israelites in a direct manner by quashing an immediate physical threat endangering their survival. It can also accomplish its purpose by precipitating providential suffering that will force the Israelites to return to a life of obedience to God so that they can once again be worthy of their own providence. Of these two expressions of inherited providence, the latter appears to be highly significant in Gersonides' reading of Jewish history in that he sees this form of providence as the factor responsible for the continuous travails of the Jewish people.

THE PRESENT EXILE

Let us now take a closer look at how divine providence affects the Jewish people in Gersonides' own period. While Gersonides never conducts an independent analysis of this question, there are numerous passages in which he attempts to give a philosophical explanation for the present exile. For example, in our last discussion we saw that Gersonides correlates both the first and second exile with specific curses in the *tokheḥah* portions of Leviticus and Deuteronomy—curses that are, in turn, attributed to providential suffering incurred by inherited providence. The hardship of the present exile is explicitly discussed by Gersonides in the following passage in his commentary on Leviticus 26:

. . . everything that is reported in these curses has happened to us and our fathers because of our sins and the sins of our fathers, as has been made known in historical accounts. My opinion is that [the phrase] "and I will make your sanctuaries desolate,"[76] refers to the destruction of the first and second Temples. The statement, "And I will scatter you among the nations, and I will unsheathe the sword against you," refers to those who died at Betar, which [was an incident that] occurred a short time after the destruction of the second Temple. The statement, "but you shall perish among the nations and the land of your enemies shall consume you,"[77] refers to the great hardships which have come to pass for us and in which many have died: for example, the destruction of some of [our] holy communities and the expulsion from France,[78] which on account of famine and disease caused the death of many times the number [of people] who left Egypt.[79]

Here Gersonides quite clearly views the suffering of the Jewish people in his own period as due to their own failings. The present exile is predicted in the *tokheḥah,* and, like all the curses reported in this portion of the biblical text, is an instance of providential suffering designed to convince the Jews to be obedient to God. The responsibility the Jews of Gersonides' own day bear for their troubles is, in fact, explicitly referred to in the above passage, when Gersonides asserts that the curses in the *tokheḥah* have come about "because of *our* sins and the sins of our fathers [italics added]."

In a number of places, however, Gersonides offers another interpretation of the suffering of the present exile that significantly differs from the one just described. The central passage for this alternative view is one to which we have also referred in an earlier discussion. We saw that in book four of the *Wars* Gersonides takes up the question of the suffering of the righteous, and that one of the reasons he offers to account for this phenomenon is that the righteous can suffer simply by circumstance; that is, a righteous person may inherit the misfortunes his ancestors have incurred through the loss of providence. Gersonides goes on to explain that this type of suffering does not imply any evil in God, since the righteous individual can still escape from these misfortunes in one of two ways. General providence may, in the long run, rectify the problem, because the constellations generally influence events for the better. Alternatively, the righteous person may be able to achieve such an extraordinary degree of perfection that he is able to overcome his unfortunate circumstances with the help of individual providence.[80]

What is significant for the present discussion is that Gersonides illustrates these principles with the exile that the Jews are experiencing in his own day:

> In a similar vein, the Prophet has said: "Our fathers have sinned and are no more; and we must bear their guilt."[81] According to my interpretation of this passage, this means: when our fathers had sinned and accordingly were punished with exile among the nations, their offspring were obliged to bear this punishment, for they are not worthy to return and repossess their land as before, unless God intervenes with His extraordinary providence.[82] And so long as the offspring do not attain that level of union [with God], they bear that punishment. But if that punishment had not been incurred by their fathers, the children would have remained in the land as before and would not have gone out unless they [themselves] had committed evil acts that required this punishment, either due to providence, as will be explained,[83] or due to the absence of providence.[84]

Gersonides informs us that the misfortunes of the Jews in his own time are due to mere circumstance in that they are suffering as a result of punishment that their ancestors brought on long ago by abandoning God. Gersonides goes on to explain that the Jews can overcome these misfortunes if they achieve a high level of conjunction with God and experience the degree of individual providence necessary to enable them to return to their homeland. As yet, Gersonides notes, the Jews are not worthy of such providence.

What Gersonides is implying in this passage is that the Jews of his own time are in a sort of providential limbo. They are apparently obedient enough to God so that their troubles cannot simply be attributed to their own sinful actions; the exile is, in fact, nothing more than an unfortunate condition that they have inherited from their ancestors. However, they are not at a sufficient level of perfection to experience providence in its most intense form—providence which would put an end to the exile altogether.

Gersonides appears to have been enamored of this explanation. He repeats it in detail in several passages in his biblical commentaries.[85] But what should be noted is that the philosophical understanding of the exile presented here is entirely different from that which we saw in his commentary on Leviticus. In the latter source, Gersonides assumes that the Jews are suffering from the hardship of the exile because of their own neglect of God's laws. In contrast, Gersonides argues in the *Wars* that the Jews of his own time are for the most part innocent of any wrongdoing, and that any suffering they are now experiencing is due to the misfortunes brought on by their ancestors.

The picture becomes even more complicated if we refer to passages in Gersonides' *Commentary on Daniel*, which also take up the subject of the exile. Let us first look at Gersonides' comments on Daniel 9:24, a cryptic verse in which the restoration of the Temple is predicted:

> The second *to'elet* is to inform us why the exile [consequent upon the destruction] of the second Temple is longer than that of the first Temple—despite what is well-known regarding the severity of the sins which the kings of Judah committed.[86] Despite this [i.e., the sins of the Judean kings], the time of the [first] exile did not extend more than fifty-two years. [Those who lived at the time of] the second Temple did not worship idols, [and yet] the exile has lasted an extraordinary length of time. The solution to this difficulty can be made clear in the following way: On account of the multiple sins committed during the [period of the] first Temple, it was decreed that the second Temple would stand only up to the completion of "seven times seventy [years]" etc.[87] After this [time], they [i.e., the Jews] would continue to bear the sin of their fathers up to the time of redemption. It is therefore evident from here that this exile which we are in today is due to the sins which Israel committed before the Babylonian exile.[88]

In this passage, Gersonides attempts to explain why the exile that the Jews are now experiencing has been of much greater duration than the first exile. His perplexity is based on the observation that the first exile was caused by grave sins, such as idol worship—a fact attested to in the biblical text—and that there is no evidence that the Jews committed sins of comparable severity to precipitate a second exile. Gersonides responds to this problem by arguing, in effect, that this question is predicated on the erroneous assumption that the second exile was caused by factors different from those which caused the first. In fact, Gersonides tells us, both were the result of the sins committed before the first exile. Those sins were of such magnitude that the Jews would have to suffer the consequences of their actions for the rest of history. Thus, the destruction of the second Temple and the suffering the Jews are experiencing during the present exile are all compensation for sins committed in the period of the first Temple. In short, the second exile is merely a continuation of the first, with the period of the second Temple being a hiatus in between.

In another passage in his *Commentary on Daniel*, Gersonides refines this explanation. In commenting on Daniel 11:36, Gersonides claims that God has spread out the punishments that resulted in the first exile over the entire duration of Jewish history in order to spare the Jews from utter annihilation. Had the full punishment been brought on during the first exile, the Jews would surely have been destroyed. Gersonides attributes this act of providence to the Patriarchal covenant. As Gersonides succinctly puts it, "God exacted compensation over a long period on account of His covenant with the Patriarchs in order to rescue Israel from annihilation."[89]

In these passages from the *Commentary on Daniel*, we see elements of both the position taken by Gersonides in the *Wars* and that which is found in his commentary on Leviticus. On the one hand, Gersonides adopts the notion presented in the *Wars* that the suffering the Jews are experiencing in Gersonides' own day is not the result of their own sins, but is due to the sins of their forefathers. On the other hand, Gersonides tells us that the covenant of the Patriarchs has had a hand to play in the suffering of the present exile, a view that is closer to the position taken in the commentary on Leviticus.

But these observations notwithstanding, the position outlined in the *Commentary on Daniel* is extremely puzzling. It is difficult, if not impossible, to harmonize what Gersonides is saying here with his philosophical views on providence. Nothing in Gersonides' philosophical or exegetical works can account for the notion that providential suffering has been "spread out" over many generations. The problem with this view becomes evident when we recall that the whole purpose of providential suffering is to chastise a person or nation so that they reestablish their connection with God. It must be presumed, therefore, that the subject who experiences this type of suffering is precisely the one who has sinned. It makes little sense to say that the subject of the punishment is someone other than the guilty party. Yet it is precisely this position that Gersonides appears to be taking when he argues that the troubles of the present exile are in compensation for the sinful behavior of the Jewish people many generations earlier.

In summary, Gersonides' views on the suffering of the Jewish people in the present exile appear to be rather unclear. Not only are his statements on this issue inconsistent with one another, some of them do not make sense within his philosophical system at all.

Rather than throw up our hands in the face of this problem, it might be worthwhile to speculate about why this issue, in particular, appears to have elicited no clear position on Gersonides' part. If we look again at the passages cited, I think we can discern the central tension lying at the root of Gersonides' confusion. The first two passages we examined offer two very different viewpoints on the problem. According to one, the Jews are suffering because of their own sins, while according to the other, their suffering is attributed to mere circumstance. Now, obviously, the second explanation has an advantage over the first in that it absolves the Jews in

Gersonides' own time of blame for their lowly condition. The advantage of this position is even more apparent when one considers that Gersonides lived his entire life in a Christian environment in which it was commonly believed that the suffering of the Jews was evidence of their damnation. Gersonides' position effectively counters that claim.

But Gersonides was perhaps not entirely satisfied with this position, given the depth of the hardship the Jews were experiencing. Surely the persecutions at the hands of the Gentile nations, to which Gersonides himself attests, were for some deeper purpose than the mere circumstance of the Jews having had sinful ancestors. In all probability, the other position was therefore formulated to respond to this challenge. Hence the suggestion that the troubles the Jews are undergoing are, in fact, due to their own sins.

Of course, there are still difficulties that cannot be easily solved. Was Gersonides aware of the inconsistency between these views? We have no clear indication one way or the other. Nor does our interpretation help account for the problematic passages in the *Commentary on Daniel*, where Gersonides offers a position on the present exile that makes little sense, at least from a philosophical standpoint.

One final issue that needs to be considered in assessing Gersonides' philosophical views on the present exile is whether he identifies his Christian overlords with the descendants of Esau. This position was not uncommon among Jewish thinkers in the Middle Ages—although there were also those who dissented from this view, including ibn Ezra, whose influence on Gersonides was considerable.[90] The reason this question is important is that in a number of places Gersonides develops an elaborate philosophical interpretation of the relationship between Jacob and Esau throughout history. If, in fact, Christendom is identified with Esau's offspring, this philosophical interpretation would have to be taken into account in our assessment of Gersonides' views on the present exile.

The most comprehensive philosophical discussion of the relationship between Jacob and Esau is contained in Gersonides' commentary on Genesis 27, the chapter in which Jacob steals Esau's blessing. Of particular interest to us is Gersonides' interpretation of the blessings Isaac confers upon Jacob and Esau. Gersonides treats these blessings as prophetic predictions about the fortunes awaiting their respective offspring.[91]

A key point in Gersonides' interpretation is that these predictions are very much contingent upon the behavior of Jacob's descendants. The wealth and prosperity promised to Jacob as well as the prediction that he will have dominion over his brother, will come about only if Jacob's offspring are worthy of individual providence. If they are not worthy, they will be dominated by the descendants of Esau.[92] The contingency of Jacob's fortunes is alluded to in Esau's blessing, when Isaac informs the latter that "when you grow restive, you shall break his yoke from your neck."[93] What this statement means in philosophical terms is that the descendants of Esau will be able to gain ascendancy when Jacob's offspring are not worthy of individual providence. Without individual providence, the fortunes of Jacob's descendants will be determined solely by the influences of general providence, a factor that can just as easily work in favor of Esau's descendants as it can for Jacob's.

Now if Gersonides indeed identifies the Christians as the descendants of Esau, it is not hard to imagine how he would use the philosophical material from his commentary on Genesis 27 to help explain the suffering of the Jews in the present exile. The subjugation of the Jews under Christendom would be a fulfillment of the predictions laid out in Isaac's blessings. Gersonides could argue that the Christians have gained the upper hand because the Jews are unworthy of individual providence and that the constellations happen to be influencing events in favor of their enemies.

This conjecture would appear to find support in a highly interesting passage in Gersonides' *Commentary on the Torah*, where the Christians are clearly identified with the descendants of Esau. After his interpretation of the episode in which the Amalekites are defeated in Exodus 18, Gersonides assesses the significance of this story for the Jews of his own period:

> Indeed, the Torah intended [that this story serve] a good purpose, since it was foreordained that, in the end, we would falter on account of deserving a much greater punishment than this, and that we would be exiled among the children of Esau who rule and dominate [us], and are "the heroes of old, men of renown."[94] So that our hearts would not melt, and our hope in God would not depart [from us], [the Torah] told us about the affair of Amalek in this story so that our hearts would be strengthened and we would believe all the promises which our prophets have promised us regarding the redemption and that He will not break us down before the children of the wicked,[95] God forbid, and so that we have hope in our God. For He will restore us as of old[96] and place us on "the highest of mountains."[97] May our eyes see the Building of our God [i.e., the Temple] speedily in our days.[98]

In unusually emotional terms, Gersonides expresses the view that the story regarding the defeat of the Amalekites was deliberately placed in the Torah in order to bolster the flagging spirits of the Jews of his own day. It was foreseen that the Jews would eventually be exiled among the children of Esau. The Torah therefore reported the defeat of the Amalekites—who are also descended from Esau—so that the Jews experiencing the future exile would never lose hope that they too would be redeemed.[99]

Nevertheless, no firm conclusion can be drawn from this passage, since there is reason to doubt that it is from Gersonides' own hand. This passage is, in fact, absent from many manuscripts.[100] Moreover, to my knowledge, there is no other place in all of Gersonides' writings in which he identifies the Christians with the descendants of Esau despite ample opportunity to do so. The sections of Gersonides' commentaries dealing with the *tokheḥah* portions would have been an ideal location to raise this issue, since, as we have seen, the philosophical meaning of the present exile is dealt with in these passages. Another place that would have been equally appropriate for Gersonides to address this matter is in his *Commentary on Daniel*, where on several occasions he discusses Christian Europe as part of his attempt to interpret Daniel's eschatological visions.[101] Yet in none of these sources does Gersonides identify Christendom with the children of Esau.[102] We must therefore conclude that there is no evidence to link Christendom with the descendants of Esau in Gersonides' thinking.

Let us review what our analysis has yielded regarding the operation of divine providence in Jewish history, from the conquest of Canaan onward. Once the Israelites settle in their new homeland, the expectation is that they will experience individual providence. By adhering to the directives contained in the Torah, they will be guided to intellectual perfection, the primary prerequisite for providential reward. Furthermore, their chances of experiencing providence will be enhanced by residing in the land of Canaan. That location is ideally suited for the reception of providential emanations. Also, the concentration of the Israelites in a single place will provide the proper communal structure for them to achieve intellectual perfection, with the Temple serving as a national focus for the study of philosophical wisdom.

Provision is also made for the possibility that the Jews will fail in their observance of the commandments and will be threatened with annihilation on account of their loss of providence. God delays the fulfillment of the Patriarchal covenant so that it will act as a protective force in these circumstances. What this means in philosophical terms is that providence inherited from the Patriarchs will continue to be available to protect the Jewish people at times when they are not worthy of providence on their own.

Inherited providence performs this function in two ways: first, by warding off immediate physical danger, and, second, by precipitating a series of providential punishments to convince the Jews to repent. In the actual historical record, inherited providence in this second form becomes a key determinant for events in Jewish history. The Jews rapidly become disobedient as they are attracted to other gods, and inherited providence comes into play to bring providential punishments which are meant to set them aright. Not heeding the warnings of these punishments, the Jews experience an escalation in the severity of these punishments until they are eventually exiled from their homeland.

Inherited providence, however, never abandons the Jews, even in the exile. It continues to protect them from destruction and will eventually work on their behalf to help them reclaim the land of Israel in the period of the Messiah. At that time, Abraham's original prophecy will be truly fulfilled, in that the Jews will gain possession of the entire land which was not fully conquered in the days of Joshua. Inherited providence will then no longer be needed, because there will be peace among nations, and the Jews will no longer be threatened with annihilation. Moreover, the Jews themselves will be devoted to worshipping God and will certainly experience divine providence in their own right.

Where Gersonides is most unclear is with regard to the activity of providence in his own period. He seems torn between two possibilities. Either the Jews are worthy of their own providence but have not achieved a sufficient degree of perfection in order to reclaim the land of Israel, or they are still mired in sin and therefore continue to feel the effects of the providential punishments designed to make them repent.

We will conclude by relating our discoveries about inherited providence in this chapter to our treatment of this issue in earlier discussions. What emerges from our analysis and is crucial for our entire study is that the role ascribed to inherited providence both before and after the conquest is entirely consistent.

In our discussion of the exodus story, we saw that inherited providence had a clearly defined role. It served as an emergency measure to rescue the Israelites from physical annihilation when they were threatened with destruction at the hands of the Egyptians but were not deserving of providence in their own right. The role of inherited providence was also a temporary one. In the course of rescuing the Israelites from slavery, it provided the necessary conditions for the Israelites to regain the capacity for achieving providence on their own. It accomplished this end by bringing miracles that would convince the Israelites to acknowledge God's existence and allow them to achieve intellectual perfection.

After the conquest of Canaan, inherited providence continues to perform a series of similar functions. It comes into play as a last resort to rescue the Jews when they have disobeyed God's commandments and are therefore threatened with destruction from harmful chance events. Its role also continues to be a temporary one. While inherited providence sometimes assists the Jews by simply warding off an immediate physical threat, its most important function in the scheme of Jewish history is that it produces providential punishments. These chastisements are designed to convince the Jews to re-establish their connection with God so that they can once again be protected by their own providence. In effect, the punishments produced by inherited providence do exactly what the miracles in Egypt did, albeit in a more painful way. Both provide the necessary conditions for the Jews to earn their own providence so that inherited providence is no longer needed.

Another feature of inherited providence that is consistent before and after the conquest is that it is clearly not as potent a form of protection as providence earned on one's own. Inherited providence softened the impact of the slavery in Egypt, but was not able to entirely prevent the suffering of the Israelites. Similarly, as we saw in Gersonides' remarks about *hester panim*, inherited providence rescues the Jews from destruction in the period of the kings, but only after they have been decimated by their enemies.

What is now evident is that providence inherited from the Patriarchs has a well-defined role for the entirety of Jewish history. It is an ever-present force available to the Jewish people when they are not worthy of any other form of divine protection. It ensures their physical survival in such circumstances, while also assisting them to achieve intellectual perfection so that they can once again earn providence on their own.

EIGHT

The Messianic Era

W e will now complete our sketch of Gersonides' interpretation of Jewish history by analyzing his conception of the projected final phase of the historical process: the messianic period. While we have already had a good deal to say about the messianic era in the course of discussion in previous chapters, our references to this subject have been fragmentary. Our task in this chapter, therefore, will be to consolidate this material into a coherent framework. We will also examine a number of issues in Gersonides' eschatology which have not yet been dealt with, such as Gersonides' views on the resurrection of the dead.

There is no place in Gersonides' writings where he deals with the messianic period in a systematic way; his thoughts on this subject are scattered throughout his exegetical works. Most important is his *Commentary on the Torah*, where he makes reference to the messianic era in a number of passages, particularly at the end of his commentary on Deuteronomy. Also important is his *Commentary on Daniel*, which, as we have already noted, treats Daniel's prophecies as predictions about events throughout Jewish history, including the messianic period. However, it would be a mistake to assume that because the messianic period is not treated systematically, Gersonides has no clear thoughts on the issue. In fact, if one examines the many references to the messianic period in his writings, there emerges a fairly well-defined picture of this era of history.

It is important to emphasize that our goal in this chapter will be to elucidate only the philosophical aspects of Gersonides' views on the messianic era, particularly as they relate to the issues of covenant and providence, which have been the focus of our study thus far. We need to make this point because a good portion of the material regarding the mes-

147

sianic period in Gersonides' commentaries—particularly that which is contained in his *Commentary on Daniel*—attempts to describe in detail the historical events leading up to the coming of the Messiah. Such material is generally not of philosophical import.[1]

One handicap that must be acknowledged from the outset is that a commentary Gersonides composed on the Book of Isaiah is lost to us.[2] Given the importance of Isaiah as a source of speculations on the messianic period in rabbinic and medieval thought, the absence of this work is a serious obstacle to a comprehensive assessment of Gersonides' eschatological views.

Much of what Gersonides has to say about the messianic period from a philosophical standpoint has already emerged in the previous chapter in the course of our analysis of inherited providence and its function in the post-conquest phase of Jewish history. The central defining feature of the messianic era in Gersonides' thinking is that it represents the fulfillment of the Patriarchal covenant. What this means in philosophical terms is that the messianic era marks the end of the influence of providence inherited from Abraham and signifies the point at which the Jews will begin to prosper in their homeland entirely on the basis of their own providence. This will be possible only in the messianic period, because in that era there will be everlasting peace, and all the nations of the world will acknowledge the God of Israel. In the absence of any threat of physical or spiritual harm from the other nations of the world, the Jews will be able to live securely in the land of Israel and pursue intellectual perfection. They will therefore perpetually experience providence which they themselves earn without having to fall back on the protection provided by inherited providence.[3]

Another important point that emerged from our previous discussion is the importance of exegetical factors in the formulation of Gersonides' views regarding the messianic era. That the Patriarchal covenant is fulfilled in the messianic period is an idea that seems to have been suggested to Gersonides by a number of biblical passages in which it is predicted that this covenant will rescue the Israelites from a future exile.[4]

While we have outlined the core issues in Gersonides' interpretation of the messianic era, there is a good deal more that needs to be said. For instance, one point of confusion that is evident in some passages in Gersonides' commentaries is the role the Jews themselves play in the process of redemption. According to the above outline, the Jews appear to have no real effect on the timing of the redemption, since it comes about as a result of a historical process beyond their control. The arrival of the messianic era appears to be determined solely by the presence of the right environmental conditions; it is only when the nations of the world worship the God of Israel that the messianic redemption will occur.

That the advent of the messianic era is a predestined event is underscored in Gersonides' attempt to adduce scriptural evidence to predict the year that the Messiah will appear. In his *Commentary on Daniel*, Gersonides singles out the year 1358 as the date of his arrival.[5] In other passages, however, Gersonides clearly supports the rabbinic notion that the Jews can hasten the redemption by diligently observing the commandments. In the previous chapter, we alluded to one of his *pinnot ha-torah*, which stresses that the advent of the messianic era is dependent on this factor.[6] We also cited a passage from the *Wars* in which Gersonides indicates that proper adherence to God's laws will bring about the end of the exile.[7]

Gersonides appears to make an attempt at resolving this conflict by arriving at a compromise between the two views in a passage in his *Commentary on Daniel*. After predicting the date of the advent of the messianic period, Gersonides adds the following remark:

> . . . and it would seem that in and around that time [of the arrival of the Messiah], God will hasten the redemption, if the Israelites improve their ways, as it is said, "I the LORD will speed it in due time."[8]

The suggestion here is that while the messianic period is the result of a necessary historical process, the Jews can ensure a somewhat earlier redemption through obedience to God's commandments.[9]

Yet, the exact timing of the redemption is a relatively minor matter compared to other factors in the messianic process that have not yet been accounted for in our discussion. In particular, we still do not have an explanation for the notion of a personal Messiah, nor for the doctrine of resurrection. In fact, according to the description we have given up to now, the implementation of the terms of the covenant could conceivably occur without these components altogether.

Gersonides certainly does not neglect these issues. In a number of passages, he comes up with the rather novel theory that the primary function of the Messiah and the resurrection miracle he performs is to redeem the non-Jewish nations. To understand what Gersonides means here, we must first look at his views on the personal Messiah. We have already dealt with this issue to some extent in our discussion of Mosaic prophecy. We saw that in a number of passages, Gersonides depicts the Messiah as a prophet of greater stature than Moses, but insists that he will not reveal a new Torah. The key prooftext for this position was Deuteronomy 34:10: "Never again did there arise in Israel a prophet like Moses." This verse was taken to mean that while no prophet of Moses' stature would arise *in Israel*, there *will* be a prophet greater than Moses who will be sent to mankind as a whole.[10]

We must now elaborate further on this comparison. Gersonides claims that the Messiah will be a greater prophet than Moses in precisely two respects. First, as we have just noted, the Messiah will be sent to all of mankind, not just to Israel, as was the case with Moses. Second, the Messiah will bring miracles that will be more impressive than those of Moses; these miracles will be more visible, will affect larger geographical areas, and will be of greater duration than the ones performed by his predecessor. These capabilities are delineated in a passage at the very end of Gersonides' commentary on Deuteronomy:

> The nineteenth *to'elet* is that to which the Torah testifies in its statement, "Never again did there arise in Israel a prophet like Moses."[11] That is, another prophet like Moses *will* arise with these things [i.e., capabilities] which are mentioned. However, he [i.e., the new prophet] will not be [sent] to Israel alone, but to Israel *and* the other nations. He will perform many signs and miracles, like those of Moses, over a very wide area [and] before a great number of people, and will constantly demonstrate "the great might" of God and [His] "awesome power"[12] before a great number of people. Since there has not yet been a prophet like this with regard to these matters in any place, we know that this will be the Messiah, son of David, who "shall be exalted and raised to great heights [italics added]."[13]

In other passages, Gersonides further explains that the miracles performed by the Messiah have a very specific function; they are designed to convince the nations of the world that the God of Israel is the one true God. Moreover, Gersonides informs us, there will be one miracle in particular which will accomplish this purpose: the resurrection of the dead. This miracle—more impressive than any performed by the prophets of Israel—will be the pivotal factor in the Messiah's program to inspire the nations of the world to believe in the God of Israel.

A passage in which these ideas are expressed in some detail is found in Gersonides' commentary on Numbers, where he begins with the now familiar explication of the verse, "Never again did there arise in Israel a prophet like Moses":

> The truth which follows from this verse is that no prophet has yet arisen like Moses who is a prophet for Israel alone; but it will come to pass that there will be a prophet, who in addition to this

[i.e., serving as a prophet for Israel], will be [a prophet] for the nations of the world as well. This is the King Messiah—as it says in the midrash, " 'Behold my servant shall prosper . . . ':[14] he will be greater than Moses."[15] It will be clear that his miracles will also be more impressive than the miracles of Moses. For Moses convinced Israel alone to worship God with the miracles that he brought; but he [i.e., the Messiah] will convince all the nations to worship God as it says, "For then I will make the peoples of pure speech, so that they all invoke the LORD by name."[16] This will occur by means of an extraordinary miracle which will be seen by all the nations throughout the world—that is, the resurrection of the dead.[17]

In another passage, Gersonides informs us that the Messiah and the miracles he performs will also be for the purpose of strengthening the faith of the Jewish people. This idea comes across in a *to'elet* in which Gersonides comments on the future exile and redemption predicted in Deuteronomy 30, a passage which we have already linked to eschatological motifs in previous discussions:

The seventh *to'elet* is that which [the Torah] informs [us] in its statement, "Then the LORD your God will open up your heart and the hearts of your offspring . . . ,"[18] [i.e.,] that God will bring signs and miracles so that Israel and their offspring will know that He is Lord and their faith[19] will be strengthened in their hearts. As a result, that covenant [i.e., in the messianic era] will be firmly established more than the covenant which God sealed with Israel when he took them out of the land of Egypt. For at that time Israel was immersed in the idolatrous practices of Egypt and had not yet been inculcated in [the ways of] the Torah. The prophets have already informed us about the truth of this [observation].[20]

However, this is the only passage in which the Israelites are the focus of concern. In all other places where Gersonides talks about the role of the Messiah, it is the non-Jewish nations who are identified as the immediate beneficiaries of the Messiah's arrival and the target of the miracles he performs.

While Gersonides never ties all the elements of his eschatology together, the picture that emerges from the pieces we have assembled is fairly clear. The implementation of the terms of the Patriarchal covenant requires that there first be a redemption for the rest of mankind; only when the nations of the world worship the God of Israel will the Jews live peacefully in their land. The Messiah secures this condition by performing prodigious miracles for all the nations of the world to witness, the most impressive of which is the resurrection of the dead.[21]

It should also be noted that for Gersonides the redemption of the Gentiles has sufficient biblical support to be termed one of the *pinnot ha-torah*, a fundamental biblical doctrine. This point is made in Gersonides' *Commentary on I Chronicles*:

> The fifth *pinnah*[22] is that all the nations will worship God, as it says, "... and it will be said among the nations that God is King"[23]—in addition to [what is said in] the continuation of this passage, as we have explained in our commentary on these words.[24] Moreover, the prophet said that God "will make the peoples of pure speech, so that they all invoke the LORD by name and serve Him with one accord."[25]

That Gersonides should see the acceptance of the God of Israel among the Gentile nations as one of the *pinnot ha-torah* should come as no surprise. He appears to have been inspired by a number of biblical passages traditionally read as a description of the messianic period and which depict a redemption that will include the non-Jewish nations. We have, for instance, the celebrated verses at the beginning of the second chapter of Isaiah in which the prophet predicts that the nations of the world will come to the Temple Mount in order to worship the God of Israel.[26] The citation of the verse from Zephaniah 3:9—ubiquitous in Gersonides' references to the messianic period—also reinforces the same theme.

More problematic is the status of the doctrine of resurrection. In a passage in his *Commentary on I Samuel*, Gersonides appears to identify this concept as one of the *pinnot ha-torah* as well. Gersonides claims that Hannah makes reference to the future resurrection in her prayer of thanksgiving after the birth of Samuel, when she states, "The LORD deals death and gives life, / Casts down to Sheol and raises up."[27] In one of his *to'aliyyot*, Gersonides refers back to this passage with the following statement: "The twenty-first *to'elet* is to inform [us] that God resurrects the dead and raises them from their graves. This is one of the *pinnot ha-'emunah*."[28]

What is perplexing here is that the doctrine of resurrection is identified as one of the *pinnot ha-'emunah*, a fundamental principle "of faith," rather than as one of the *pinnot ha-torah*. Now there may be no significance in this change of terminology. In listing a number of *pinnot ha-torah* in a passage in his *Commentary on I Chronicles*, Gersonides refers to these doctrines collectively as *pinnot ha-torah ve-ha-'emunah*, "fundamental principles of the Torah and faith."[29] This latter passage seems to treat principles of the Torah and principles of faith as equivalent.

One problem, however, is that there does not seem to be enough scriptural support to justify the elevation of the resurrection doctrine to the status of a fundamental biblical principle. Certainly, there are a number of passages in Scripture that Gersonides interprets as references to the future resurrection. We have already seen that I Samuel 2:6 is one such passage. The statement in Deuteronomy 32:39, in which God declares "I deal death and give life" is also taken by Gersonides as proof for the resurrection doctrine.[30] Gersonides also finds support for the resurrection in what is perhaps the only truly explicit reference to this concept in the biblical text: Daniel 12:2-3.[31] But to call the resurrection doctrine a fundamental biblical principle on the basis of these few verses would seem unwarranted. Gersonides' reference to the resurrection as one of the *pinnot ha-'emunah* may therefore reflect a reluctance on his part to identify this concept as a fullfledged biblical principle.

Nevertheless, it is important to point out that Gersonides at times will identify a doctrine as one of the *pinnot ha-torah* only because it supports another similar principle. Thus, for instance, Gersonides identifies the notion of creation as one of these *pinnot* because it is a necessary prerequisite for the belief in miracles.[32] The doctrine of resurrection may therefore qualify as a fundamental biblical principle because of a similar reason. The resurrection event is viewed by Gersonides as a necessary precursor to the redemption of the Gentile nations—and the latter idea, as we saw above, is specifically identified as one of the *pinnot ha-torah*.

We should also be reminded of the historical context. The resurrection doctrine was at the center of a heated debate in Gersonides' period on account of the ongoing controversy surrounding Maimonides' views on this subject. This controversy undoubtedly had an effect on Gersonides' own position, though there is not enough material in Gersonides' commentaries to make any firm determinations in this regard.[33] In sum, there is evidence that Gersonides considers the resurrection doctrine as one of the *pinnot ha-torah*, though the evidence is not clear.

One final issue that should be dealt with is the return of the kingship to the Davidic line in the messianic period. This issue is discussed in a number of places in Gersonides' biblical commentaries. In all such passages Gersonides does little more than refer to the various biblical sources in which God formulates a covenant with David and guarantees him the kingship over Israel for all time.[34] This approach is exemplified in one of Gersonides' *to'aliyyot* in his *Commentary on II Samuel*:

The eleventh [*to'elet*] is to inform [us] that God in lovingkindess gave the kingship [over Israel] to David's offspring for all time[35] as [embodied] in the covenant that He accorded to David with regard to this matter; [God made this covenant] because of the righteousness and uprightness that He found in him. It [i.e., the kingship] will extend perpetually in his offspring when Israel does what is right in the eyes of God; He will then be able to bring about "all success" and "every desire"[36]—even when evil is ready to afflict them as a result of [the failure of] general providence. However, when this is not the case [i.e., when Israel is not obedient to God], and the kingship ceases in Israel, it will not completely depart from the House of David; rather, it will be "secured"[37] for him. This is explained [in the passage which says that], ". . . A shoot shall grow out of the stump of Jesse, / A twig shall sprout from his stock,"[38] and [that] he will rule and be established over Israel. For it is impossible that the kingship will depart from his offspring completely. This is further explained in the words of the prophets, as it says, "[He] deals graciously with His anointed, / With David and offspring evermore."[39] It [also] says, "For He has granted me an eternal pact, / Drawn up in full and secured. / Will He not cause all my success / And [my] every desire to bloom?"[40]

Drawing from standard biblical sources, Gersonides informs us that the kingship in Israel has been promised by God to David for eternity. Even when Israel loses its sovereignty as a result of sinful behavior, the line of David will be maintained so that it can be reconstituted in the messianic era.[41]

What is somewhat surprising is that Gersonides does not at any point offer a philosophical explanation for the Davidic covenant. Gersonides could have easily justified the eternity of kingship in the Davidic line on the basis of inherited providence. That is, David bequeaths individual providence to his descendants in the same way that Abraham passes on providence to the Jewish people as a whole.

While there is, in fact, one passage in which Gersonides invokes the concept of inherited providence in connection with David's offspring, it stops short of drawing a firm link between inherited providence and the eternity of the Davidic dynasty. We are referring here to Gersonides' reading of I Kings 11:11-13. In this biblical passage, God informs Solomon that, as punishment for his sins, his offspring will lose control of the greater portion of the Israelite kingdom. The biblical text goes on to explain that it is only out of consideration for David that God will delay the breakup of the kingdom until after Solomon's death and that a part of the kingdom will be preserved for Solomon's descendants. Gersonides offers the following interpretation of God's decision to soften the punishment:

FOR THE SAKE OF MY SERVANT DAVID:[42] this tells [us] that the providence over the father extends to the son. For the sake of David His servant, He exercised providence over Solomon so that the kingdom would not be torn away from him in his lifetime. Also, for the sake of David His servant, He exercised providence over the offspring of Solomon in order that the kingdom would not depart from them altogether.[43]

In this passage, Gersonides informs us that the influence of providence inherited from David is responsible for preventing the kingdom from being taken away from his descendants in its entirety; but there is no explicit mention of the notion that inherited providence sustains the Davidic line until the messianic period.

Gersonides is clearly a disciple of Maimonides in his conception of the messianic period. Both believe that the messianic period will be continuous with world history, except for the fact that the Jews will again be sovereign in their own homeland and the dead will be resurrected.[44] However, Gersonides' views on the messianic period are only properly understood in relation to his reading of Jewish history. The key to Gersonides' interpretation of the messianic era is that it represents the fulfillment of the Patriarchal covenant. In philosophical terms, this means that the messianic period will be inaugurated when providence inherited from Abraham will provide the conditions that will allow the Jewish people to live peacefully in the land of Israel and perpetually earn providence on their own. These conditions will be secured by the Messiah, who will convince Israel's enemies to worship the God of Israel, thereby neutralizing the primary physical and spiritual threats to Israel's well-being. He will accomplish this goal by performing extraordinary miracles, most notably the resurrection of the dead.

Our analysis of Gersonides' account of the messianic period once again underscores the centrality and significance of the Patriarchal covenant in Jewish history. It is now apparent that Gersonides understands all of Jewish history as a process leading towards the fulfillment of this covenant. It is process that begins with Abraham's prophetic vision in Genesis 15 and reaches its conclusion only in the final, climactic phase of Jewish history.

NINE

The Language of Providence in Gersonides' Biblical Commentaries

There is one more topic that needs to be considered briefly before we draw conclusions from our study. So far, we have analyzed the content of Gersonides' philosophical views regarding divine providence over the Jewish people; we must now turn our attention to the style of discourse in which those views are expressed.

To appreciate the importance of this issue, let us first be reminded of the basic philosophical premises of Gersonides' position on divine providence. Gersonides does not believe in a personal God who responds to human concerns or interacts with human events. All providential activity is to be explained in terms of static, impersonal laws. Gersonides therefore consistently translates the descriptions of God's actions in the biblical text into philosophically acceptable terms. Throughout our study we have seen how such categories as miracles, reward and punishment, and covenant are creatively interpreted in this way.

The problem is that one cannot avoid being struck by the many passages in Gersonides' biblical commentaries—including a number that we have cited in the course of our study—in which he himself describes God's providential activity in terms very much characteristic of a personal God. Frequently, Gersonides unabashedly adopts the discourse of biblical and rabbinic literature in which God is depicted as directly responding to and interacting with events in the world below. These types of descriptions, at least in terms of Gersonides' philosophical system, appear to be nothing

short of anthropomorphic in that they seem to be modeled on human behavior rather than on a philosophically 'correct' conception of God.

Perhaps this type of language should be no cause for concern. Gersonides may have simply expected that his audience would be philosophically adept and would therefore understand the true philosophical
meaning of his anthropomorphic language. However, there is also the possibility that Gersonides deliberately used anthropomorphic terminology
in his biblical commentaries in order to make these writings more palatable to a popular, traditional audience. Gersonides might have seen this
choice of discourse as particularly appropriate for his exegetical works,
given that these writings were more likely to be read by a traditional
reader than his philosophical works.

As we have already argued, there is no evidence to suggest that Gersonides went so far as to adopt an esoteric style of writing in his commentaries. Still, we cannot rule out a more subtle attempt on Gersonides' part
to appease the traditional reader. In describing divine activity in terms that
strongly suggest the notion of a personal God, Gersonides could very well
have been trying to preempt any criticism of his unorthodox philosophical views.

The question of Gersonides' style of writing is thus important not only
for the immediate philosophical issues we have discussed, but also for assessing the overall character of his exegetical writings. In this chapter we
will therefore take a close look at this problem. We must, however, acknowledge our limitations here. A comprehensive study of Gersonides'
use of language in describing divine action is beyond the scope of our project. A complete examination of this question would involve a thorough
analysis of Gersonides' theory of divine attributes developed in the *Wars*,
as well as an analysis of all the passages in the biblical commentaries in
which Gersonides deals with descriptions of God in the biblical text. Thus,
while the following discussion will attempt to address the concerns we
have raised, the conclusions will be, at best, preliminary.

Let us begin by seeking a clearer definition of the problem. There are
a number of expressions that Gersonides frequently employs throughout
his biblical commentaries that suggest a direct and intentional intervention
on God's part in human affairs.[1] For example, Gersonides often refers to
God as "saving" the righteous from harm (*hizil, yazil*),[2] or "bringing evil"
(*mevi' ra'ot*)[3] for providential purposes.

There are also instances in which God is described as personally responding to human concerns or interacting with human events. An example of this type of depiction can be found in Gersonides' commentary on
Exodus where he explains why God at first instructed Moses to coax
Pharaoh into letting the Israelites go:

. . . God wanted at first to determine if Pharaoh would agree to send the Children of Israel willingly. After he [i.e., Pharaoh] did not agree to this, God extended His hand to strike him with every one of the plagues. [He did] this in incremental fashion; for He brought upon him plagues, pestilence and afflictions that were, at first, light, and later, harsh, as we shall explain after this, God willing.[4]

According to this passage, God is described as first testing Pharaoh to determine whether he will free the Israelites and then as responding to Pharaoh's stubbornness by punishing him with afflictions of increasing severity.

Striking anthropomorphic descriptions of divine action are contained in a series of passages in Gersonides' commentary on Exodus which emphasize that God has the freedom to alter the course of nature and perform miracles whenever He so desires. A description of this sort appears, for example, in Gersonides' interpretation of Exodus 9:14, where God declares, "There is no one like Me in all the world." Gersonides understands this assertion to mean that God has complete control over the whole of the sublunar world, as opposed to each of the Separate Intellects, who have jurisdiction over only a portion of the events in the world below. As Gersonides puts it, God has dominion over the natural order "to move it to [do] whatever He wishes."[5]

In another passage, Gersonides expands on this conception:

The first to'elet is [that the Torah] announces and makes widely known God's awesome power to alter the nature of existence for the sake of providence, so that He brought these plagues miraculously and took them away at the time that He wished. There also occurs from His awesome power that the hearts of men are moved and diverted in whichever [direction] He wishes.[6] He hardened Pharaoh's heart not to let the people go, despite the many factors which He arranged which should have taken away[7] the hardness of his heart.[8]

The notion that God does "whatever He wishes" in the performance of miracles gives the impression that God acts freely and directly in the sublunar realm. This conception if taken literally is in marked contrast to the emphasis in the *Wars*, where Gersonides consistently maintains that even in the performance of miracles God acts through a fixed series of impersonal laws.[9]

It would be a mistake to assume, however, that all descriptions of divine activity in the biblical commentaries are of this sort. A careful examination of the commentaries will show that in many passages Gersonides adopts a style of discourse that is more philosophical in tone. For example,

Gersonides often attributes providential action to the impersonal influences of providence itself rather than to God, a mode of expression that better reflects Gersonides' philosophical principles. Thus, for example, in one passage where he sums up his thoughts about divine providence over the Israelites in Egypt, Gersonides describes God's providential action as follows: ". . . divine providence watches over those who receive such providence to cause them to acquire spiritual goods and to save them from spiritual harm. . . ."[10]

Another example of philosophically sensitive language is Gersonides' frequent use of the verb, *sibev*, "to cause" or "to bring about," in his descriptions of divine action. The use of this philosophically significant verb suggests that God's actions are indirect and mediated by natural causes. Thus, in his description of the splitting of the Red Sea, Gersonides tells us that God "caused" or "brought about" that Moses would follow behind the Israelites when they crossed the Red Sea so that his superior level of providence would confer protection on them.[11] God also "caused" the east wind to blow which parted the Red Sea.[12]

There are even instances in the biblical commentaries in which Gersonides moves freely between anthropomorphic and philosophical descriptions of divine activity in the very same passage. A superb example of this tendency is a *to'elet* in Gersonides' commentary on Exodus in which he sums up the purpose of the first of the Ten Commandments:

> The first *to'elet* is with regard to the commandments. That is, [the Torah] said that [one must] believe[13] that there is a God who has dominion over all the existents to move them to [do] whatever He wishes and that He upsets the order which is ordered by the stars so as to bestow good upon those conjoined to Him. That is why it says, "I, the LORD, am your God who brought you out of the land of Egypt, the house of bondage."[14] Now the benefit [to be derived] from this command is in theoretical knowledge. . . . [15] For when it is not believed that there is an efficient cause, there can be no science whatsoever. For the sciences investigate the causes on account of which a thing exists. When there is no efficient cause, there is no final cause[16] whatsoever as it has already been explained in [other] sources. Similarly, when it is not believed that there is a [Being] watching over individuals in the species of man[17] in this manner, one is deprived of a great fundamental principle of theoretical knowledge as we have explained in the fourth [book] of the *Wars*, in addition to its being one of the great fundamental Torah principles.[18]

The entire first half of this passage describes divine activity in terms appropriate for a personal Deity. The notion that God "moves" the stars and "upsets" the celestial order to do "whatever He wishes" is reminiscent of examples we quoted earlier.[19] But note that in the second half of the passage the same descriptions are restated in more technical, philosophical terms. Thus, God's ability to move the stars and to do as He wishes is translated into the philosophical concept of efficient causation.

It is therefore more accurate to say that the biblical commentaries contain a mixture of styles. At times, the language Gersonides adopts to describe divine action is of the anthropomorphic variety characteristic of the biblical and rabbinic traditions; at other times, it is more philosophical in tone.

These observations, however, do not entirely address our original question. Even if Gersonides does not always adopt anthropomorphic terminology in his descriptions of divine activity, we could still argue that this type of language is used sporadically in the biblical commentaries in order to lend a more traditional flavor to this particular body of writing.

A strong argument against this suggestion comes from a careful examination of the language used in Gersonides' major philosophical work, *The Wars of the Lord*. While we have shown that Gersonides intended for the *Wars* to be accessible to a range of readers—including those with traditional beliefs—it would certainly be stretching the point to say that this work is 'popular' in any sense. The difficulty and complexity of the philosophical arguments presented in the *Wars* leave little doubt that it was intended for a reader with at least some degree of philosophical background. And, yet, one finds in a number of passages in the *Wars* descriptions of God's providential activity that evoke the image of a personal God no less forcefully than the examples we have cited from his commentaries.[20]

In the *Wars*, the inspiration for describing God in anthropomorphic terms is in some instances clearly based on a biblical prooftext associated with the discussion. Thus, in book four, when Gersonides takes up the question of providential suffering and its effect on the Jewish nation as a whole, descriptions of direct divine action follow naturally from the biblical references which Gersonides cites in the same passage. For instance, in his interpretation of Leviticus 26:18, where God promises "I will go on to discipline you sevenfold for your sins," Gersonides explains in the following terms why this verse must refer to a case of providential suffering:

If this were merely for the sake of punishment [i.e., retribution without any aim toward moral rehabilitation], this would be an obvious evil [with respect to God]. On the other hand, if this is providential, it is proper; that is, when God (may He be blessed) brings afflictions upon them to reprove [them], and they are not chastened but persist in their crimes, it is proper that He chastise them seven times for theirs sins.[21]

In this example, Gersonides appears to be following the lead of the biblical text when he states that God "brings affliction" upon the Jews in order to "reprove" them (yagia' lahem ha-yisurin 'al zad ha-tokhahat) and that He "chastises them" (yeyasrem) for their sins.

Similarly, in the passages where Gersonides gives a philosophical interpretation of the doctrine of hester panim—the hiding of the divine countenance—he tends to adopt the language of the biblical text. Gersonides explains that God "hides His countenance" when the righteous have sinned so much that they are no longer deserving of individual providence. At that point, God "abandons them to the contingencies of time and does not consider their deeds." Once again, the notion that God "abandons" (ya'azov) the righteous and does not "consider" (yifkod) their deeds are descriptions that are no doubt prompted by the biblical sources on which he is commenting.[22]

At times, however, the tendency to use this type of language does not seem to come from a particular biblical source. Note how Gersonides explains providential suffering that afflicts the righteous man to save him from greater spiritual harm:

> . . . sometimes God brings evil upon the righteous for the sake of providence in order to save them from a minor sin that they have begun to be implicated in. . . . For if God (may He be blessed) tries to save them in this manner [i.e., dispensing lesser evils for the purpose of avoiding greater evils] from sensuous evils that are not [properly] human, all the more so is it proper for Him to dispense these evils providentially in order to save them from spiritual evils that are [truly] human.[23]

In this passage, Gersonides describes God as reacting to the sinful deeds of the righteous and intervening to prevent them from further sin. Most significant, Gersonides uses the same anthropomorphic terms to describe divine action that are used in the Commentary on the Torah. God "brings evil" (mevi' ra'ot) upon the righteous and thereby "tries to save them" (yishtadel le-hazilam) from greater evil.[24]

Another significant example supporting the same point is a passage that appears in book four of the Wars, in which Gersonides comments on the hardening of Pharaoh's heart in the exodus story:

> This passage[25] indicates that the hardness of heart [afflicted upon] Pharaoh was [designed] for the purpose of increasing the

wonders of God and that the latter were designed to make known throughout Israel and succeeding generations that *there is a God who does whatever He wishes* [italics added].[26]

Note that according to the description of divine activity in the last phrase of this passage, God "does whatever He wishes" (*po'el kol mah she-yirzeh*). This phrase is practically identical with a series of anthropomorphic expressions which, as we noted earlier, appear in the *Commentary on the Torah*.[27]

Thus, anthropomorphic descriptions of divine activity also appear in the *Wars*, an observation that calls into question any suspicion that Gersonides was motivated by political concerns in using these types of descriptions in his exegetical works. This conclusion leaves us with one more question: why is it then that Gersonides uses this anthropomorphic language at all? One possibility is that he may have simply adopted this style of discourse unconsciously. Given Gersonides' thorough familiarity with biblical and rabbinic sources, it is not surprising that the language of this literature would unwittingly invade his vocabulary. Another possibility is one that we suggested at the beginning of our discussion; he may have assumed that a philosophically trained audience would understand the true meaning of this language.

There is, however, another approach that we must consider. There is reason to believe that Gersonides, in fact, viewed such anthropomorphic descriptions as philosophically legitimate. Support for this interpretation can be found by first looking at Gersonides' position on divine attributes in book three of the *Wars*.[28] For Gersonides, divine attributes are ambiguous terms. An ambiguous term is a predicate that applies to more than one subject; however, it applies to one subject in a more primary sense than it does to the others. Thus, for example, the word 'man' can be applied to a human being and to a statue of a man. Yet the former application is obviously the primary instance of the term, while the latter application is a secondary instance.

With regard to divine attributes, a similar line of reasoning can be used. The term 'knowledge,' for example, is an ambiguous term when applied to God and man. Both God and man have knowledge. However, this predicate more truly applies to God than it does to man. For one, God's knowledge is far superior to human knowledge in that He has complete knowledge of all that exists. Moreover, God's knowledge is the source of our knowledge, since it is only through Him that we can have cognitions in the first place. Therefore, according to this theory, God's attributes are different from human attributes not in kind but only in degree.

We should note that Gersonides' position on divine attributes follows the major medieval Arabic philosophers and is an explicit rejection of Maimonides. According to Maimonides, divine attributes are equivocal terms. That is, when predicates are applied to God and man, they have only the word in common, since there is no commonality whatsoever between God and man. Maimonides therefore believes that the difference between divine and human attributes is more than one of degree; it is a difference of kind.

Gersonides, however, follows Maimonides in one respect. Gersonides believes that not all human attributes are to be found analogously in God. Gersonides goes along with Maimonides in insisting that only attributes that constitute perfections are appropriate for God. Thus, corporeal attributes of any kind would be ruled out.[29]

The important point here is that since the difference between divine and human attributes is considered by Gersonides to be one of degree and not one of kind, he may not have seen anything philosophically untenable in describing God's actions in human terms. It is perhaps for this reason that Gersonides does not hesitate to use terminology to describe divine activity that strongly evokes the conception of a personal God.

Support for this line of thinking can be found by probing more deeply into Gersonides' discussion of divine attributes. Important for our purposes are two lists of predicates that appear in the *Wars*, in which Gersonides enumerates what he considers to be acceptable divine attributes. One of these lists is to be found in a passage in book three where Gersonides mentions the following attributes: substance, being, one, intellect, living, knowing, provident, beneficent, powerful and willing.[30] In another passage in book five, a more complete list of attributes is provided. Those attributes not included in the first list are as follows: joyful, existing, agent, gracious, emanating, good, telos, everlasting, permanent, righteous, just, strong, governing, and powerful.[31]

What is important to note is that many of the attributes in these lists are precisely the same as those which Gersonides himself uses for describing divine activity. We can illustrate this point by looking again at a passage cited earlier from the *Commentary on the Torah*:

> The first *to'elet* is [that the Torah] announces and makes widely known God's awesome power to alter the nature of existence for the sake of providence, so that He brought these plagues miraculously and took them away at the time that He wished. His awesome power also causes the hearts of men to be moved and diverted in whichever [direction] He wishes. He hardened Pharaoh's heart not to let the people go, despite the many factors which He arranged which should have taken away the hardness of his heart.[32]

What initially troubled us about this passage was that the language Gersonides uses here seems to evoke a conception of God who is personally and directly involved in human affairs. Yet it is important to note that at least two of the predicates describing divine activity in this passage appear in Gersonides' lists of acceptable attributes in the *Wars*. God's "power" (*yekholet*) and his discretion to do what He "wishes" (*yirzeh*) can both be found among the attributes enumerated in books three and five of the *Wars*.[33] Thus, terminology that appears to clash with Gersonides' philosophical principles is, upon closer examination, legitimate philosophical language.

The lists of attributes in books three and five of the *Wars* do not account for all the anthropomorphic terms we cited earlier from Gersonides' writings. However, in at least some of these cases, those terms can be easily interpreted as variations or extensions of those attributes in the *Wars*. For instance, in a passage quoted earlier from the *Commentary on the Torah*, Gersonides refers to God as having "dominion" (*shalit*) over all existents. This predicate can easily be related to the attribute, "governing" (*memshalah*), which appears in the list of attributes in book five in the *Wars*.

Furthermore, as Touati argues, there is evidence to suggest that neither of the lists of attributes in the *Wars* is seen by Gersonides as exhaustive. First of all, the two lists are substantially different, an indication that Gersonides' attitude is flexible with regard to the divine attributes he is willing to consider. Second, in discussing the attributes in the first list, Gersonides makes passing reference to "these predicates and the like," a phrase which implies that his first list, at least, is not necessarily complete.[34]

Further evidence to support Touati's observations is that some of the attributes in the second list appear to be synonymous with each other. For example, the attributes "permanent" and "enduring" (*nizhi, kayyam*) are grouped together and appear to refer to the same quality. Similarly, the attributes "strong", "governing", and "powerful" (*'oz, memshalah, yekholet*) are listed together and again, may simply be different expressions for the same conception.[35] Therefore, we should not be surprised if Gersonides uses a somewhat wider range of terms to describe divine activity in his own writing than those listed in books three and five of the *Wars*. These lists appear to be far from complete.

There is another passage in the *Wars* that bears even more directly on the whole question of Gersonides' use of language in describing divine activity. The relevant remarks appear in book six of the *Wars* in Gersonides' discussion of miracles. In the middle of this discussion, Gersonides arrives at the conclusion that God is not the proximate cause of miracles, but is rather their remote cause. Why then, Gersonides asks, does the biblical text frequently describe God as performing miracles directly? Gersonides responds to this difficulty by claiming that there is nothing philosophically incorrect with this type of depiction. His reasoning is as follows:

> . . . [with regard to] what is found in the biblical text, [i.e.,] that God is equated with the agent of miracles—[this] does not necessitate [the conclusion] that God is the proximate cause [of miracles]. For you find that everything generated is attributed to God—even those matters that originate from human free will, as it says, ". . . because the LORD told him to abuse David";[36] indeed, it was so, for God is the origin of all things that are generated as has been explained, but He is not their proximate cause.[37]

Gersonides explains that the biblical text is justified in ascribing miraculous actions directly to God. Even if God is not the proximate cause of miracles, He is certainly the source of these events in functioning as a remote cause. The same reasoning explains why the biblical text attributes events of every variety directly to God; God is ultimately responsible for everything that occurs in the world below.[38]

The relevance of these remarks for our problem is clear. When Gersonides himself describes God as performing some action directly—such as saving the righteous or bringing evil upon the wicked—he is not lapsing into discourse that is at variance with his philosophical views. Rather, Gersonides is using idioms that he would consider to be philosophically meaningful. Since God is the source of all activity, ascribing actions in the world directly to Him is within the bounds of legitimate philosophical discourse.

Our discussion began with the observation that in the biblical commentaries Gersonides often uses anthropomorphic terminology to describe God's providential activity, language that seems out of character with his philosophical principles. The question was raised as to whether this style of discourse was adopted by Gersonides as a deliberate attempt to make his biblical commentaries more palatable to a popular audience.

Our analysis has shown that there is no support for this hypothesis. The same tendency to use anthropomorphic language is also present in Gersonides' major philosophical work, *The Wars of the Lord*. Moreover, this style of discourse can be fully justified according to principles within Gersonides' own philosophical system. Gersonides' general position on divine attributes implies that there is a certain degree of commonality between God and man. Therefore, as long as one does not attach corporeal attributes to God, one can refer to God in anthropomorphic terms. Moreover, with regard to the more specific question of God's activity in the sublunar realm, Gersonides tells us in an important passage in the *Wars* that there is nothing wrong with ascribing actions directly to God, since He is, in fact, the ultimate cause of all events.

Our discussion is at best a preliminary examination of a more complex issue.[39] Yet, one point is clear; the highly Aristotelian character of Gersonides' philosophical system did not stop him from speaking about God in personal terms. Even though Gersonides believed in a God who does not know particulars as particulars, who is not able to experience a change of will, and who is for the most part detached from the world of human events—Gersonides still managed to preserve in spirit, if not in letter, the personal God of the Bible.

TEN

Conclusions

In my introduction, I set out a number of reasons for exploring the theme of the Chosen People in Gersonides' thought. First and foremost, this doctrine is one of Judaism's cardinal principles and is therefore a key issue in any comprehensive philosophy of Judaism. An examination of Gersonides' views on this subject would therefore undoubtedly enrich our understanding of this major medieval Jewish thinker.

I also argued that the question of Jewish chosenness was of particular significance in the study of Gersonides. For one, the concept of the Chosen People is one of the more formidable philosophical challenges that classical Judaism presents for Gersonides on account of the highly Aristotelian character of his thought-system. The notion that there is an ongoing, covenantal relationship between God and the Jewish people throughout history is not easily harmonized with Gersonides' conception of an impersonal God. Second, an analysis of Gersonides' position on the concept of the Chosen People would allow for a careful examination of the philosophical material in his biblical commentaries, an area of his corpus that has received little attention from scholars of medieval Jewish philosophy. It was our hope that we would gain insight into the role that Gersonides' exegetical writings play in the development of his philosophical thought and that we would arrive at a better understanding of the relationship between these writings and *The Wars of the Lord*, his major philosophical work.

Before we address these concerns, let us first review and consolidate what we have discovered in our study. What has emerged from our analysis is that in Gersonides' thinking there is in fact a fairly coherent position regarding the special status of the Jewish people. The concept that was consistently the key factor in our discussion was the Patriarchal covenant first formulated with Abraham in Genesis 15. For Gersonides, this covenant is a metaphor for a special manifestation of divine providence that an individual of unusual perfection can pass on to his descendants for generations to come.

Providence inherited from Abraham in effect guides the entire process of Jewish history up to the messianic period. Its task is to ensure that Abraham's descendants experience maximum material and spiritual reward. Yet, inherited providence does not accomplish its purpose directly. It is perhaps best described as a catalyst for providence, rather than a providential force in its own right. It exerts its influence by furnishing a series of conditions that in turn allow the Jews to achieve perfection and earn providential reward on their own. The most important of these conditions is the acquisition of the land of Israel which provides an ideal environment for achieving moral and intellectual perfection. This location is especially receptive to providential emanations. Moreover, the settlement of the Jewish people in one geographical area provides the proper social framework for pursuing intellectual perfection.

But according to Gersonides, at no time in their history did the Jews actually take full possession of the land of Israel as predicted in Abraham's prophecy; the acquisition of the entire land will occur only in the messianic era. In the meantime, the role of inherited providence is to provide a series of secondary conditions guaranteeing that the Jews will have the requisite level of providence for inheriting the land of Israel when the messianic redemption finally occurs. The most important of these secondary conditions is the Torah, which serves as a philosophical guidebook for the inculcation of moral and intellectual perfection.

We should emphasize that for Gersonides the acquisition of the land of Israel is certainly not the sole purpose of observing the Torah's directives. Gersonides assumes that by learning from the Torah's instruction the Jews can experience individual providence even before the messianic redemption occurs. It is also assumed by Gersonides that the Jewish people will continue to observe the Torah's instruction even after they have settled in their homeland in the messianic era. The Torah is therefore independent in some degree from the Patriarchal covenant. But it should be kept in mind that the initial purpose of the revelation of the Torah is, quite specifically, to make it possible for the Jews to earn the right to take possession of the land of Israel, and this continues to be one of its purposes throughout history. The notion that adherence to the commandments results in inheriting the land of Israel is, in fact, identified by Gersonides as one of the *pinnot ha-torah*, a fundamental biblical principle.[1]

The Torah is not the only secondary condition provided by inherited providence for ensuring that the Jews will acquire the land of Israel. Another major function of inherited providence is to guarantee the physical survival of the Jewish people throughout history. Obviously, the Jewish people cannot take possession of the land of Israel if there *is* no Jewish people when the messianic redemption finally occurs. Inherited providence performs this task by functioning as an emergency measure to save the Jews from annihilation when they are not worthy of individual providence and when general providence is not working in their favor. It is for this reason that inherited providence rescues the Israelites from Egypt. During this period in their history, the Israelites are not worthy of individual providence, nor is general providence available to alleviate their suffering. They therefore need inherited providence to save them from destruction at the hands of the Egyptians.

After the first—but incomplete—conquest of Canaan, inherited providence continues to guarantee the physical survival of the Jewish people when they are disobedient to God and are no longer worthy of providence. It sometimes saves the Jews from utter destruction by directly intervening in historical events. But even more important, it is capable of bringing a series of incremental providential punishments designed to encourage the Jews to observe the Torah's directives once again so that they can achieve perfection and experience individual providence. The curses and threats in the *tokheḥah* portions of Leviticus and Deuteronomy are interpreted by Gersonides as punishments of this sort. These sections of the biblical text are also extremely important in Gersonides' interpretation of actual events in Jewish history. They become the basis for explaining the continual hardships the Jewish people has experienced throughout its history.

At the time of the messianic redemption, inherited providence will also provide the proper conditions for the Jews to inherit the land of Israel by exerting its influence on the non-Jewish nations. In order to create an environment that is physically and spiritually secure for the Jews to live in their homeland, inherited providence will ensure that a personal Messiah is sent who will convince the non-Jewish nations to worship the God of Israel.

What may be somewhat confusing is the way the different forms of providence depend on one another in Gersonides' reading of Jewish history. Inherited providence sets in motion a series of interlocking conditions and safeguards that allow for increasing providential reward for the Jewish people. Until the messianic era, the most immediate benefit inherited providence provides is the opportunity for the Jewish people to earn their own providential reward through the observance of the Torah's instruction. But providence earned in this way, in turn, functions as a means for the Jews to inherit the land of Israel—which is itself a condition for earning even greater providential reward. The pinnacle of this process is the messianic period, when the Jews will achieve maximum providential reward by observing the Torah's directives in their homeland.

An important implication of this reading of Jewish history is that the Jews are always protected by individual providence of one form or another; they are never entirely abandoned to the unreliable protection of general providence. Put in other terms, at no time do the Jewish people experience the full effects of *hester panim*, the biblical concept Gersonides equates with this lesser form of protection. In instances in which the Jews on their own are not worthy of individual providence and are threatened with harm from chance events, individual providence inherited from Abraham protects them from destruction—though, as Gersonides implies in some passages, the protection of inherited providence is not as great as that provided by individual providence earned by the Jews themselves.[2] That the Jewish people are constantly protected in this way is the basis for Gersonides' interpretation of the famous talmudic statement, *'ein mazal le-yisra'el*, "there is no star for Israel," a dictum he frequently quotes.[3] What this statement means in philosophical terms is that Israel's providence is dictated by individual providence, not by general providence which comes from the constellations.[4]

But perhaps the most the important conclusion to draw here is that providence inherited from Abraham more than any other factor in Gersonides' thinking accounts for the chosen status of the Jewish people. This force constitutes the backbone of the relationship between God and the Jews throughout history in that it is directly or indirectly responsible for all of the major events in Jewish history up to the messianic era.

GERSONIDES ON JEWISH CHOSENNESS: ANALYSIS AND ASSESSMENT

In evaluating Gersonides' views on Jewish chosenness let us begin by noting that in his reading of Jewish history, Gersonides has attempted in a most creative manner to resolve the tension between two major types of covenantal formats that appear in the Bible and that have been the subject of much recent scholarship. The biblical text often depicts the covenantal relationship between God and the Jewish people in conditional terms. The most important covenant of this type is, of course, the covenant at Mount Sinai, in which God promises reward to the Israelites in return for their obedience to His commandments. But in other places in the biblical text, the covenantal relationship between God and the Jewish people is described as unconditional. Perhaps the primary example of a covenant of this sort is the one formulated with Abraham in Genesis 15. Here God promises reward to Abraham's descendants but without requiring anything in return.

These two types of covenantal agreements define the relationship between God and the Jewish people throughout the biblical history but are never fully brought into harmony. Scholars have shown that the two formats have their origin in different types of treaty arrangements in Ancient Near Eastern culture.[5] The tension between them can therefore be explained by referring to the respective models of treaty arrangements upon which these covenants are based.

Gersonides, of course, has to make sense of this tension within his own philosophical framework. What he in effect proposes in his reading of Jewish history is that the two types of covenants perform different but complementary roles throughout Jewish history. As we have seen, the conditional covenant at Sinai is equated by Gersonides with normal individual providence. Individual providence is 'conditional' in the sense that one earns this type of providential reward on condition that one achieve moral and intellectual perfection. The function of the revelation at Mount Sinai is to provide the Israelites with the opportunity to fulfill this condition by offering convenient instruction in moral and theoretical wisdom. We have also shown that the unconditional covenant with Abraham in Genesis 15 is equated with inherited providence. This form of providence is 'unconditional' because the recipient is able to benefit from providence that has already been earned by a righteous ancestor. Thus the Jews benefit from Abraham's providence even when they themselves are not worthy of providential reward.

For Gersonides, these two covenants are intimately linked. The conditional covenant at Sinai is seen by Gersonides as an outgrowth of the unconditional covenant with the Patriarchs. In philosophical terms, this means that providence inherited from the Patriarchs is responsible for the revelation at Sinai, which in turn allows the Jews to earn providential reward on their own. Inherited providence also supports the covenant at Sinai after the Torah is given by providing providential punishments when the Jews are not obedient to the Torah's instruction.

Gersonides has therefore made room for both types of covenants in his reading of Jewish history. Neither is sufficient for explaining the relationship between God and the Jewish people. The unconditional Patriarchal covenant is a catalyst for the conditional covenant at Sinai, but the unconditional component does not outlive its usefulness once the conditional component has come into effect.

The biblical text, of course, describes other covenantal agreements between God and the Jews, such as those formulated in Genesis 17, Joshua

24, and Nehemiah 9. While modern scholars analyze these covenants as independent agreements, for Gersonides they are extensions of the Sinai
covenant. The commandment of circumcision in Genesis 17 is a covenant
in the same way that all other commandments in the Torah are. The only
difference with this commandment is that it had to be given to Abraham
and his offspring before the revelation at Sinai in order to safeguard them
from the licentious practices of their Canaanite neighbors.[6] The covenantal agreements in Joshua 24 and Nehemiah 9 are interpreted by Gersonides
as confirmations of the original Sinai pact.[7] The only covenantal agreement
that is never really given adequate treatment by Gersonides is the Davidic
covenant. As we saw, Gersonides tends to justify this covenant exegetically and at no point provides a sound philosophical explanation for the
choice of David's descendants as the sole legitimate heirs to the kingship
in Israel.[8]

   We can further enrich our understanding of Gersonides' theory of
Jewish chosenness by exploring possible antecedents for his views in the
philosophy of Judah Halevi, the renowned eleventh century Spanish Jewish thinker and poet. There are striking similarities between Gersonides'
notion of inherited providence and Halevi's *amr ilāhi*, or "divine thing," a
conception of central importance in the latter's major philosophical work,
the *Kuzari*. In that work, Halevi justifies the special status of the Jewish
people on the basis of a genetic trait only the Jews possess and which is inherited from one generation to the next. The *amr ilāhi* is the factor responsible for the capacity of the Jews to receive prophecy and experience
miracles. Yet, these capabilities, though genetic in origin, do not emerge
spontaneously; the *amr ilāhi* must be cultivated by proper observance of
the divine commandments and by living in the land of Israel.[9]

   There is much that Halevi's *amr ilāhi* and Gersonides' inherited providence share in common. Both are the exclusive property of the Jewish
people; both are inherited genetic principles; and both account for the
providential relationship between God and the Jewish people. Yet, neither
the *amr ilāhi* nor inherited providence is sufficient in itself; both principles
require that the Jews observe the divine commandments and live in the
land of Israel. In Halevi's philosophy, these actions cultivate the genetic
principle that in turn brings divine providence. For Gersonides, these
same actions are conditions made possible by the genetic principle that en-
hances the capability of the Jews to earn divine providence on their own.

   There are also important differences between the two conceptions.
The *amr ilāhi* is a racial principle that is carried internally by the Jews. Inherited providence, in contrast, is a providential law in the divine mind
which exerts its influences on the Jewish people from without.[10] However,
the difference between Gersonides and Halevi on this point is reduced

somewhat if one takes into account an observation made by Herbert Davidson in his analysis of Halevi's *amr ilāhi*. Davidson claims that while there are many passages in the *Kuzari* in which the *amr ilāhi* is depicted as an internal genetic principle, there are also instances in which it is seen as functioning as an external aura that envelops the Jewish nation or the land of Israel. In this alternative sense, the *amr ilāhi* functions in a manner quite similar to Gersonides' inherited providence.[11]

Another difference between the *amr ilāhi* and inherited providence is with respect to the duration of their influence. Halevi's *amr ilāhi* is present in mankind from Adam onward. Adam is the first one to possess this genetic trait, which is then passed on to select individuals in each generation until it becomes the property of the entire Jewish people after the time of Jacob.[12] The duration of Gersonides' inherited providence is more circumscribed. It begins to exert its influence only with the advent of Abraham. Gersonides also makes it clear that inherited providence will no longer be needed in the messianic period once the Jews settle in the land of Israel, a restriction that in no way applies to Halevi's *amr ilāhi*.

But perhaps the most important difference between these two principles is with regard to the respective philosophical premises upon which they are based. Halevi's *amr ilāhi* is a doctrine formulated in conscious opposition to Aristotelian philosophy. What Halevi is arguing is that it is not intellectual perfection that allows one to experience prophecy and miracles as the Aristotelians claim; rather, these capabilities result from a genetic trait that only the Jewish people possesses.[13] Gersonides' conception of inherited providence, in contrast, is based firmly on Aristotelian foundations. Abraham earns his providence by means of intellectual perfection. In subsequent generations this providence is inherited by Abraham's descendants, but only as an extension of Abraham's original providence.

Yet, despite the differences between Halevi's *amr ilāhi* and Gersonides' inherited providence, I believe that there is a connection between the two conceptions. What I will argue is that the idea of inherited providence in fact represents a deliberate attempt on Gersonides' part to adapt Halevi's *amr ilāhi* to an Aristotelian mode. This transformation may seem odd given that the *amr ilāhi*, as we have just noted, is a concept formulated in direct opposition to Aristotle. However, with reflection it is not hard to understand why Gersonides would have been drawn to this motif in Halevi's thought. The major Jewish philosopher who exerts the greatest influence on Gersonides is without doubt Maimonides. However, one weakness in Maimonides' philosophy is that it does not provide a clear theory of Jewish chosenness nor a philosophy of Jewish history.[14] Halevi's philosophy, by contrast, places these issues at the very center of his thought-system. In fact, his concern for such issues was one of the major factors that made his philosophy so appealing to Jewish thinkers from the medieval period onward. Therefore, despite Halevi's anti-Aristotelian bias, it would have made sense for Gersonides to look to Halevi's philosophy in order to establish a position with regard to Jewish chosenness. The chief problem for Gersonides was to reinterpret Halevi's philosophy so that it would fit into his Aristotelian thought-system, a problem he seems to have confronted with characteristic creativity and ingenuity.

In sum, scholars have traditionally seen Maimonides and Averroes as the primary influences on Gersonides' philosophy, an assessment that is certainly justified. But with respect to the issues of Jewish chosenness and Jewish history, it would appear that the primary influence is Judah Halevi.

From what we have said thus far, it is clear that in grappling with the concept of the Chosen People, Gersonides demonstrates great originality in his reading of the biblical text, in his interpretation of Jewish history, and in the manner in which he draws from Halevi's philosophy. But we still have not confronted the central question: has Gersonides successfully explained the chosenness of the Jewish people from a philosophical standpoint? In particular, does Gersonides manage to formulate a convincing position on Jewish chosenness even though he believes in an impersonal God?

We can conclude that Gersonides is indeed successful to the extent that he has managed to define the Patriarchal covenant and the covenant at Sinai as manifestations of impersonal providential laws. There is no question that Gersonides is aware of the philosophical difficulties that the concept of the Chosen People presents for him, and that he attempts to deal with these difficulties with the kind of ingenuity that characterizes his philosophy as a whole.

There are, however, a number of problems here that must be noted. One difficulty, for example, is Gersonides' inadequate explanation for the extension of the Patriarchal covenant to the messianic period. This was a pivotal component in Gersonides' interpretation of Jewish history in that it accounted for the special relationship between God and the Jewish people after the conquest of Canaan. Yet Gersonides never clearly explains whether the extension of the covenant was part of Abraham's original prophecy or whether the providential plan described in that prophecy has somehow changed in midstream. Given the philosophical difficulties with the latter alternative, one is tempted to opt for the former explanation; but Gersonides does not provide enough information for us to be sure of his exact position here.[15]

There are other, more fundamental difficulties in Gersonides' theory of Jewish chosenness. Most important, Gersonides fails to provide a metaphysical mechanism to explain how inherited providence functions; indeed, his metaphysics would appear to preclude the possibility of such a phenomenon.[16] The implications of Gersonides' silence on this matter are now fully evident, for without an adequate explanation of inherited providence, the philosophical foundation of Gersonides' position on Jewish chosenness is of questionable soundness.

It should be pointed out, however, that this problem is not unique to inherited providence. In our analysis of other forms of providence in which events in the sublunar realm are directly affected—i.e., providential suffering and miracles—we noted that Gersonides is similarly reticent about the metaphysical mechanisms that control such processes.[17] Thus, in all fairness, it is not inherited providence per se that is the problem here, but a more basic flaw in Gersonides' handling of providence.

Another difficulty with Gersonides' theory of Jewish chosenness is that it is questionable whether the phenomenon of inherited providence really provides justification for the uniqueness of the Jewish people. The problem is that inherited providence is a providential law that can affect the descendants of *any* individual who has achieved an unusually high degree of perfection. While the instantiation of this law may be a rare occurrence, there is nothing to rule out the possibility that another person, Jew or non-Jew, would bequeath providence to his descendants in the same way that Abraham did. Thus, from a theoretical standpoint, there *could* be another Chosen People besides the Jews.

Gersonides does not seem to have entertained this possibility. He appears to have believed that Abraham was the only individual to have been capable of passing providence on to his offspring throughout history. However, Gersonides never explains why Abraham is unique in this regard.

Gersonides' lack of explanation on this point has to be seen as a crucial gap in his philosophical reading of history. Abraham's providence, after all, affects not just the entirety of Jewish history, but eventually non-Jewish history as well; it is providence inherited from Abraham that serves as a catalyst for the messianic redemption of the Gentile nations as well. Without an explanation for the long-lasting influence of Abraham's providence, the force of Gersonides' reading of history is therefore seriously weakened.

It is interesting to note that if the problem of the uniqueness of the Jewish people emerges anywhere in Gersonides' thinking, it is not in his treatment of inherited providence but in his discussions of Mosaic prophecy. It is with this issue that Gersonides seems to have perceived the difficulties that his Aristotelian principles present for the concept of Jewish chosenness. We saw that in a number of passages in the *Wars* and in his biblical commentaries, Gersonides struggles with Mosaic prophecy in an apparent attempt to preserve the uniqueness of the Torah and, by implication, the uniqueness of the Jewish people. A number of interpretations are proposed for Mosaic prophecy; but in the end Gersonides never really gets around the central problem that this phenomenon has to be understood as a manifestation of impersonal providential laws that can operate on behalf of anyone who has achieved the requisite state of perfection. Even Gersonides' boldest solution that Mosaic legislation is a non-repeatable miracle does not eliminate the difficulty. Miracles are also controlled by impersonal laws operating on behalf of a worthy recipient who has achieved the proper degree of perfection. There is thus no reason why another Moses could not come along and produce another Torah.[18]

Yet, while these problems should not be minimized, they should not cause us to lose sight of what I believe to be the main point. Our study has shown that Gersonides is indeed concerned about Jewish chosenness and that he develops a defined position on this issue with the same ingenuity that characterizes his philosophy as a whole. If Gersonides is unable to provide a tight fit between his Aristotelian principles and the thought-world of the Bible, he is certainly not the only medieval philosopher to have had this problem.

Our study provides a glimpse into a side of Gersonides that has not been sufficiently appreciated. Scholars of Gersonides have focused for the most part on the abstract dimensions of his philosophy, an emphasis that has tended to obscure the more human aspects of his thought-world. The effort Gersonides expends to make philosophical sense of the concept of Jewish chosenness clearly indicates that he was not only a philosopher concerned with abstract matters, but also a Jew attempting to come to terms with his environment, with the suffering of the Jewish people, and with the meaning of Jewish history.

THE PLACE OF THE BIBLICAL COMMENTARIES
IN GERSONIDES' PHILOSOPHY

Besides exploring Gersonides' conception of Jewish chosenness for its philosophical value, we were also interested in this question because of its methodological significance. An examination of this theme would allow us to assess the biblical commentaries as sources of insight into Gersonides' philosophical system and to evaluate their relationship to his major philosophical work, *The Wars of the Lord*. Our study leaves little doubt that Gersonides' biblical commentaries can provide important insight into his philosophical thought. For a proper understanding of Gersonides' position on Jewish chosenness, the biblical commentaries have proven to be indispensable. We have shown that it is primarily in these writings that Gersonides formulates his philosophical views on this issue.

The more difficult question is the nature of the relationship between the biblical commentaries and the *Wars*. Let us first define the problem more sharply. There is no doubt that with regard to some issues, Gersonides consciously chose to express his views in the biblical commentaries rather than in the *Wars*. As we noted in the course of our study, there are two subjects of this kind: ethics and the divine commandments. According to Gersonides, neither of these lends itself to demonstrative reasoning. The only certain knowledge that one can achieve in these matters is through the scriptural record produced by prophetic revelation. Thus, it is no surprise to find that Gersonides does not discuss ethical questions or the explanations for the commandments in his major work of systematic philosophy; these topics are dealt with exclusively in his commentaries on the biblical text.[19]

But for Gersonides the most exalted of the philosophical disciplines is metaphysics, and in this important area of enquiry the relationship between the *Wars* and the biblical commentaries is rather ambiguous. According to Gersonides, this discipline is certainly subject to systematic philosophical treatment, but it is also revealed in the biblical text as well. It is for this reason that Gersonides discusses issues in metaphysics both in the *Wars* and throughout his biblical commentaries.[20]

What is not entirely clear is the precise relationship between these two genres of literature in their respective treatments of metaphysical questions. Does Gersonides merely repeat in the biblical commentaries what he has discovered through systematic argument in the *Wars*? Or do the philosophical and exegetical modes of writing each make a distinctive contribution?

One possibility we have ruled out is that the biblical commentaries represent an attempt by Gersonides to offer a traditional version of his philosophical views in order to appease a popular audience. While Gersonides appears to have acknowledged the need for esoteric discourse in some circumstances, there is no evidence that he adopted this style of writing in his exegetical works or in any of his other works.

There are other possibilities. One is that from the standpoint of content there is no substantial difference between the philosophical material in the *Wars* and that contained in the biblical commentaries. In dealing with metaphysical questions in both, perhaps Gersonides' intention was to strengthen his philosophical system by showing that it could be derived by systematic reasoning *and* through interpretation of the biblical text. Another possibility is that the two genres somehow serve different functions in the development of Gersonides' philosophical thought. That is, Gersonides chose intentionally to discuss some metaphysical issues in the *Wars* while leaving others for his biblical commentaries.

An additional factor that needs to be taken into account here is one that we noted in our introduction. We must keep in mind that most of Gersonides' biblical commentaries were composed after his completion of the *Wars*. Thus, when we deal with the relationship between these bodies of writings, we must keep in mind that we are attempting to determine what the commentaries add to the discussions in the *Wars*, not the reverse.

Another point that we also mentioned in our introduction is that we must recognize our limitations in trying to settle these questions. We cannot provide a comprehensive answer to the problems raised here on the basis of our study alone, because we have focused on only one issue that the *Wars* and the biblical commentaries share in common. However, it is certainly possible to make an assessment regarding the material we have examined, an assessment that may at least provide a basis for a broader evaluation of the relationship between Gersonides' systematic philosophy and his biblical exegesis.

With respect to our topic, it would seem that the exegetical and philosophical modes of discourse do, in fact, serve different but complementary functions. We began our analysis by examining Gersonides' views on divine providence in the *Wars* and discovered that in this work Gersonides makes use of systematic analysis to postulate the existence of a number of manifestations of divine providence. But we noted that the discussions in the *Wars* tend to remain in the realm of the abstract. This work does not provide a theory of God's ongoing covenantal relationship with the Jewish people throughout history. In the remainder of our study, we then went on to find that it is in the biblical commentaries that Gersonides grapples with this issue. It is in these writings that he shapes and organizes the various components of his theory of providence in order to construct a coherent reading of Jewish history.

But it is important to emphasize that the biblical commentaries do more than just interpret the events of Jewish history in light of the philosophical positions in the *Wars*. In the process of explicating the biblical text, Gersonides frequently offers valuable new insights regarding his views on providence that are not contained in the *Wars*. In sum, while the *Wars* works out basic philosophical positions on providence, the biblical commentaries apply these positions to Jewish history and, in the process, clarify and refine them.

No example in our study better illustrates these observations than Gersonides' treatment of inherited providence. This concept is given only brief attention in the closing passages of the *Wars*, and there is no indication here that it is a doctrine of any significance. Yet in the biblical commentaries this concept is highly important as it becomes the basis for explaining the covenantal relationship between God and the Jewish people throughout history. Here, inherited providence is developed into a significant philosophical conception as Gersonides works out its nuances against the background of the biblical narrative.

The concept of providential suffering provides a similar if less impressive illustration. Providential suffering is dealt with in the *Wars* more extensively than inherited providence. As with inherited providence, however, the biblical commentaries significantly enrich our understanding of this idea. For one, the biblical commentaries inform us about the importance of this manifestation of providence in Gersonides' reading of Jewish history. The concept of providential suffering is used to explain the manifold hardships the Jewish people has experienced throughout history. It is in the commentaries that we also get a better understanding of the circumstances which bring about providential suffering and the way in which this form of punishment expresses itself.

There are many other examples of this sort that we could call upon from our study to support our position. Now as we have already suggested in our Introduction, one might argue that if the biblical commentaries provide new philosophical insights not found in the *Wars*, it is because of their later date of composition. While there is certainly some truth in this suggestion, I do not believe that this reason alone explains the substantial insight the biblical commentaries provide with regard to such questions as covenant and Jewish chosenness. More likely, it was by conscious choice that Gersonides confronted these issues in his exegetical writings. Gersonides seems to have felt—and understandably so—that a direct explication of the biblical narrative was the ideal medium for shaping and defining his views on matters relating to Jewish chosenness. After all, the biblical text in Gersonides' mind contains the authoritative record of God's relationship with the Jewish people not just for the biblical period but for all of Jewish history. As we saw in the course of our study, Gersonides treats a number of portions of the biblical text—such as the *tokheḥah* sections in Leviticus and Deuteronomy, and parts of the Book of Daniel—as authoritative prophecies for events in Jewish history up to the messianic period.

We must again emphasize that what we are saying here about the relationship between the biblical commentaries and the *Wars* may not apply to all issues. Still, the fact that we have demonstrated a complementarity between these bodies of writings on themes as central as divine providence and Jewish chosenness is evidence of the benefit of our approach to Gersonides' writings. Furthermore, it should be noted that at least three of the

six books in the *Wars* are concerned with matters relating to divine providence.[21] Our findings therefore affect a substantial portion of the material
in this treatise.

There is one point of caution which should be added here. If our
study has underscored the value of Gersonides' biblical commentaries as
sources of insight into his philosophical thought, it has also pointed up
the difficulties that this type of literature presents when used in this way.
The biblical commentaries were remarkably consistent on most of the
philosophical issues that we examined in our study. However, there were
at least two occasions when these writings were anything but consistent.
More precisely, in the treatments of Mosaic prophecy and the present
exile, we discovered that Gersonides presents widely differing viewpoints
in his exegetical writings, depending on which passages one consults.

That there are inconsistencies in Gersonides' thinking should not
trouble us greatly; after all, there is no philosopher who is free of such difficulties. But the inconsistencies that we find in Gersonides' exegetical
writings are particularly problematic because, unlike the *Wars*, these writings are by their very nature unsystematic and therefore more elusive
when it comes to dealing with philosophical issues. As we have seen
throughout our study, philosophical views on the same subject can appear
in widely scattered sources and in widely different contexts in Gersonides'
vast exegetical corpus. All is fine as long as the sources agree or comple-
ment one another; but this is not always the case.

The approach we tended to follow in our study was to find a way of
explaining such inconsistencies either by reconciling them or by comprehending the tension which might have produced alternative perspectives
in Gersonides' thinking. In both examples just cited, the latter method was
used with a fair degree of success.[22] Still, the problems inherent in using
Gersonides' exegetical writings as sources for his philosophical views
need to be noted here and must be taken into account in any further study
of these works.

In closing, I would like to offer one last series of comments about Gersonides' exegetical writings. One factor that may help explain the neglect
of Gersonides' biblical commentaries by students of medieval philosophy
is the style in which they are written. These works tend to read much more
easily than the dense and difficult *Wars of the Lord*. There is, therefore, the
temptation to view the exegetical writings as simplistic compositions that
are at best an adjunct to the more complex philosophical discussions in the
Wars. This impression is only reinforced by the fact that in his biblical commentaries Gersonides rarely cites the rabbinic and medieval sources from
which he consistently draws. A cursory reading of these commentaries
leads one to feel that Gersonides is skipping merrily through his explica-

tion of the biblical text without much thought for the tradition of interpretation that precedes him.

It is my hope that the present study has dispelled these impressions. If anything has become clear in the course of this analysis, it is that Gersonides' biblical commentaries are anything but simplistic. While on a superficial level these writings may be easier to read than the *Wars*, this is certainly not the case when one subjects them to a more careful examination.

Throughout our study, we have seen that the biblical commentaries are designed to challenge the reader on a number of levels. For one, Gersonides will often refer to doctrines in the *Wars* by doing nothing more than citing the section in which they are to be found. Gersonides therefore assumes that his audience has thorough familiarity with this treatise. Moreover, even when Gersonides makes explicit reference to doctrines in the *Wars*, he does not always fully explain the connection between these doctrines and the biblical text. Most often it is left to the reader to take brief allusions and references to the *Wars* and apply them to the biblical text on his own. Indeed, most of our study has been occupied with this very exercise. We consistently came across brief references to the *Wars* in Gersonides' exegetical writings which required substantial effort to interpret.

Gersonides also seems to expect his readers to have knowledge not just of his philosophical treatise but of his other biblical commentaries as well. We had instances in which philosophical material in one portion of Gersonides' exegetical writings could only be properly understood by reference to material in his other commentaries. This was especially evident in our explication of the covenant in Genesis 15. Gersonides' interpretation of this chapter could be fully clarified only by looking at remarks in commentaries on other books of the Pentateuch, in particular his commentary on Exodus.

A proper reading of Gersonides' philosophical exegesis also requires more than just a sensitivity to the immediate philosophical issues being discussed. We saw that Gersonides' explication of the biblical text often incorporates and reinterprets material from rabbinic aggadah and previous medieval exegetes, even though he rarely identifies his sources. In a number of instances, an awareness of these sources was necessary for understanding Gersonides' reading of the biblical text.

Thus, one should not be deceived by the unadorned quality of Gersonides' exegetical writing. It is in these works, more than in any other portion of his corpus, that we see the integration of Gersonides' many talents as scientist, philosopher, rabbinic scholar and biblical commentator. Indeed, it is here that the complexity and originality of this remarkable medieval thinker most clearly emerges.

Appendix

THE *PINNOT HA-TORAH* IN GERSONIDES' THOUGHT

A concept that has surfaced at several key junctures of our study is the *pinnot ha-torah*, or fundamental principles of the Torah. For instance, we saw that Gersonides identifies the immutability of the Torah as one of the *pinnot ha-torah*, a point that was significant in our discussion of Mosaic prophecy. We also argued that Gersonides effectively treats the extension of the Patriarchal covenant to the messianic period as one of these *pinnot*.[1] It is therefore important that we devote a separate discussion to the *pinnot ha-torah* in order to define precisely what they are.

There are many other doctrines that Gersonides identifies as *pinnot ha-torah* throughout his major philosophical work, *The Wars of the Lord*, and his biblical commentaries. The major problem is that he never clarifies how these principles are derived nor what function they serve. Charles Touati—to my knowledge, the only scholar to address the issue—contends that the *pinnot ha-torah* are effectively articles of faith modeled on Maimonides' thirteen principles in the introduction to *Perek Ḥelek*. Touati lists seven such *pinnot*, which are scattered throughout Gersonides' writings.[2]

The discovery of articles of faith in Gersonides would be of no small significance. A whole series of questions would immediately be raised that bear on Gersonides' philosophy as a whole. Why are these particular principles chosen? What does their selection teach us about Gersonides' philosophical system? To whom are they directed?

It is my contention, however, that Touati's conclusions are problematic. I will try to show that the *pinnot ha-torah* are indeed significant in the overall scheme of Gersonides' thought, but not as articles of faith. I will argue that the *pinnot ha-torah* are key concepts for determining the nature of the relationship between philosophical truth and the Bible. They are doctrines derived primarily from Scripture, the function of which is to set limits for the direction of philosophical enquiry. I will also attempt to demonstrate that Gersonides' conception of *pinnot ha-torah* originates with Maimonides, not from his discussion in *Perek Ḥelek*, but from his position on creation in the *Guide*.

I should point out that a thorough examination of each and every one of the *pinnot ha-torah* will not be attempted. As we shall soon see, Touati has greatly underestimated the number of *pinnot ha-torah* in Gersonides' writings. The complete list covers an impressive range of doctrines that touch on all the major aspects of Gersonides' philosophical and religious thought. An exhaustive discussion of the *pinnot* would therefore not be feasible here. I will instead attempt to highlight the basic features of these principles while demonstrating their significance in Gersonides' thinking.

Before discussing the fundamental principles of the Torah in Gersonides' thought, we must first review Gersonides' position on the Bible as a source of philosophical speculation.[3] The key statement with respect to this issue is contained in the introduction to the *Wars*. There Gersonides states that the Bible must be interpreted to conform to demonstrative truths discovered in the course of philosophical investigation, a position he acknowledges is drawn from Maimonides.[4] Gersonides goes on to explain that, like Maimonides, he is prepared to interpret the Torah to affirm the eternity of the universe if reason were to require us to believe in that doctrine.[5] Gersonides therefore plans in the *Wars* to adopt the method of first conducting a thorough philosophical investigation of various issues and then showing how those views can be confirmed in the Torah.[6]

Gersonides expresses confidence in the ultimate identity between the philosophical conclusions in his own treatise and the doctrines found in Scripture. In fact, the name of the treatise, *The Wars of the Lord*, is derived from the notion that the false views of his predecessors have been refuted in the course of demonstrating philosophically that his own views accord with the "view of our Torah."[7]

This method of harmonizing philosophy and Scripture invites an obvious question. If Scripture is always interpreted to conform to truths arrived at by philosophy, is there really any need for Scripture? Has its role not become superfluous?

Gersonides responds to these questions with the affirmation that the Bible indeed serves a positive, active role in philosophical speculation. With some philosophical problems—especially the difficult ones—the Bible itself has guided him towards the truth. The Bible, therefore, does not serve an exclusively passive role in philosophical investigation, but itself becomes part of the enquiry by furnishing valuable clues to solve philosophy's most difficult problems.[8] Touati has astutely focused on Gersonides' notion of the Torah as *haysharah*, or "guide," as a central motif in his attitude towards the Torah. As *haysharah*, the Torah leads the philosopher in the correct path of investigation without necessarily providing clear and explicit answers.[9]

In his discussion of creation in the *Wars*, for example, Gersonides includes a lengthy exegesis of the biblical account that he claims was instrumental in guiding him toward his theory.[10] Even more noteworthy is his analysis of miracles at the very end of the treatise, which is based entirely on the data provided in biblical sources.[11] The value of prophetic revelation is therefore upheld as an essential source that helps lead one to proper philosophical conclusions and not merely as a text to be interpreted once the investigation is complete.

This function, however, is not the only active role that Scripture plays. Gersonides also alludes in several passages to *pinnot ha-torah*, or "fundamental principles of the Torah," biblical doctrines that play an important role in philosophical discourse.

In the *Wars*, Gersonides says very little about how these principles function. At first, they seem to have no active role in philosophical speculation. While summing up the main points of his introduction, Gersonides claims that in the course of settling the philosophical problems he has chosen to discuss, "the fundamental principles of the Torah [*ha-pinnot ha-toriyyot*] will in their entirety have been established."[12] In another passage, Gersonides alludes in passing to the "fundamental principles of the Torah" (*ha-pinnot ha-toriyyot*) which are based upon the topics of discussion in his treatise.[13] Gersonides thus envisions a set of fundamental principles of the Torah which are confirmed in the course of his philosophical discussions.

Gersonides' position on these principles takes a new turn in book three of the *Wars*. While trying to show how his position on divine knowledge is identical to that of the Torah, Gersonides depicts the fundamental principles of the Torah as functioning in a more active role. He repeats his contention that when a literal understanding of the Torah conflicts with what has been proven philosophically, one must interpret the Torah to conform to truths derived from philosophy. Yet, he then adds that one follows this procedure "so long as none of the fundamental principles of the Torah [*pinnah mi-pinnot ha-torah*] is destroyed." Gersonides claims that Maimonides also followed this practice in many cases in his *Guide of the Perplexed*.[14]

A more explicit statement that affirms the active role of these principles is to be found in Gersonides' *Commentary on Proverbs*:

> INCLINE YOUR EARS TO THE WORDS OF THE *ḤAKHA-MIM*:[15] to learn their philosophy. But also PAY ATTENTION TO MY WISDOM[16] and do not rely exclusively on the words of the philosophers. [Heed their words] only in that which agrees with what I have made known to you as founded upon the fundamental principles of the Torah.[17] For the Torah guides [one] to comprehend what can be comprehended of Me by way of wisdom.

Here again the fundamental principles of the Torah appear to exercise what amounts to a veto power over the conclusions arrived at by philosophy.

These passages conflict with Gersonides' introductory remarks in the *Wars* for two reasons. First, in the introduction to the *Wars*, the principles of the Torah were seen as being confirmed from the consequences of philosophical enquiry; now, they are antecedent to philosophical enquiry and function as a significant factor in controlling the whole direction of philosophical discussion. Second and more important, the notion that the *pinnot ha-torah* set limits to what philosophical reasoning can prove contradicts the position, also voiced in the introduction to the *Wars*, that one must always interpret the Torah to conform to truths arrived at through philosophical speculation.

Whether Gersonides was aware of these conflicts or saw them as true inconsistencies is not clear. He makes no attempt to reconcile his various statements. We will proceed with the assumption that there is an active role for the *pinnot ha-torah* in Gersonides' method. Certainly, the two passages in the *Wars* and in the *Commentary on Proverbs* are evidence enough that the *pinnot ha-torah*, at least in some instances, exert decisive influence on philosophical speculation. The validity of this assumption will also be confirmed, I hope, in the course of further investigation.

The major problem is that Gersonides says so little about the precise character and function of these principles. Gersonides never explains how these principles are derived, nor does he clarify why they exert such influence on philosophical discussion. Touati argues that they are articles of faith modeled on those of Maimonides, an interpretation that could explain their centrality for philosophical speculation.[18] However, Gersonides never actually compiles these principles into an independent list as Maimonides does and never once identifies them as articles of faith. Furthermore, Touati compiles a list of only seven *pinnot* scattered throughout Gersonides' philosophical and exegetical writings. In fact, this list is far from complete.[19] I have found no less than twenty-two *pinnot ha-torah* in Gersonides' writings covering an impressive range of doctrines. This number of principles would appear to be rather unwieldy to serve as a series of basic dogmas or beliefs.

The following is a list of doctrines referred to as *pinnot ha-torah* in Gersonides' writings:[20]

1. God's existence[21]
2. God's oneness[22]
3. creation[23]
4. the Sabbath[24]
5. events in the sublunar realm are controlled by movements of the spheres[25]
6. human actions are contingent, man has free will[26]
7. general providence[27]
8. individual providence[28]
9. all good comes from God[29]
10. God judges man according to his deeds[30]
11. miracles[31]
12. prophecy[32]
13. God's promises are fulfilled[33]
14. God emanates goodness into the world by virtue of kindness and mercy, not by virtue of necessity[34]
15. ultimate joy is in being close to God[35]
16. the commandment to love God[36]
17. the Torah is immutable[37]
18. the Torah is everlasting[38]
19. the appointment of judges to adjudicate matters regarding the laws of the Torah[39]
20. the reasons for the commandments are fully known only to God[40]
21. through observance of commandments the Jews are worthy of inheriting the land of Israel in the messianic period[41]
22. all nations will eventually worship the true God in the messianic period[42]
(23. resurrection of the dead[43])

In order to gain some insight into the *pinnot ha-torah*, we should start with a basic observation. Implicit in Gersonides' remarks is that the *pinnot ha-torah* are distinguished by their being based in Scripture as opposed to philosophical reasoning. His approach, as we have described it up to now, is predicated on the distinction between the fundamental principles of the Torah, on the one hand, and doctrines derived by philosophical method, on the other.

Gersonides uses terminology in his biblical commentaries that formalizes this distinction. On occasion, Gersonides refers to his major philosophical positions in the *Wars* as "fundamental principles of philosophy," or *pinnot ha-ʿiyyun*.[44] Therefore, it is clear that there are principles which are derived from philosophical discourse, *pinnot ha-ʿiyyun*, and those which in contrast are derived from Scripture, *pinnot ha-torah*.

There is a good deal of overlap between the two sets of principles. In his biblical commentaries Gersonides will often refer to a principle as belonging simultaneously to both philosophy and the Torah.[45] The same principle can belong to either category depending on whether philosophical or exegetical means happen to be used in formulating a particular doctrine. These observations fall in line with Gersonides' assertion in the introduction to the *Wars* that the *pinnot ha-torah* are confirmed by philosophical discourse.

It should also be noted that the *pinnot ha-torah* are not doctrines derived exclusively from the Pentateuch. Many of these principles are drawn from the Prophets and the Writings. When referring to the fundamental principles of the Torah, Gersonides therefore uses the term *torah* rather loosely to refer to all parts of the Bible.

That the *pinnot ha-torah* are scripturally based still does not tell us very much. We still do not know why specific biblical doctrines are selected, nor do we know why they have such an important role to play in the process of philosophical enquiry. Perhaps the best clue for understanding the *pinnot ha-torah* is the reference cited earlier from book three of the *Wars*. Recall that Gersonides names Maimonides' *Guide* as the source of his position that one must interpret Scripture to conform to philosophical truth so long as none of the fundamental principles of the Torah are destroyed.[46] Maimonides' writings do indeed contain frequent references to fundamental principles of the Torah. The entire first book of the *Mishneh Torah*, in fact, is devoted to that issue: *Hilkhot Yesodey ha-Torah*. In *The Guide of the Perplexed* there are also numerous references to the *qawāʿid al-shariʿa*, a phrase translated by Ibn Tibbon as either *yesodey ha-torah* or *pinnot ha-torah*.

Maimonides seems to have used this concept in a flexible fashion. In the introduction to *Perek Ḥelek*, for example, Maimonides applies the phrase *qawāʿid al-shariʿa* to the thirteen principles of belief. In this context, the fundamental principles of the Torah are synonymous with the basic dogmas of Judaism.[47]

However, in the *Guide* there is evidence that the concept of principles of the Torah takes on new meaning. In the celebrated discussion of creation in the second part of the *Guide*, there emerges a distinctly hermeneutical function for these principles. In *Guide* II:25, Maimonides explains why he does not resort to interpreting the biblical account of creation to support the Aristotelian conception of an eternal universe. Biblical interpretation, after all, was used earlier in the *Guide* in response to the problem of biblical anthropomorphism.

Maimonides offers two reasons for his reluctance to interpret the biblical sources according to Aristotle's view. First, there is demonstrative proof for God's incorporeality, while such proof is lacking for the theory of an eternal universe. Second—and this is the point that interests us most—reinterpreting the anthropomorphic references in the Bible in no way destroys "the foundations of the Law" (qawā'id al-sharī'a); however, the reinterpretation of the creation story "destroys the Law in its principle." Maimonides goes on to explain that the notion of an eternal universe would assume that God performs all his activities by virtue of absolute necessity; consequently, basic biblical concepts, such as willful divine intervention in the form of miracles, and reward and punishment, would be reduced to sheer nonsense.[48]

What is most important here is that Maimonides is using the phrase, "foundations of the Law," in a manner very different from that in *Perek Ḥelek*. Here they no longer represent basic dogmas of Judaism, but take on a hermeneutical character. In the introduction to *Perek Ḥelek*, the belief in God's incorporeality is a foundation of the Law by virtue of being one of the articles of faith. In the *Guide*, however, Maimonides explicitly rejects the belief in God's incorporeality as one of these foundations. Instead, the foundations of the Law are such concepts as miracles, reward, and punishment—concepts that must be upheld in order to preserve the intelligibility of the Torah. Since God's incorporeality does not serve this function, it does not qualify. Clearly, the foundations of the Law are seen in our passage in the *Guide* as playing an exclusively interpretive role and are not to be identified with the thirteen articles of faith.[49]

Maimonides' position, however, is not the focus of our concerns.[50] What is central for us is that Gersonides appears to adopt Maimonides' conception of "foundations of the Law" as a hermeneutical device. In the key passage in the *Wars*, Gersonides explicitly names the *Guide* as his source for the notion that one can interpret the Bible "so long as none of the fundamental principles of the Torah is destroyed"—a position that appears to be based on Maimonides' discussion of creation. Like Maimonides, Gersonides is stating that the Bible should be interpreted to conform to philosophical truth, but not at the expense of robbing Scripture of its basic intelligibility. The *pinnot ha-torah* would be those doctrines that minimally preserve the contents of the Torah in this regard.

Some of the terminology used by Gersonides in reference to the *pinnot ha-torah* is reminiscent of that used in the *Guide* when Maimonides refers to such principles. Moreover, this terminology reflects the very function that the *pinnot* are designed to serve according to Maimonides' formulation in the discussion on creation. For instance, providence—one of the more important *pinnot*—is described by Gersonides as a doctrine "upon which the Torah in its entirety is built."[51] Similar language is used to describe the doctrine of free will, which is "one of the great principles of the Torah upon which it is built."[52] This imagery is borrowed directly from a passage in the *Guide*, where Maimonides refers to individual providence as "one of the fundamental principles of the Law, which is built upon it. . . ."[53] Thus, the *pinnot* are envisioned literally as foundations upon which the structure of the Torah is supported. This conception is extended by Gersonides into another metaphor. Gersonides will sometimes refer to one of the *pinnot* as a doctrine without which "the Torah in its entirety would collapse" (*tipol ha-torah bi-khlalah*), an image that again calls upon the analogy of a building standing upon its foundation.[54]

There is another feature in Gersonides' conception of the *pinnot* that can be traced to Maimonides. In several of Gersonides' references, some of the *pinnot ha-torah* are dependent on other *pinnot*. For instance, Gersonides explicitly states that the belief in prophecy is dependent on the notion that God's promises to the prophets are fulfilled.[55]

In fact, some doctrines appear to qualify as *pinnot ha-torah* only because they support other doctrines central to the Bible, not because they are themselves essential. For instance, it is not immediately apparent why Gersonides includes as one of the *pinnot ha-torah* the notion that events in the sublunar world are controlled by the movements of the spheres. However, Gersonides is careful to explain in the passage that describes this *pinnah* that this conception is necessary for the denial of dualism and for upholding the oneness of God. That is, it is important to recognize that the realm of the spheres and the sublunar world are not controlled by separate deities but by one God. The oneness of God is itself one of the *pinnot ha-torah*, and it is clear, therefore, that believing in the influence of the spheres upon the sublunar world becomes one of the *pinnot* by virtue of its association with this central biblical doctrine.[56]

There are other principles that can be understood through a similar type of interdependence. The notion that God emanates goodness into the world out of mercy and kindness, not necessity, is another principle that in itself seems to be a rather odd choice as one of the *pinnot ha-torah*. Yet, it is important to take note that Gersonides introduces this notion as one of the *pinnot* in explicit connection with the doctrine of creation. Gersonides points out that if emanation were to occur by virtue of blind necessity, the Aristotelian view of an eternal universe would necessarily follow.[57]

What about creation itself? Why does *this* concept qualify as one of the *pinnot ha-torah*? Gersonides appears to have viewed it as one of the fundamental principles for the same reason Maimonides does. At the very beginning of his commentary on Genesis, Gersonides points out that belief in creation is a necessary prerequisite for the belief in miracles.[58] Here we have an example where a chain of three *pinnot* are dependent on each other; non-necessary emanation supports the doctrine of creation, which in turn supports the doctrine of miracles. The inclusion of certain commandments only makes sense in light of these observations. The Sabbath, for instance, is seen as one of the *pinnot ha-torah* because it too supports the notion of creation.[59]

The notion that some of the *pinnot ha-torah* are dependent on each other is also a concept that can be traced to Maimonides. We have already seen that creation is one of the fundamental principles of the Torah because it is a necessary prerequisite for the concept of miracles. In another passage in the *Guide*, Maimonides specifically sees the belief in the existence of angels—which is elsewhere identified as one of the fundamental principles of the Torah—as a necessary prerequisite for believing in prophecy, another such principle.[60]

It is important to point out that these observations have important implications for the philosophical status of these principles. Earlier, we said that the *pinnot ha-torah* are in harmony with the conclusions of philosophical speculation because they have to be; the fundamental principles of the Torah place limits on the direction of philosophical enquiry. According to this formulation, the *pinnot ha-torah* are independent of and antecedent to the process of philosophical investigation.

Yet it is evident from what we have just said about the dependence of some *pinnot* on others that the issue is more complex—more so than Gersonides himself may have intended. Some of these fundamental principles can be properly understood only by approaching the biblical text with the help of prior philosophical knowledge. It is noteworthy that in all these cases one principle is linked to another on the basis of insights only the philosopher can provide. Thus the notion that creation is one of the *pinnot ha-torah* because it allows for miracles, presumes that the philosophical connection between creation and miracles is evident. The same goes for the concept that the movements of the heavens are responsible for events in the sublunar realm. That this concept is one of the *pinnot* because it supports the notion of God's oneness again assumes that one is acquainted with basic issues in metaphysics. Thus, the notion that the *pinnot ha-torah* can be derived purely from Scripture does not always hold true.

In some instances Gersonides appears to depart from Maimonides' position in subtle but important ways. There are indications that some doctrines are designated as *pinnot ha-torah* because they are necessary for the very possibility of revelation itself. Here, it is not so much the intelligibility of the Torah which is at stake, but the historical fact of revelation that allows for a Torah to exist in the first place. For instance, in one passage where Gersonides refers to prophecy as one of the *pinnot ha-torah*, he adds the following remark: "... and this [i.e., prophecy] is a great fundamental principle [*shoresh*] and a mighty pillar for affirming the giving of the Torah from God by means of prophecy, for without this belief [in prophecy] the Torah in its entirety would collapse."[61] The suggestion here is that prophecy is one of the *pinnot ha-torah* because without it there could be no revelation to Moses and therefore no Torah.

Other doctrines which Gersonides views as *pinnot ha-torah* could be seen as serving a function similar to that of prophecy. The belief in God, for instance, is obviously necessary for believing in the possibility of a revelation at Sinai. The belief in providence could also be seen as having a similar status. Since providence and prophecy are closely identified in Gersonides' philosophy, it is possible that Gersonides sees the belief in providence as serving the same purpose as prophecy. Without such belief, the possibility that God would give the Torah to the Jews would be precluded. Only a God who exercises providence would be interested in providing the Jewish people with a revealed text to guide them in their relationship with God.[62]

An instance in which Gersonides applies the concept of *pinnot ha-torah* in a rather novel way is with regard to the doctrine that the reasons for the divine commandments are known fully only by God. The explanation for this position is as follows:

> The fifth *to'elet* which is one of the most important of the fundamental principles of the Torah [*pinnot ha-torah*] is that God commanded us to obey the words of the Torah only with regard to that which is overt in them. We are commanded to do this for all generations to come. But that which is concealed in the words of the Torah—that is, the underlying meanings towards which the Torah intended the commandments to guide [us]—is something which cannot be known completely except by God alone. This [notion] is what safeguards men from sinning to some extent with regard to a commandment—[i.e.,] in [their] thinking that they have understood the reason that the Torah intended that commandment and that therefore one need not observe this particular commandment. [The Torah] therefore erected with this [principle] a fortified wall to protect the Torah so that one will not say that its words are [to be observed] according to that which is concealed and not according to that which is overt.[63]

Here a doctrine is considered one of the *pinnot ha-torah* not because of any hermeneutical issue but to safeguard the actual observance of the commandments. If men were to have complete knowledge of the reasons for the commandments, such knowledge would be used as a pretext for circumventing them.[64]

Still, most of the *pinnot* appear to function according to the original model set by Maimonides' discussion of creation. Most often these doctrines are concepts that are so commonly expressed in Scripture that the denial of them would threaten the intelligibility of its contents. The notion of free will, for instance, is necessary for making sense of the whole notion of divine command.[65]

What emerges from our analysis is that the *pinnot ha-torah* are doctrines that stand at the very interface between philosophy and revelation in Gersonides' thought. They are inviolable biblical principles the philosopher must take into account in the course of philosophical enquiry.

Our major handicap in evaluating the place of the *pinnot ha-torah* in Gersonides' thought is that he provides little information about how they are derived and the function they serve in philosophical discourse. Nevertheless, we have been able to formulate some notion of his position on the basis of the evidence he provides in the *Wars* and his exegetical writings. Most important in our investigation were conceptual and terminological parallels between Gersonides and Maimonides with regard to this issue. It would appear that Gersonides formulates his conception of *pinnot ha-torah* from Maimonides' discussion of creation.

Gersonides' reliance on Maimonides may in fact explain why he provides so little theoretical information about the function of these principles. He may have simply assumed that all his readers were thoroughly familiar with the *Guide* and that they were all interpreting Maimonides precisely as he was. Gersonides may have regarded his own method of using the *pinnot ha-torah* in philosophical enquiry as an obvious extension of Maimonides' methodology set forth in the *Guide*, one that did not require further explanation.

The major problem with the *pinnot ha-torah* is that the whole concept of a fundamental biblical principle is not well-defined by Gersonides. For one, he does not spell out—nor does Maimonides for that matter—how basic a biblical concept has to be in order to qualify as one of the *pinnot ha-torah*.[66] Certainly, little justification is needed to include the existence of God or the notion of prophecy as a fundamental principle of the Torah. These concepts permeate the entire body of Scripture. However, the list of *pinnot* also includes a good many doctrines which appear to be nothing more than concepts that are frequently stated in the Bible. Does this mean that all concepts frequently mentioned in the Bible are *pinnot ha-torah*? Gersonides provides no criteria to distinguish between concepts that are included under that rubric and those that are not.

A related problem is that the list of *pinnot ha-torah* could potentially include just about any philosophical principle in Gersonides' thought. Recall that Gersonides sometimes includes as *pinnot ha-torah* those philosophical doctrines which lend support to central biblical conceptions even if they themselves are not fundamental to the Torah. Is there then any limit to the number of fundamental principles? Given the range of doctrines in the list of *pinnot ha-torah*, one could practically include any number of philosophical concepts that support one or another of these principles. Yet if all philosophical concepts can be included, the *pinnot ha-torah* effectively become so diffuse as to lose all meaning.

Despite these problems, there are important conclusions to be drawn from our discussion which concern Gersonides' thought as a whole. First, our analysis demonstrates the important role Scripture plays in Gersonides' philosophical thought. There are no fewer than twenty-two fundamental principles of the Torah. If our theory is correct, these principles exert a decisive influence on Gersonides' philosophical positions and must therefore be taken into account for a full exposition of Gersonides' thought. Moreover, our discussion highlights the importance of Gersonides' biblical commentaries as resources for his philosophical views, a recurrent theme in our study. As we have seen, the overwhelming majority of references to the *pinnot ha-torah* are contained in the biblical commentaries.

It should be emphasized that our enquiry into the *pinnot ha-torah* is preliminary. We have attempted to delineate the general character of these principles while demonstrating their potential importance. Only further research will determine the precise function of each of the various *pinnot ha-torah* in Gersonides' thought.

Notes

1. According to the acronym for his full name, Rabbi Levi ben Gershom.

2. This is the designation by which he is known in modern scholarship, and it will be the one used in this study.

3. Further details about Gersonides' life and writings are contained in the following studies: Moritz Steinschneider, "Levi ben Gerson," *Gesammelte Schriften* 1 (Berlin, 1925): 233–70; Ernst Renan and Adolph Neubauer, *Écrivains juifs français du XIVème siècle* (Vol. 27 of the *Histoire littéraire de la France*) (Paris, 1893), pp. 240–298 (586 –644); Joseph Shatzmiller, "Gersonides and the Jewish Community of Orange in his Day" (in Hebrew), *University of Haifa Studies in the History of the Jewish People and the Land of Israel* 2 (1972): 111–26; idem, "Some Further Information about Gersonides and the Orange Jewish Community in his Day" (in Hebrew), *University of Haifa Studies in the History of the Jewish People and the Land of Israel* 3 (1972): 139-43; idem, "Gersonide et la société juive de son temps," *Gersonide en son temps*, Gilbert Dahan, ed. (Louvain: Peeters, 1991), pp. 33–43; Anne-Marie Weil-Guény, "Gersonide en son temps: Un tableau chronologique," *Studies on Gersonides—A Fourteenth Century Jewish Philosopher-Scientist*, Gad Freudenthal, ed. (Leiden: E. J. Brill, 1992), pp. 355–65; Touati, pp. 33–82; Feldman, *WL* 1, pp. 3–30.

4. Several studies deal with the history and intellectual life of Provençal Jewry in this period: Richard W. Emery, *The Jews of Perpignan in the Thirteenth Century* (New York: Columbia University Press, 1959); Salo W. Baron, *A Social and Religious History of the Jews*, vol. 10 (New York: Columbia University Press, 1965), pp. 82–91; Isadore Twersky, "Aspects of

the Social and Cultural History of Provençal Jewry," *Jewish Society Through the Ages*, H. H. Ben Sasson and S. Ettinger, eds. (New York: Schocken Books, 1972), pp. 185–207; idem, *Rabad of Posquières* (Cambridge, MA: Harvard University Press, 1962). Touati devotes the first chapter of his book to the intellectual and historical setting of the period in which Gersonides lived. See, also, Feldman, *WL* 1, pp. 31–42.

5. The reactions to Gersonides' writings after his death are treated by Touati, pp. 541–59, and by Menachem Kellner, "Gersonides and his Cultured Despisers: Arama and Abravanel," *Journal of Medieval and Renaissance Studies* 6 (1976): 269–96.

6. In fact, some of Gersonides' writings on astronomy seem to have been commissioned by these churchmen; see Touati, p. 43; Shatzmiller, "Gersonides and the Jewish Community," pp. 120–3. The relationship between Gersonides' philosophy and Christian scholasticism has been explored in a number of studies by Shlomo Pines: "Scholasticism after Thomas Aquinas and the Teachings of Hasdai Crescas and his Predecessors," *Proceedings of the Israel Academy of Sciences and Humanities* 1, no. 10 (1966): 1–101; "Saint Thomas et la pensée juive médiévale: quelques notations," *Aquinas and Problems in His Time*, G. Verbeke and D. Verhelst, eds. (Louvain: University Press and The Hague: Martinus Nijhoff, 1976), pp. 126–28; "Appendix: Problems in Teaching Gersonides," appended to "On Certain Subjects Included in the Book Ezer ha-Dat by Isaac Polkar and Parallels to Them in Spinoza" (in Hebrew), *Studies in Kabbalah, Jewish Philosophy and Ethical Literature in Honor of Isaiah Tishby* (in Hebrew) (Jerusalem: Magnes Press, 1986), pp. 447–57.

7. For details about the composition and style of the *Wars*, see Touati, pp. 76–82, and Feldman, *WL* 1, pp. 55–61.

8. The exceptions are his commentaries on Ecclesiastes and the Song of Songs.

9. *CT*, pp. 2a–d. We will be discussing this classification in chapter five. The general characteristics of Gersonides' exegetical works are discussed in Touati, pp. 63 –72, and in Feldman, *WL* 1, pp. 11–16. Besides the *to'aliyyot*, there are other structural features that distinguish Gersonides' commentaries from other medieval Jewish exegetical works. For instance, in some of his commentaries, Gersonides adopts a tripartite scheme of interpretation. He first provides an explanation of specific words and phrases in a given section of the biblical text (*be'ur ha-millot*). He then gives a summary of that section (*be'ur divrey ha-parashah* or *be'ur divrey ha-sippur*). Finally, he lists his *to'aliyyot*. This scheme, however, is not consistent throughout the commentaries. It is most prominently utilized in the Genesis and Exodus portions of the *Commentary on the Torah*.

10. Julius Guttmann, *Philosophies of Judaism*, David Silverman, trans. (New York: Schocken Books, 1964), p. 237.

11. His views were expressed in "Les idées philosophiques et théologiques de Gersonide (1288–1344) dans ses commentaires bibliques," *Revue des sciences religieuses* 27 (1954): 335–67.

12. See Touati's remarks, pp. 70–72, regarding the value of the commentaries for a proper explication of Gersonides' philosophy. Note Touati's vigorous denial of Guttmann's position (p. 71 n. 104).

13. Seymour Feldman has recently dealt with Gersonides' exegesis in several articles: "Appendix: Gersonides and Biblical Exegesis," *WL* 2, pp. 213–47; "The Binding of Isaac: the Test-Case of Divine Omniscience," *Divine Omniscience and Omnipotence in Medieval Philosophy*, Tamar Rudavsky, ed. (Dordrecht: D. Reidel, 1985), pp. 105–135; "The Wisdom of Solomon: A Gersonidean Interpretation," *Gersonide en son temps*, pp. 61–80. See also Jacob Staub, *Creation of the World According to Gersonides* (Chico, CA: Scholars Press, 1982), which deals with Gersonides' explication of the creation story in Genesis; Amos Funkenstein, "Gersonides' Biblical Commentary: Science, History and Providence," *Studies on Gersonides*, pp. 305–15; Menachem Kellner, "Gersonides' Commentary on Song of Songs: For Whom Was It Written and Why?" *Gersonide en son temps*, pp. 81–107.

14. In the introduction to his *Commentary on the Torah*, Gersonides claims that he will not adduce interpretations according to *derash* in the course of his commentary, but will only be concerned with "interpreting the words of Torah according to what they themselves teach" (*CT*, p. 2c). Gersonides' proviso obviously does not mean that he will not rely on aggadic material at all; rabbinic sources are quoted frequently by him. Gersonides merely limits his use of rabbinic materials to those sources that address a reading of the text according to the *peshat*.

15. One reason that Gersonides' commentaries have received so little attention is that there has been little scholarship done in the area of Jewish biblical exegesis in general. A couple of reliable surveys are M. H. Segal's *Biblical Exegesis* (in Hebrew) (Jerusalem: Kiryat Sefer, 1943) and the *Hebrew Encyclopedia* article, edited by Moshe Greenberg, which was published as a book entitled, *Jewish Biblical Exegesis: an Introduction* (in Hebrew) (Jerusalem: Magnes Press, 1983). Gersonides is dealt with briefly in both of these works; see Segal, pp. 104–5 and Greenberg, p. 95. Gersonides' use of rabbinic aggadah is addressed in Warren Zev Harvey's "Quelques réflexions sur l'attitude de Gersonide vis-à-vis du Midrash," *Gersonide en son temps*, pp. 109–16.

16. Touati devotes a short discussion to this aspect of Gersonides' thought; see pp. 506-14. See also Eli Freiman, "A Passage from Gersonides' *Commentary on the Torah*" (in Hebrew), *Me-ʿAley ʿAsor* (Yeshivat Birkat

Mosheh Tenth Anniversary Volume) B. Braner, O. Kafiḥ, and Z. Shimshoni, eds. (Maʿaleh Adumim: Maʿaliyot, 1988), pp. 162–89.

17. The *Wars* was written between 1317 and 1329, while the biblical
commentaries were composed roughly between 1325 and 1338. For details,
see Touati, pp. 49–53, and Feldman, *WL* 1, pp. 55–8.

18. A whole section of Gersonides' writings that we will not be dealing with in the course of our study is his commentaries on Averroes, another much neglected portion of Gersonides' corpus. The commentaries on
Averroes are not relevant to our concerns, since the philosophical issues
relating to Jewish chosenness are nowhere discussed in these works. Also,
in general there appears to be no strong relationship between Gersonides'
commentaries on Averroes and his exegetical works. In his biblical commentaries, Gersonides does refer to the commentaries on Averroes, but not
with any great frequency; the exegetical works, to my knowledge, are
never cited in the commentaries on Averroes. In fact, Touati claims to have
discovered only two occasions where the biblical text itself is quoted in
these commentaries (Touati, p. 75). For details about the commentaries on
Averroes, see Touati, pp. 72 –5 and Feldman, *WL* 1, pp. 27–30.

19. Menachem Kellner is at present working on a critical edition and
English translation of Gersonides' *Commentary on the Song of Songs*. The introduction to this work was published in *Daʿat* 23 (1989): 17–26. An English
translation of this introduction has appeared in *From Ancient Israel to Modern Judaism: Intellect in Quest of Understanding: Essays in Honor of Marvin
Fox*, vol. 2, Jacob Neusner, Ernest S. Frerichs and Nahum M. Sarna, eds.
(Atlanta: Scholars Press, 1989), pp. 187–205.

20. The only exception to this rule is the introduction to Gersonides'
Commentary on the Song of Songs, translated by Menachem Kellner.

21. Some of the issues in the discussion that follows are dealt with by
Eli Freiman in a recently published article, "Le commentaire de Gersonide
sur la Pentateuque," *Gersonide en son temps*, pp. 117–32.

22. Why there are two versions of manuscripts is uncertain. It is possible that they represent earlier and later stages in Gersonides' composition of the commentary. The other possibility is that at some point copyists
or publishers edited material out of the commentary because of its daunt-
ing length.

23. As the present study was being completed, the first volume of this
edition—Gersonides' commentary on Genesis—appeared in print under
the title *Ḥamishah Ḥumshey Torah ʿim Be'ur ha-Ralbag*, edited by Eli Freiman and Baruch Braner, (Maʿaleh Adumim: Maʿaliyyot, 1993).

24. This copy can be found in the National Library of the Hebrew University of Jerusalem under the call number R79 A6661 MS 94. Freiman believes that this emended Venice text was most likely annotated in the

eighteenth century by David Franco-Mendes (1713–1792), a scholar who specialized in this type of work. A second author whose corrections also appear in the text has not yet been identified. It is possible, according to Freiman, that these annotations were done with the hope of publishing a new edition of the commentary. For information on Franco-Mendes, see *Encyclopedia Judaica*, vol. 7 (Jerusalem: Keter Publishing House, 1972), p. 51.

25. *Perushey Ralbag 'al ha-Torah*, Yaacov Leib Levi, ed. (Jerusalem: Mossad ha-Rav Kook, 1992).

26. See Levi, *Perushey Ralbag*, pp. 22–5, where the editor discusses these sources.

NOTES TO CHAPTER TWO

1. We will not discuss Gersonides' *Commentary on Job*, which is devoted to the question of providence. The views expressed in this commentary are for the most part consonant with those in the *Wars*.

2. When we refer to Aristotle here and elsewhere, we are of course referring to Aristotle as understood by medieval philosophers and thus at times several steps removed from the original.

3. The cosmology Gersonides adopts is in broad outline similar to that of most medieval philosophers. In the center of the universe is the sublunar world that we inhabit. Rotating around the world are a series of concentric celestial spheres, the movements of which are determined by a corresponding series of Separate Intellects emanating from God. The Active Intellect is the Separate Intellect which resides closest to the sublunar realm and plays a major role in the operations of nature. Gersonides' cosmology is developed in book five of the *Wars* (*MH*, pp. 101–7). For a comprehensive analysis of Gersonides' cosmology and the points where he departs from his medieval contemporaries, see Touati, pp. 301–58.

4. The problem of God's knowledge is dealt with in a number of studies. See Touati, pp. 129–60, and two articles by Norbert Samuelson: "The Problem of Free Will in Maimonides, Gersonides and Aquinas," *CCAR Journal* 17 (1970): 2–20, and "Gersonides' Account of God's Knowledge of Particulars," *Journal of the History of Philosophy* 10 (1972): 399–416. See also Samuelson's introduction to his translation of book three of the *Wars* in *Gersonides on God's Knowledge* (Toronto: Pontifical Institute for Mediaeval Studies, 1977); Tamar Rudavsky, "Divine Omniscience and Future Contingents in Gersonides," *Journal of the History of Philosophy* 21 (October 1983): 513–536; idem, "Divine Omniscience, Contingency and Prophecy in Gersonides," *Divine Omniscience and Omnipotence in Medieval Philosophy*, Tamar Rudavsky, ed. (Dordrecht: D. Reidel, 1985), pp. 161–181; Sarah Klein-Braslavy, "Gersonides on Determinism, Possibility, Choice and

Foreknowledge" (in Hebrew), *Da'at* 22 (1989): 5–53. For discussion of the related problem of divine will, see Touati, p. 201f.; Menachem Kellner, "Gersonides on the Problem of Volitional Creation," *HUCA* 51 (1980): 111–128.

5. *MH*, pp. 124–5, 138–9, 239; *WL* 2, pp. 96–7, 117–8.

6. *MH*, p. 138f.; *WL* 2, p. 117f. The impetus for the inclusion of particulars and historical events in the realm of divine knowledge seems to stem from a desire on Gersonides' part to fashion the God of Aristotle into a biblical mold. Still there is much in Gersonides' theory of divine knowledge that remains unclear. The notion that God does not know particulars except through the universal order in the divine mind is not entirely coherent. It is therefore not surprising that Gersonides' position on divine knowledge has come under fire from medieval and modern critic alike. For a discussion of this problem, see Tamar Rudavsky, "Divine Omniscience and Future Contingents in Gersonides" and references on p. 533.

7. Actually, the term Gersonides uses is '*behirah*,' or "choice," which is Aristotelian in origin.

8. We will be dealing with Gersonides' views on prophecy shortly.

9. *MH*, pp. 142–3, 147–9; *WL* 2, pp. 122–3, 135–7.

10. Much of what has been said about God's knowledge and will applies with equal validity to the Active Intellect. The Active Intellect also contemplates the universal order; its knowledge and will are also immutable; and it knows particulars only through the universal order. However, the Active Intellect in some respects does not have knowledge that is as extensive as that of God. For example, its knowledge of the Separate Intellects is weaker than God's, because the Active Intellect is itself an effect of the Separate Intellects while God is their cause. See *MH*, pp. 37–8, 106f., 446, 448; *WL* 1, p. 151; *WL* 2, p. 52f.

11. Gersonides' position on providence is discussed by Touati, pp. 361–92; Moïse Ventura, "Belief in Providence According to Gersonides" (in Hebrew), *Minhah le-Avraham* (Jerusalem, 1959), pp. 12–21; Menachem Kellner, "Gersonides, Providence and the Rabbinic Tradition," *Journal of the American Academy of Religion* 42 (1974): 673–685. See also the introduction to J. David Bleich's translation of book four of the *Wars* in *Providence and the Philosophy of Gersonides* (New York: Yeshiva University Press, 1973); Idit Dobbs-Weinstein, "The Existential Dimension of Providence in the Thought of Gersonides," *Gersonide en son temps*, pp. 159 –78.

12. *MH*, pp. 95–8, 181; *WL* 2, pp. 33–7, 200.

13. The terms 'chance' and 'accidental' are used here in the technical, philosophical sense. In fact, the events that cause harm in the sublunar realm are no less law-like than other events in the natural order. They are

chance-like or accidental in that they are not related *essentially* to the natural order which is designed to produce the maximum possible good.

14. *MH*, pp. 164–5; *WL* 2, pp. 174–5.

15. *MH*, pp. 104, 165–7; *WL* 2, pp. 48, 176 –9; Gersonides' example is talmudic in origin. See *BT Niddah* 31a. The rabbinic doctrine of *yisurin shel 'ahavah* appears in a number of talmudic passages. See the discussion of this concept in Ephraim Urbach's *The Sages: Their Concepts and Beliefs*, Israel Abrahams, trans. (Jerusalem: Magnes Press, 1979), pp. 444–8.

16. *MH*, p. 174; *WL* 2, p. 188.

17. Gersonides' views on prophecy have been analyzed by Touati, pp. 366–75, 451–68, and "Le problème de l'inerrance prophétique dans le théologie juive du Moyen Age," *Revue de l'histoire des religions* 174 (1968): 169–187; David W. Silverman, *The Problem of Prophecy in Gersonides* (Ph.D. diss., Columbia University, 1975); Howard Kreisel, "Veridical Dreams and Prophecy in the Philosophy of Gersonides" (in Hebrew), *Da'at* 22 (1989): 73–84; Tamar Rudavsky, "Divine Omniscience, Contingency and Prophecy in Gersonides," pp. 161 –181.

18. *MH*, pp. 98–106, 111; *WL* 2, pp. 38–51, 59.

19. *MH*, pp. 108–9; *WL* 2, pp. 55–7.

20. *MH*, pp. 460–2.

21. *MH*, p. 169; *WL* 2, pp. 180–1.

22. Norbert Samuelson, "The Problem of Free Will in Maimonides, Gersonides and Aquinas," pp. 2–20.

23. *MH*, p. 169; *WL* 2, p. 181.

24. Touati, pp. 366–8, 385–7. It is surprising that in the scholarship on Gersonides little attention has been paid to providential suffering. As we shall see in later chapters, providential suffering plays a major role in Gersonides' explication of events throughout Jewish history.

25. There is also a passage in the *Wars* which we will be discussing shortly where Gersonides clearly contrasts harmful chance events in the general providential order with events that are the result of providential suffering. The two types of events, therefore, cannot be identified with each other as Touati tries to do.

26. One should not be confused by the terminology here. Just because individual providence can affect a whole nation does not make it any less 'individual.' That is, the individual affected by this form of providence can be a single person or a single nation.

27. *MH*, pp. 180–1; *WL* 2, pp. 198–9.

28. Gersonides sometimes employs religious language in order to express philosophical concepts in the *Wars* and the biblical commentaries. Thus, for instance, severing one's ties with the Active Intellect is equated

with 'sin' by Gersonides. This use of language will be the subject of a lengthy discussion in chapter nine.

29. *MH*, p. 181; *WL* 2, p. 200.

30. *MH*, p. 182; *WL* 2, pp. 201–2. It is here that Touati's interpretation of providential suffering runs into its greatest difficulty (supra, pp. 19–20). In this passage, it is evident that Gersonides does not treat providential suffering as a chance event in the general providential order, as Touati claims, but that he sees providential suffering and chance events as entirely different types of occurrences. Gersonides informs us quite clearly that the loss of providential suffering results in vulnerability to chance events. See Touati, pp. 385–7, where he attempts to deal with this problem with a highly forced interpretation.

31. *MH*, p. 183; *WL* 2, pp. 202–3. We will be conducting a more detailed analysis of this passage in the coming chapter.

32. *MH*, pp. 168–74, 179; *WL* 2, pp. 180–88, 196. The nature of the divine punishment here is unclear. It could refer either to providential suffering or harmful chance events that are consequent upon the loss of providence altogether. We will be dealing more extensively with this passage in chapter seven.

33. *MH*, pp. 169–70; *WL* 2, pp. 182–3. For a discussion of the phrase *hazlaḥah nafshit*, see Feldman's note on p. 182. Feldman translates this phrase as "spiritual happiness." Gersonides deals with the metaphysics of immortality in book one of the *Wars*. For an analysis of Gersonides' views on this matter, see Touati, pp. 434–42.

34. Though the scholarly literature on the subject of miracles in Gersonides' philosophy is not extensive, this issue has been briefly dealt with by Touati, pp. 469–77; Guttmann, pp. 247–8; Howard Kreisel, "Miracles in Medieval Jewish Philosophy," *JQR* 75, no. 2 (October 1984): 122-6. An interpretation differing significantly from that offered by these three scholars is that of Menachem Kellner in "Gersonides on Miracles, the Messiah and Resurrection," *Da'at* 4 (1980): 5–34. My presentation supports the interpretation of the first group.

35. Why Gersonides chooses to discuss miracles at the end of this treatise and not in book four, where he treats the issue of providence, is a question that need not preoccupy us. He seems to have believed that the issue of miracles is closely tied in with the subject of creation, the topic to which the final book of the *Wars* is devoted. Touati briefly discusses this connection (p. 477).

36. It should be noted that our discussion does not follow the order of Gersonides' exposition. I have chosen to rearrange some of the elements of his presentation for the sake of greater clarity.

37. *MH*, pp. 441–2.

38. *MH*, pp. 442–3.

39. *MH*, pp. 443–51.

40. *MH*, pp. 450–1.

41. Gersonides actually makes reference both to God and the Active Intellect when posing this dilemma. For the sake of simplicity, I will be making reference only to God here.

42. *MH*, pp. 447–8.

43. *MH*, pp. 451–2.

44. *MH*, p. 459.

45. It is not absolutely clear whether the intermediary steps are skipped over altogether, or whether they are traversed at great speed. The passage could have either interpretation.

46. Touati, p. 474.

47. *MH*, pp. 183–4; *WL* 2, pp. 202–3.

48. See also C. *Esther*, pp. 39a, 43b, 43c, 43d, 50a to. 1, where Gersonides again identifies events as miraculous that do not exhibit any obvious contravention of nature.

49. Touati, p. 472. Guttmann comes up with another formulation that makes the same point. He refers to a "natural law of miracles" which is a series of conditions in the universal order responsible for producing particular miracles (pp. 247–8).

50. *MH*, pp. 451–2. Gersonides also points out that miracles, like all other events, remain contingent even if they can be predicted. The recipient can always circumvent a miracle that is foreordained by exercising his free will and contravening the predicted order.

51. *MH*, pp. 455–6.

52. *MH*, pp. 454–5.

53. *MH*, p. 452.

54. *MH*, p. 456f.

55. Supra, p. 19.

56. Actually, Gersonides does say at one point that miracles cannot affect the heavenly bodies, because that would have a deleterious effect on events in the sublunar realm (*MH*, p. 456; supra, p. 26). However, in this passage he is specifically referring to miracles which occur in the movements of the heavenly bodies themselves—such as the cessation of the movement of the sun in Joshua 10—not to the participation of the heavenly bodies in the production of miracles in the sublunar realm.

57. Supra, n. 34.

58. Supra, p. 24.

59. *MH*, pp. 453–4. This position is somewhat inconsistent with earlier statements. Gersonides had earlier stated that prophets are present when miracles occur because it is unlikely that providence of so great a

measure could extend to anyone of lesser stature (*MH*, pp. 451–2). Gersonides seems to soften this view in the passage we are now considering. A man may achieve enough intellectual perfection to warrant a miracle without being a prophet.

60. The term 'inherited providence' is not one that Gersonides actually uses, but is my own coinage for providing a convenient reference.

61. Touati, pp. 447–8. Touati's analysis is brief but points in a direction similar to that of my own.

62. This phrase is added here in order to complete the comparison Gersonides is drawing between individual and general forms of inherited providence. Otherwise, the analogy would not make sense. We will see in the discussion which follows that this analogy is more clearly drawn in passages in the biblical commentaries.

63. Read with MSS: *ha-min ha-sheni*.

64. Gen. 15:14.

65. Read with MSS: *ha-'av ha-nivḥar bo*.

66. Read with MSS: *ki 'ein zeh yoter zar*.

67. *MH*, p. 463.

68. There are other places where Gersonides emphasizes that one should not degrade the righteous by burying them with others of lesser stature. See, for instance, *CT*, p. 49d, where Jacob's request to be buried in the land of Israel reflects this concern.

69. One detects that Gersonides is not satisfied with his explanation. He immediately adds that there may have been someone nearby who performed this miracle, even though there is no evidence of this in the text. Cf. *CT*, p. 111c–d, where Gersonides mentions the incident with Elisha in order to help explain how the oil used for anointing High Priests had miraculous effectiveness beyond Moses' lifetime.

70. Gen. 26:2–6.

71. *CT*, p. 34d.

72. Supra, p. 21.

73. *MH*, pp. 172–3; *WL* 2, pp. 186 –8.

74. Supra, p. 31.

75. *CT*, p. 115a.

76. *MH*, p. 181; *WL* 2, p. 200.

77. *CT*, p. 210c to. 18. The rest of this passage also contains a comprehensive summary of how inherited providence is responsible for the redemption of the Israelites from Egypt. We shall leave this portion of the passage for our next chapter.

78. *CT*, p. 29a to. 18.

79. *CT*, p. 23c to. 7.

80. *CT*, p. 30a; cf. C. *II Kings* 25 to. 3.

81. *C. 1 Kings* 22 to. 20 and 21.

82. Touati argues that individual providence is transferred only in the sense that the righteous man can protect his relatives and friends by providing them with prophetic predictions. By predicting the future, the prophet can warn his loved ones about any calamity that may be ordained to befall them (pp. 446–7). The evidence we have adduced would suggest that Touati's interpretation is too narrow. Gersonides does not limit the transfer of providence to the sharing of prophetic predictions and does indeed believe that the direct transfer of providence is possible. Inherited providence provides the strongest evidence to back this claim. Here the prophet is not even alive to provide prophetic predictions to his descendants; therefore, in this case, the transfer of providence must be of a direct nature if it is to occur at all. Gersonides' one example of inherited individual providence in the *Wars* makes this point clear; Abraham's providence allows the Israelites in Egypt to experience miracles long after his death.

83. *CT*, pp. 23c to. 7, 29a to. 18 and 21, 34c to. 2, 40b to. 27, 113a, 113d to. 4, 191a to. 7.

84. We will be discussing the rabbinic sources pertaining to the role of *zekhut 'avot* in the exodus in the coming chapters. For an analysis of how the phrase *zekhut 'avot* is used in rabbinic literature, see Solomon Schechter, *Aspects of Rabbinic Theology* (New York: Schocken Books, 1961), pp. 170 –1. The development of this doctrine and its relationship to early Christian teachings is discussed by W. D. Davies, *Paul and Rabbinic Judaism* (Philadelphia: Fortress Press, 1980), pp. 268–73; E. P. Sanders, *Paul and Palestinian Judaism* (Philadelphia: Fortress Press, 1977), pp. 183–98; Rimon Kasher, "Miracles, Faith and Merit of the Fathers: Conceptual Development in the Sages' Writings" (in Hebrew), *Jerusalem Studies in Jewish Thought* 5 (1986): 15–23.

85. *BT Berakhot* 27b; cf. *'Avot* 2:2; Urbach, pp. 499–500; Schechter, pp. 171–7.

NOTES TO CHAPTER THREE

1. In this chapter, we will not be dealing with the covenant of circumcision in Genesis 17. This covenant is different in character from the one formulated in Genesis 15 and will be dealt with in a separate discussion in chapter five.

2. *CT*, pp. 18c–d, 20c. The notion that God exercises providence over the human species as a whole is an idea that appears in other passages in Gersonides' biblical commentaries. Divine care for the entire human race is the reason given by Gersonides for the long life spans in Genesis (*CT*,

p. 18b). Since human scientific knowledge was relatively undeveloped at that time, long lives were necessary to allow for a greater period of time to achieve intellectual perfection. Gersonides describes this example of providence as a miracle similar to the giving of the Torah to the Israelites. Both were designed to allow a human collective to achieve intellectual perfection. Divine providence over the human race is also responsible for the destruction of the tower of Babel (*CT*, p. 22a). The notion that providence can be operative for the human race as a whole is not mentioned in the *Wars*. Yet this concept follows easily from Gersonides' position that God can exercise providence over entire nations in the same way that He does over a single individual. If providence can protect any defined collective of individuals, there is no reason why its protection cannot extend to humanity as a whole.

3. I have deviated from the NJPS translation here in order to capture Gersonides' understanding of the text. The NJPS version translates the phrase *ve-hakimoti 'et beriti* "I will establish My covenant . . ."—a reading implying that God is referring to a covenant that has not yet been formulated. As we will see, Gersonides clearly interprets this phrase to mean that God is reaffirming a covenant that already exists. I have therefore rendered the phrase, "I will *fulfill* My covenant."

4. Gen. 6:18–9.

5. The reference here is to *CT*, p. 13b f. which discusses Gen. 2:1–3. In the first lines of this passage, I have adopted the reading of *F* over *EVE*. While the two readings say essentially the same thing, the reading in *F* is far more coherent. According to *F*, read: *ve-zeh ha-brit 'asher zakhar hu le-fi mah she-'eḥshov mah she-'asahu ha-shem ba-yom ha-shvi'i le-kayyem ha-'olam. . . .*

6. *CT*, p. 19c.

7. *Supra*, p. 17. In other passages in the biblical commentaries that deal with these types of dialogues, Gersonides sometimes states these philosophical premises explicitly. In his commentary on Exodus, for example, Gersonides explains that Moses' dialogue with God prior to the revelation at Sinai is the product of Moses' imagination (*CT*, pp. 74b, 75a to. 4).

8. *Supra*, p. 17.

9. Somewhat puzzling is the other, less preferred interpretation which Gersonides suggests. At the very end of the passage quoted above, Gersonides provides an alternative explanation when he adds that "perhaps God made a covenant with Noah beforehand, even though it was not mentioned." Gersonides does not inform us what the content of this previous covenant with Noah might have been.

10. Gen. 9:10–17.

11. *CT*, p. 20b. Note, however, that Gersonides does not adequately account for the fact that God specifically promises that He will not destroy the world again *by flood*.

12. Gen. 15:8.

13. *CT*, pp. 24c, 24d–25a.

14. *CT*, pp. 24c, 24d, 25a–b.

15. *CT*, pp. 22b, 22c to. 4. Throughout his biblical commentaries, Gersonides makes reference to the notion that some locations are especially susceptible to receiving divine emanation. See, for instance, *CT*, pp. 36b, 54c. Echoes of Judah Halevi are evident here. We will be discussing the special qualities of the land of Israel more extensively in a later chapter.

16. *MH*, pp. 460–1.

17. Ibid.; *CT*, p. 40d. Cf. *BT Berakhot* 4a.

18. *CT*, p. 25b to. 5.

19. Supra, p. 21.

20. *MH*, pp. 180–1; *WL* 2, pp. 198–9.

21. *MH*, p. 183; *WL* 2, pp. 202–3.

22. *MH*, pp. 183–4; *WL* 2, p. 203.

23. Ex. 10:1–2.

24. There is a passage in Rashi's commentary on the Torah that seems to foreshadow Gersonides' interpretation. In explicating Exodus 7:3, where God promises to harden Pharaoh's heart for the sake of performing miracles, Rashi says as follows:

> Since he has wickedly resisted Me, and it is manifest to Me that the heathen nations find no satisfaction in setting their whole heart to return to Me penitently, it is better that his heart should be hardened in order that My signs may be multiplied against him so that you may recognize My divine power. Such indeed is the method of the Holy One, blessed be He: He brings punishment on the nations so that Israel may hear and fear [Him], as it is said: "I wipe out nations; / Their corners are desolate ... And I thought that she [i.e., Israel, according to Rashi; the text actually reads "you"] would fear Me, / Would learn a lesson"[Zeph. 3:6–7].

Rashi's view appears to be an interpretation of a talmudic source in *BT Yevamot* 63a: "Punishment comes into the world only on Israel's account. ..." The prooftexts cited for this view are Zeph. 3:6–7, the same one used by Rashi. Note, however, that Gersonides transforms Rashi's position into a philosophical one. While Rashi refers to the notion that Israel will "hear and fear" God as a result of the miracles, Gersonides sees the miracles as producing intellectual perfection.

25. We should note, incidentally, that in this particular chapter, the biblical text is quite explicit in describing Abraham's dialogue with God as occurring in a "vision," a detail that does not go unnoticed by Gersonides (Gen. 15:1). Gersonides comments on the specific use of the term, "vision," by noting that a vision is a higher order of prophecy than a veridical dream (CT, p. 24b).

26. Gersonides' understanding of the allegory here is based on midrashic sources adopted by some of his exegetical predecessors. See Bereshit Rabbah, J. Theodor and Ch. Albeck, eds. (Jerusalem: Wahrmann Books, 1965), 44:18, vol. 1, pp. 435–40, and commentaries of Rashi and Radak ad loc.

27. Gen. 15:18.

28. CT, p. 25b.

29. Gen. 15:14.

30. Supra, p. 30 and discussion which follows.

31. CT, p. 210c to. 18. Another similar exposition is given in CT, p. 216a to. 11.

32. In this passage, the Torah is also mentioned as a crucial factor in bringing the Israelites towards perfection. We shall discuss the role of the Torah in chapter five.

33. Ex. 2:24.

34. Ex. 2:25.

35. CT, p. 56a to. 2. Cf. also CT, pp. 54c, 55b, 114d. The notion that the Israelites are saved before the appointed time will be explained in a later discussion.

36. This is the opinion of Shemu'el in BT Nedarim 32a.

37. Bereshit Rabbah 44:18, vol. 1, p. 435; Midrash Rabbah, vol. 1, trans. by H. Freedman (New York: Soncino Press, 1983), p. 369. For references to the full range of views on this question, see Louis Ginzberg's Legends of the Jews, vol. 5 (Philadelphia: Jewish Publication Society of America, 1962), p. 227 n. 110.

38. Commentaries of ibn Ezra and Naḥmanides on Gen. 15:7.

39. Gen. 15:6.

40. Ex. 4:31. Mekhilta de-R. Ishmael, Horowitz-Rabin, ed. (Frankfurt: J. Kauffmann, 1931), massekhta de-va-yehi 3, p. 99; translation from the edition of Jacob Z. Lauterbach (Philadelphia: Jewish Publication Society, 1976), vol. 1, p. 220.

41. Ibid., massekhta de-va-yassa' 2, p. 160.

42. The classification of views delineated here is based on a similar scheme in Arthur Marmorstein's The Doctrine of Merits in Old Rabbinical Literature (London: Oxford University Press, 1926), pp. 139–46. Of help here were also Solomon Schechter, Aspects of Rabbinic Theology (New York:

Schocken Books, 1961), pp. 170–99, where an entire chapter is devoted to the concept of inherited merit, and Ephraim E. Urbach, *The Sages: Their Concepts and Beliefs*, Israel Abrahams, trans. (Jerusalem: Magnes Press, 1979), pp. 496–511.

43. *Midrash Tehillim*, S. Buber, ed. (Vilna: Rom Family, 1891), 114, pp. 268, 473; Urbach, p. 499; Marmorstein, pp. 84, 91, 139.

44. *Shir ha-Shirim Rabbah* 2:19; Marmorstein, pp. 56, 143.

45. *Ba-Midbar Rabbah* 3:4; *Shir ha-Shirim Rabbah* 4:24; Marmorstein, pp. 141–2.

46. *Mekhilta de-R. Ishmael, massekhta de-pisḥa* 5, p. 14; Marmorstein, pp. 143–4.

47. This approach is also foreshadowed in a couple of rabbinic sources according to Urbach (pp. 497–8). However, the examples which Urbach quotes do not appear to anticipate Gersonides' specific formulation.

NOTES TO CHAPTER FOUR

1. *CT*, p. 55b.

2. Supra, pp. 16–17.

3. Ex. 2:12–14.

4. The biblical text does not actually report these activities. Gersonides is obviously basing his interpretation on the juxtaposition of Ex. 2:14, in which one of the Israelites accuses Moses of the murder, with Ex. 2:15, where it is reported that Pharaoh heard about the incident and sought to punish Moses.

5. *CT*, p. 54b to. 8. Gersonides' interpretation of the incident between Moses and the quarreling men is based on rabbinic sources. Gersonides also follows a passage in *Shemot Rabbah* in his suggestion that the behavior of the participants in the quarrel is evidence of Israel's sinfulness and that the Israelites therefore deserved the punishment received at the hands of Pharaoh. See *Midrash Shemot Rabbah*, 1:30; Cf. *BT Sanhedrin* 43b; Rashi on Ex. 2:14.

6. *CT*, ibid. We should also note incidentally that this passage affords an important insight into Gersonides' general doctrine of providence. One question which Gersonides does not take up explicitly in the *Wars* is the effect of actions dictated by free will on the subsequent order of events in the world. If human acts of free will can contravene what has been foreordained by the stars, does this mean that the course of events which follows is permanently and irreversibly upset? In our passage, Gersonides appears to answer this question in the negative. The Israelites are in fact able to contravene the divine order temporarily by their righteous action until the death of Joseph. However, once they cease to be righteous,

the order of events as predetermined in the divine mind goes back into effect. Thus, the remaining period of the slavery runs its course. Touati assumes that Gersonides supports this view, but offers no explicit proof for this observation (p. 147).

7. Ibid.

8. This interpretation is also given in *CT*, p. 26a. Cf. *Bereshit Rabbah* 46:10, vol. 1, p. 460; Rashi on Gen. 17:1; Maimonides, *Guide* I:63, p. 155.

9. In line six, after *be-'avot ha-kedoshim*, insert with *EVE*, *ve-'im lo' yitakhen*. This entire sentence is missing in *F*; however, its absence does not affect the meaning of the passage.

10. *CT*, p. 57c.

11. Ex. 1:7, 1:12, 1:20.

12. Read with *EVE*: *mah she-yi'ad ha-shem*.

13. Ex. 1:7.

14. *CT*, p. 53c to. 1.

15. Ex. 3:7–9.

16. *CT*, pp. 54c, 55b. Again, one must keep in mind that, as with all prophetic visions, Gersonides would view the conversation between Moses and God as one produced by Moses' imagination. The terms and imagery in that vision when properly understood represent deeper philosophical truths. As in Abraham's vision the term 'covenant' refers to inherited providence.

17. *CT*, p. 24c–d; cf. *CT*, p. 63a. In his interpretation of Genesis 15, Gersonides claims that the 400-year period in Egypt begins at the time of Jacob's birth. With detailed genealogical calculations Gersonides shows that the bondage ends somewhere between 30 and 45 years earlier than it should have. Gersonides, like most commentators, is also troubled by the discrepancy between Gen. 15:13, where the slavery in Egypt is predicted to last 400 years, and Ex. 13:40, where it is reported to have lasted 430 years. Gersonides manages to settle this difference with the suggestion that the passages refer to different starting points.

18. *CT*, pp. 54c, 55b.

19. An allusion to Ex. 6:2–3.

20. *CT*, pp. 58b to. 1; cf. pp. 54c, 55b, 56a to. 2. A key phrase for Gersonides is *va-yeda' 'elohim* in Exodus 2:25. The verb *yada'*, which is commonly translated as "to know," creates obvious problems for Gersonides due to the limitations he places on divine knowledge. Gersonides therefore interprets it to refer to the operations of divine providence—in this case, inherited providence. Cf. *CT*, p. 27a, where Gersonides interprets the verb *yada'*, in similar fashion.

21. One might detect a slight inconsistency here. We said before that inherited providence initially softens the impact of the slavery by allow-

ing the Israelites to multiply despite the oppression of the Egyptians. In the passage we have just quoted, the Israelites have to be rescued from slavery because they are in danger of complete annihilation. If inherited providence protected the Israelites from the worst effects of the slavery in its initial stages, it can be asked why they are then threatened by complete destruction later on. Gersonides does not address this problem.

22. Ex. 34:9–10.

23. Supra, p. 40.

24. Again, there is no actual dialogue taking place between God and Moses. Rather, the dialogue is the product of Moses' imagination, which has concretized the providential laws affecting the Israelites in imaginative form.

25. Ex. 32:11–14.

26. *CT*, pp. 113a, 113d to. 2 and 4. The notion that providence guards the righteous man's relatives and friends is discussed above on pp. 34–35. It is interesting to note that despite Moses' reference to the Patriarchal covenant in his attempt to convince God to withdraw his threat, Gersonides does not bring inherited providence into his interpretation here.

27. Ex. 32:30f.

28. Ex. 32:34.

29. *CT*, p. 113c.

30. Ex. 33:15f.

31. *CT*, p. 114a–b.

32. Ex. 3:11–2.

33. *CT*, pp. 54c–d, 55b–c.

34. Ibid.

35. Ex. 3:12.

36. *CT*, p. 54d. Note that in Gersonides' interpretation, Moses' question about the worthiness of the Israelites is practically identical with Abraham's query in Genesis 15 and invites an almost identical response; cf. supra, p. 43. A similar interpretation of this dialogue can be found in *Shemot Rabbah* 3:4, and Rashi.

37. Read with *EVE*: *le-kabel zot ha-torah*.

38. *CT*, p. 71d to. 1; cf. *CT*, p. 72c where the same idea is reiterated.

39. Read with *EVE* and *F*: *'im ha-mizvot ha-nilvim lah*.

40. *CT*, p. 64b to. 3. Gersonides bases his interpretation on aggadic sources. See, for instance, *Shemot Rabbah* 16:2–3. We also see the influence of Maimonides here. Maimonides frequently explains the commandments as negating the various practices of idol worshipers (*Guide* III:37, pp. 540ff.). Gersonides' approach towards the commandments and his relationship to Maimonides on this question will be dealt with in chapter five.

41. *CT*, pp. 60c–61d, 64b to. 3, 64c to. 5.

42. Ex. 3:13–4.

43. Gersonides in many respects follows Maimonides' interpretation of this passage in *Guide* I:63, pp. 153 –6.

44. Read with *EVE* and *F*: *she-limadeta 'oto*.

45. *CT*, p. 57c.

46. *CT*, p. 57c–d.

47. Ex. 14:4. See also Ex. 9:14, in which the miracles are also depicted as convincing the Egyptians of belief in the one true God.

48. *CT*, p. 68a–b.

49. Ex. 8:14–5.

50. *CT*, p. 59a.

51. *CT*, p. 71d to. 1. In line five of the paragraph, read with *EVE* *bede'ot* instead of *mi-ra'ot* and *'ad* instead of *'im*.

52. Ex. 10:10.

53. According to the NJPS translation, Pharaoh is directing the comment at Moses, and it is taken to mean: "Clearly, you are bent on mischief."

54. *CT*, p. 60a. It is interesting to note that even though Rashi quotes a similar explanation, Gersonides does not identify Rashi as his source. There is also an aggadic source for this interpretation in *Shir ha-Shirim Rabbah*, quoted in Ginzberg, *Legends*, vol. 5, p. 431 n. 196.

55. Ex. 32:12.

56. Ibid.; *CT*, p. 70c.

57. *CT*, p. 68b.

58. *CT*, p. 71c–d. Here Gersonides is able to rely on a similar interpretation which appears in ibn Ezra and originates in *Mekhilta de-R. Ishmael, massekhta de-va-yassa'* 6, pp. 174–5.

59. *Kuzari*, D. H. Baneth, ed. (Jerusalem: Magnes Press, 1977), I:97, pp. 29–32.

60. *CT*, p. 112c.

61. *CT*, p. 112d. There are other places, however, where Gersonides equates the sin with idol worship. See *CT*, p. 113b. Halevi also suggests the possibility that the golden calf was some sort of "talisman" (*talasim*). See *Kuzari* I:97, p. 30.

62. An allusion to Ex. 13:17.

63. Num. 14:4. *CT*, p. 188a to. 4.

64. That is, the manna and other forms of sustenance which are reported in Deut. 8:3–4, 29:4–5.

65. *CT*, p. 215d to. 7.

66. See, also, p. 240a to. 10, where the same point is made. Gersonides bases his interpretation on a couple of passages in Deuteronomy emphasizing the positive value of the forty years of wandering without any mention of its punitive aspect; see Deut. 8:2–6, 29:4–5. Similar interpreta-

tions in rabbinic sources appear to be based on these same passages; see *Mekhilta de-R. Ishmael, massekhta va-yehi be-shalaḥ, petiḥta*, p. 76; *Sifre De-varim* 32, pp. 56–7.

NOTES TO CHAPTER FIVE

1. The term Gersonides often uses when discussing the value of the Torah as a source for philosophical guidance is *haysharah*, or 'guide.' See, for example, how this term is used in Gersonides' introduction to his *Commentary on the Torah* (*CT*, p. 2a–c).

2. Helpful for our analysis in this chapter were Touati's chapters on the Torah, pp. 478–85; the commandments, pp. 492–505; and ethics, pp. 514–9.

3. Supra, pp. 16–18.

4. *MH*, p. 4; *WL* 1, pp. 94–5.

5. Ibid.

6. *MH*, p. 4; *WL* 1, p. 95, my italics.

7. *MH*, pp. 4–5; *WL* 1, pp. 94-6. Touati points out that Gersonides' rejection of the notion that the prophet has intuitive knowledge superior to that of the philosopher is in direct opposition to Averroes (p. 453). Gersonides' view also appears to differ from that of Avicenna, who believed that the prophet has privileged access to philosophical truth through intuitive knowledge. For Avicenna's view, see Herbert Davidson, "Alfarabi and Avicenna on the Active Intellect," *Viator* 3 (1972): 167.

8. *MH*, pp. 101–105; *WL* 2, pp. 42–7.

9. *MH*, p. 119; *WL* 2, p. 72; *CT*, pp. 184d, 209d–210a to. 8, 248a to. 15. We will be discussing these sources in greater detail below.

10. Menachem Kellner, "Maimonides and Gersonides on Mosaic Prophecy," *Speculum* 52 (1977): 62–79. Touati also has a short section on Mosaic prophecy in his major work on Gersonides (pp. 466–8). However, it is only Kellner who has noted the inconsistencies in Gersonides' position.

11. Maimonides' central discussions on Mosaic prophecy are contained in the seventh article of faith in the introduction to *Perek Ḥelek* in the *Commentary on the Mishnah, Seder Nezikin*, ed. and trans. into Hebrew by J. Kafiḥ (Jerusalem: Mossad ha-Rav Kook, 1963), p. 213; *Mishneh Torah, Hilkhot Yesodey ha-Torah*, 7:6; *Guide* II:35, pp. 367–9.

12. Kellner, p. 74.

13. *MH*, pp. 110–1; *WL* 2, pp. 57–9. These characteristics are reminiscent of those enumerated by Maimonides. We need not dwell on these psychological aspects of Mosaic prophecy. Our main focus will be on Moses as legislative prophet and giver of the Torah. One question that arises here is how Moses was able to achieve such extraordinary intellectual perfec-

tion. A passage in Gersonides' commentary on Exodus appears to address this problem by suggesting that he learned his wisdom from Egyptian science while growing up in Pharaoh's palace. While Gersonides emphasizes the deficiency of Egyptian knowledge, Moses was able to glean enough from their science to become Israel's greatest prophet. See *CT*, p. 54a, and references to previous sources upon which this theory is based, in Touati, p. 466 n. 65.

14. Deut. 34:10. *MH*, p. 119; *WL* 2, p. 72.

15. Supra, p. 17.

16. Kellner, pp. 73–4.

17. Num. 12:8.

18. Read with *EVE* and *F*: *kemo she-'amar*.

19. Deut. 34:10.

20. Gersonides' Hebrew is somewhat unclear here.

21. Literally, "a prophet of the Torah."

22. *CT*, p. 184d.

23. Deut. 4:26.

24. I.e., the assumption that Moses' prophecy *was* due to natural disposition.

25. *CT*, p. 209d to. 8.

26. Recall that in Gersonides' thinking the Israelites settle in the land of Israel because of its special qualities for enhancing providence for those who live there. Thus if Moses had already achieved the highest level of providence imaginable, his living in the land of Israel would confer no added benefit.

27. *CT*, p. 198a to. 2. (P. 198 appears after p. 194 due to a mix-up in the Venice printing.)

28. *CT*, p. 209d to. 8. Cf. Gersonides' commentary on Deuteronomy 34:10 in *CT*, pp. 247a–b, 248b to. 18. The various qualities of Moses' prophecy enumerated at the end of Deuteronomy according to Gersonides' reading are three: Moses' ability to experience prophecy without the help of the imagination; the performance of miracles affecting large geographical areas; and the performance of miracles that are long in duration. The Messiah will have all three of these qualities. We will be discussing Gersonides' views on the Messiah more extensively in chapter eight.

29. Incidentally, it is interesting to note how Gersonides construes the crucial prooftext from Deuteronomy, "Never again did there arise. . . ." In passages we cited earlier, Gersonides seems to understand the verse quite literally: it supports the special nature of Mosaic prophecy by asserting that a prophet of similar stature never arose again in Israel (supra, pp. 78, 80). Note how Gersonides has given it an entirely new twist in the passage we have just cited. The same prooftext is converted from a descriptive

statement about the past to a predictive statement about the future. It is now taken to mean that no prophet will ever rise again in Israel like Moses. Moreover, the whole sense of the passage is turned inside out. It is now understood to mean that while there may be no new Moses "in Israel," another prophet of Moses' stature will arise whose mission will be to Israel *and* the other nations of the world.

30. *CT*, p. 248a to. 15.

31. Supra, pp. 24–26.

32. Deut. 5:3. The verse continues, ". . . but with us, the living, every one of us who is here today."

33. Deut. 5:26.

34. Deut. 6:2.

35. Mal. 3:6: *CT*, p. 211c to. 4.

36. Maimonides also characterizes the immutability of the Torah as a fundamental Torah principle; see *Guide* II:39, pp. 378–9. See my appendix for a general discussion of the *pinnot ha-torah* in Gersonides' thought. There are references to twenty-two such principles scattered throughout the *Wars* and the biblical commentaries.

37. *CT*, p. 240d; cf. p. 216c to. 23. See Gersonides' reading of II Kings 17:37 (*C. II Kings*, ad loc.) which he also takes as proof that the Torah is immutable.

38. *CT*, p. 2a. The phrase "true felicity" is undoubtedly a reference to immortality. In an earlier chapter, we saw that in the *Wars*, Gersonides uses a similar phrase, "spiritual felicity" (*hazlahah nafshit*), in reference to immortality. See supra, p. 22.

39. Deut. 30:15, 30:19–20.

40. *CT*, p. 240d. The term "spiritual life" is somewhat ambiguous in this passage; but on p. 241c to. 10, in his summary of this passage, Gersonides clearly identifies "spiritual life" with "eternal life" (*ha-hayyim ha-nizhiyyim*)—i.e., immortality.

41. Ibid. Cf. *CT*, p. 210b to. 11. Other passages making reference to these two types of reward include *CT*, pp. 167b, 197a, 211d, 213d to. 14.

42. *CT*, p. 240d. See also *CT*, p. 171a. In the course of discussing the Feast of Weeks in his commentary on Leviticus, Gersonides refers to the Torah as a divine gift that allows the Israelites to attain "eternal life," in addition to providing the means for achieving "material goods, such as the inheritance of the land of Canaan." Here there is clear reference to both the material and spiritual rewards consequent upon observing the Torah's laws and learning from its instruction.

43. *CT*, p. 2a–d.

44. Supra, p. 4.

45. To a large extent, this conclusion also applies to his treatment of the biblical text as a whole. However, it is most evident in his *Commentary on the Torah*.

46. *CT*, pp. 16d, 34 a to. 21. There are a number of instances in which Gersonides interprets passages in the Torah as an attempt to preempt doubts or incorrect philosophical arguments that might arise in the mind of the reader. See, for example, Gersonides' explanation for what he perceives to be the improper ordering of the Genesis narrative in *CT*, p. 13d. In these examples, Gersonides applies a method discussed in the introduction to the *Wars*, where he claims that a good philosophical treatise first disproves an incorrect viewpoint before arguing for the correct position (*MH*, p. 9; *WL* 1, p. 102).

47. See, for example, *CT*, pp. 30c to. 2, 205c to. 1. Other examples abound in the Gersonides' commentaries. In some places the historical details are directed specifically at the Israelites in Moses' time, who will recognize the landmarks or customs mentioned in the narrative; see, for example, *CT*, pp. 30c to. 7, 40c to. 36. Most of the historical information, however, is directed at all readers, not just those in Moses' time.

48. Touati provides a short but comprehensive discussion of Gersonides' position on the commandments to which the present analysis is indebted: see pp. 492–505. Yitshak Heinemann also deals with this topic in *Reasons for the Commandments in Jewish Literature*, vol. 1 (in Hebrew) (Jerusalem: World Zionist Organization, 1954), pp. 97–102. A thorough explication of this subject is well beyond the scope of this project. The large body of material in Gersonides' biblical commentaries regarding the commandments deserves separate study. Furthermore, as noted in our introduction, a good portion of the material regarding the commandments was not included in the standard printed editions of the biblical commentaries. That material can be found in a number of manuscripts that did not serve as the basis for the Venice edition. See our discussion, supra, pp. 9–10.

49. *CT*, p. 134c f. Cf. Maimonides' discussion in *Guide*, III:48, pp. 598–601.

50. *CT*, p. 80a. Maimonides, who rejected astrology, would of course find such an explanation unacceptable.

51. *Guide* III:37, pp. 540f.

52. Gersonides' discussion on this and other forbidden mixtures in Leviticus 19 is to be found in *CT*, p. 162a-c. As we shall see later, even this type of explanation grows out of historical considerations regarding the pedagogical needs of the Israelites at the time of the giving of the Torah.

53. The seven levels of forms are as follows: the elements, the homoeomerous bodies, the vegetative soul, the animal soul, the intellectual

soul, the Separate Intellects, and God. These seven levels are alluded to in a number of passages. See for example *CT*, p. 80a.

54. Gersonides' explanation of each part of the Tabernacle is in *CT*, p. 104b f. The Tabernacle provides knowledge in allegorical fashion not just about the hierarchy of forms but also about a host of other issues in natural science, astronomy, and metaphysics.

55. *CT*, pp. 9a, 104b. Thus, according to this interpretation, Moses preempted Aristotle as the first one to provide a comprehensive and accurate metaphysics in response to the pre-Socratic philosophers and Plato. See Touati, p. 479 n. 13, for references to the views of other medieval philosophers regarding the state of knowledge among the Israelites in the time of Moses. We might mention that Gersonides interprets not just the philosophical message according to its historical context, but sometimes the style of the prophet's discourse as well. In a number of cases, Gersonides will explain an anomaly in the biblical text as the product of the prophet's mode of discourse. See *CT*, p. 116c, for example, where Gersonides uses this type of explanation to deal with the repetition of detail regarding the building of the Tabernacle.

56. *CT*, pp. 104b–105a. For examples of other commandments which are explained this way, see *CT*, pp. 162a, 231d.

57. *CT*, p. 9a.

58. *Guide* III:32, p. 525f.

59. A similar argument is made by Naḥmanides in his commentary on Lev. 1:9.

60. *CT*, pp. 21a–b, 117b, 122b, 198c. Halevi, ibn Ezra, and Naḥmanides also believed that the sacrifices helped one achieve prophecy, as noted by Touati, p. 503 n. 52.

61. *CT*, p. 132d.

62. *CT*, p. 130b ff.

63. *CT*, pp. 138b ff., 193d ff.

64. *CT*, p. 2c–d.

65. I have adopted the reading in *F* here: *ve-zeh mi-mah she-yishmor ha-ʾadam me-ḥet bi-kẓat ha-mizvot*.

66. *CT*, p. 241c to. 5. Note that Gersonides even designates the unknowability of the ultimate reasons for the commandments as one of the *pinnot ha-torah*. See also *CT*, p. 240c for a lengthier exposition of this point, and *C. Prov.*, in *beʾur ha-devarim* on verse 3:8.

67. *CT*, p. 2a–b.

68. *CT*, pp. 243a, 244d to. 1.

69. *CT*, p. 2b–c. The second distinction Gersonides makes here is problematic. There are also portions in the biblical narrative that teach philosophical lessons with the use of parables. For example, the Garden of Eden

episode is read by Gersonides as a philosophical allegory. Therefore, the narrative material on occasion also relates philosophical teachings indirectly. Gersonides, however, generally frowns upon reading the biblical text allegorically; see *CT*, pp. 16d, 28b, and Touati, pp. 30, 483–4.

70. *CT*, p. 2a–b.

71. *CT*, pp. 2b, 9a.

72. Supra, p. 90.

73. *CT*, p. 16c; *C. Prov.* 29:18; Aristotle, *Nichomachean Ethics* I, iii; Maimonides, *Treatise on Logic*, Israel Efros, ed. and trans. (New York: American Academy of Jewish Research, 1938), p. 47; *Guide* I:2, pp. 23–6. The notion that ethics is not a demonstrative science is alluded to in the first book of the *Wars* during Gersonides' attempt to explain why it is that the Active Intellect relays knowledge with different gradations of clarity. One factor is the subject matter: ". . . for if the subject matter is imperfect so will the knowledge of it be defective, as is the case in political philosophy and related subjects" (*MH*, pp. 50–1; *WL* 1, pp. 168–9).

74. The Torah does not really provide a system of ethics for Gersonides, as Touati points out, but only a series of guidelines (pp. 517–9). The notion that the Torah furnishes the only sure guidance in ethics is adopted from Maimonides, who expresses this view in the *Guide* II:39–40, pp. 378–85.

75. Throughout his introduction to that work, Gersonides makes clear that he intends to settle each of the questions he discusses with demonstrative certainty; see especially *MH*, pp. 4–5; *WL* 1, pp. 94–7.

76. It is also telling that Gersonides seems to have left no commentaries on any of Averroes' works dealing with political philosophy or ethics, even though he composed extensive commentaries on other works by Averroes on natural science and metaphysics. Once again, Gersonides seems to have seen the Torah as the sole source of guidance in the areas of politics and ethics.

77. *MH*, pp. 6–7; *WL* 1, p. 98.

78. Ibid.; *Guide* II:25, pp. 327–8.

79. *MH*, p. 6, 441; *WL* 1, p. 98.

80. *MH*, pp. 6–7, 419; *WL* 1, p. 98; *C. Prov.* 30:4.

81. *MH*, pp. 418–41.

82. *MH*, pp. 441–2; supra, p. 23.

83. See our appendix for a full discussion of this issue.

84. We should be aware that there is much here that Gersonides does not adequately clarify. The main difficulty is that Gersonides provides no standards by which one can recognize how a given piece of biblical information is to be used. We are never told how to distinguish between a biblical source that has to be interpreted in light of the results of philosophical

enquiry and one that becomes part of the investigation itself. Moreover, when a biblical source does become part of the investigation, we are not given any insight into how one decides whether that source merely furnishes a specific point of information, or whether it embodies some essential principle that guides the whole direction of the enquiry. We therefore have a series of guidelines, but no clear indication as to how they are to be applied.

85. *CT*, p. 74a.
86. Gen. 17:9–14.
87. *CT*, p. 26a–b.
88. Ibid.; *C. Josh.* 5:1–9, 8 to. 4.

NOTES TO CHAPTER SIX

1. Supra, p. 4.
2. Touati, in a couple of brief statements, declares emphatically that there is no support for esotericism in Gersonides' writings (pp. 93–4, 95–6). Touati rejects Guttmann's position on p. 71 n. 104. The most in-depth treatment of Gersonides' attitude towards esotericism is contained in Menachem Kellner's, "Gersonides' Commentary on Song of Songs: For Whom was it Written and Why?" *Gersonide en son temps*, pp. 87–101. This article, which was recently brought to my attention, deals with some of the same questions which will be discussed in this chapter and shows an appreciation for the subtleties in Gersonides' position. Kellner's article, however, is mostly concerned with the issue of esotericism as it relates specifically to Gersonides' *Commentary on the Song of Songs*. The discussion below deals with Gersonides' position on esotericism in much broader terms. Leo Strauss briefly discusses Gersonides in his book, *Philosophy and Law*, Fred Baumann, trans. (Philadelphia: Jewish Publication Society of America, 1987), pp. 71–78. Strauss's analysis, however, does not draw clear conclusions on the issue of esotericism. Moreover, his discussion is far from complete, since he does not take into account many of the sources which we will be citing.
3. Supra, pp. 88–89.
4. *Guide*, Introduction, pp. 6–7, 8–9. See also *Guide* I:5, pp. 30–1, in which Maimonides criticizes the elders of Israel who in Ex. 24:10–1 are said to have caught a glimpse of God. According to Maimonides' reading, the elders went beyond their intellectual capacities in an attempt to comprehend the nature of God and were later punished for this misdemeanor.
5. Menachem Kellner, "Gersonides' Introduction to His *Commentary on the Song of Songs*" (in Hebrew), *Da'at* 23 (1989): 21, and English transla-

tion in *From Ancient Israel to Modern Judaism: Intellect in Quest of Understanding*, p. 195.

6. Ibid., p. 22 (Hebrew); pp. 195–6 (English). It is important to emphasize that Gersonides is not suggesting that there is no material reward whatsoever for observing the commandments, but only that the true reward for their observance is spiritual. See supra, pp. 85–86.

7. Ibid.

8. *CT*, p. 211d.

9. *CT*, p. 122b to. 1. See also Gersonides' explanation for the pouring of blood at the base of the altar on p. 131a.

10. Supra, p. 85–6.

11. I have deliberately deviated from the NJPS translation by rendering the term *rokhel* as "tale-bearer," not "base fellow." It is the former meaning that Gersonides seems to have in mind.

12. See also *C. Prov.* 20:19, where a similar warning is given about revealing philosophical truths to the masses.

13. This approach is in contrast to that of Maimonides. We will be drawing a comparison between Gersonides and Maimonides later on in our discussion.

14. Supra, p. 102.

15. The Tetragrammaton was believed by Gersonides to embody the notion of God's necessary existence, a philosophical truth that could only be understood properly by those trained in philosophy. See *MH*, pp. 136–7; *WL* 2, p. 115.

16. *CT*, p. 218c to. 6.

17. In an earlier discussion, we saw that Moses also taught the Israelites the philosophical truths contained in the divine name as part of God's program to redeem them from Egypt. See supra, p. 65.

18. What we are arguing here helps explain why Gersonides, alongside his support for esotericism, also places a good deal of emphasis on the value of proper pedagogy in his *Commentary on Proverbs*. See, for example, his remarks on Proverbs 11:24–6.

19. *MH*, pp. 5–6; *WL* 1, p. 97. Cf. *C. Prov.*, 11:24–26.

20. *MH*, pp. 7–10; *WL* 1, pp. 99–103. These principles appear to be modeled on Maimonides' list of principles in the introduction to the *Guide*, which delineate the different kinds of contradictions that authors utilize in their work (*Guide*, Introduction, pp. 17–8). It is tempting to see Gersonides' list as designed to be in deliberate opposition to that of Maimonides. Maimonides' principles seem to deal with contradiction and obscurity, while those of Gersonides emphasize clarity and order. However, this is a simplistic assessment. The two lists are not always at odds. For instance, at least one of Maimonides' principles is designed for pedagogical pur-

poses similar to those discussed by Gersonides. Maimonides' fifth principle allows the author to contradict himself when he must first explain an obscure matter in simple terms before offering a more comprehensive explanation later on. Moreover, Gersonides' seventh principle appears to reflect the influence of Maimonides, as we shall soon see. A full comparison between the two lists deserves separate study.

21. *MH*, p. 8; *WL* 1, p. 101.

22. *MH*, pp. 9–10; *WL* 1, pp. 102–3.

23. Gersonides' method of gradual education seems to have been inspired by Maimonides' explanation for the sacrifices. In the continuation of the passage just quoted from the *Wars*, Gersonides explains that sometimes an author can wean his reader away from an erroneous belief by taking "the sustenance" of his incorrect view and utilizing it to support a correct one. This echoes Maimonides' theory that God transformed the idolatrous sacrificial practices of the Israelites into proper divine worship. An explicit connection between Maimonides' explanation for the sacrifices and the pedagogical principle of gradual education is made in *CT*, p. 132d.

24. Feldman translates the term *'emunah* variously as "religious faith," "faith," and "religious convictions." I have consistently translated it as "religious faith." Justification for this translation will be discussed shortly.

25. *MH*, p. 91; *WL* 1, p. 226, with adjustments to the translation.

26. Touati, p. 93; cf. Isaac Husik, *A History of Medieval Jewish Philosophy* (Philadelphia: Jewish Publication Society of America, 1958), pp. 330–31; Shalom Rosenberg, "Biblical Interpretation in the *Guide*" (in Hebrew), *Jerusalem Studies in Jewish Thought* 1 (1981): 154-5. Touati's position is not clear. At first, he identifies the term *'emunah* in our passage with belief in the fundamental principles of the Torah. Yet, a short time later he seems to construe *'emunah* as dependent on the reading of specific passages in Scripture:

> Encore faut-il entendre le terme *croyance religieuse, 'emunah*, dans le sens le plus fort, comme doctrine biblique fondamentale . . . on doit admettre que le penseur, qui, au terme de sa libre investigation, se heurte à un texte biblique rebelle à toute interprétation harmonisatrice, est obligé de reprendre la question à nouveau.

Touati therefore blurs the distinction between the *pinnot ha-torah* which are *general* principles derived from Scripture and the reading of *individual* passages in the biblical text that may require philosophical interpretation.

27. Some definitions of *'emunah* in medieval Jewish thought are dealt with in Shalom Rosenberg's "The Concept of *Emunah* in Post-Maimonidean Jewish Philosophy," *Studies in Medieval Jewish History and*

Literature, vol. 2, Isadore Twersky, ed. (Cambridge, MA: Harvard University Press, 1984), pp. 273–309.

28. *MH,* pp. 3–4; *WL* 1, p. 94, with some adjustments to the translation.

29. The verb *ya'aminu,* is from the same root as the term *'emunah.*

30. This is not to say that Gersonides always equated *'emunah* with dogmatic belief. One would have to conduct a thorough study of Gersonides' philosophical and exegetical writings to see if he is consistent in his use of this term. However, the passage we have just cited provides evidence that at least in some cases it can be understood in this way. Cf. *CT,* p. 211d, where Gersonides also contrasts rational understanding and dogmatic belief in his interpretation of Deut. 6:4, "Hear O Israel! The LORD is our God, the LORD is one." For the elite, this verse commands that the Israelites "rationally understand" (*yavinu*) God's existence, while for the masses the command is to "believe" (*ya'aminu*) by instruction.

31. *MH,* pp. 88, 90–1; *WL* 1, pp. 222, 225.

32. Supra, p.107.

33. Even in Maimonides' lifetime this issue had erupted into open controversy. Reactions to his position on resurrection and the world to come had forced Maimonides to compose his *Treatise on Resurrection.* For a discussion of the debate on resurrection and the related issues of immortality and the world to come, see Joseph Sarachek, *Faith and Reason: The Conflict over the Rationalism of Maimonides* (Williamsport: Bayard Press, 1935), pp. 39–65; Daniel J. Silver, *Maimonidean Criticism and Maimonidean Controversy* (Leiden: E. J. Brill, 1965), pp. 64–6, 109–35; Bernard Septimus, *Hispano-Jewish Culture in Transition: The Career and Controversies of Ramah* (Cambridge, MA: Harvard University Press, 1982), pp. 39–61. One point of contention was Maimonides' alleged denial of the resurrection of the dead in the messianic era. Another was his view that the rabbinic concept of the world to come (*'olam ha-ba'*) referred to immortality and not to a future world associated with the messianic period.

34. Supra, p. 107.

35. *Treatise on Resurrection,* J. Finkel, ed. *PAAJR* 9 (1939): 9.

36. *Treatise on Resurrection,* pp. 8–9; *Guide* I:5, pp. 30–1; I:22, pp. 50–1.

37. Supra, p. 107.

38. *Guide,* Introduction, pp. 6–7.

39. Ex. 3:6; *Guide* I:5, pp. 29–31.

40. Ex. 3:3.

41. *CT,* pp. 56b to. 6, 210a to. 9. The dispute between Maimonides and Gersonides appears to be based on a debate in the Talmud, *BT Berakhot* 7a, in which there is a similar division of opinion about Moses' reaction to the burning bush.

42. Kellner suggests historical reasons to explain these differences between Maimonides and Gersonides. Kellner claims that Gersonides is not

afraid of revealing philosophical truths to the masses because these truths had already been revealed in the previous generation by a number of Maimonidean disciples, such as Samuel Ibn Tibbon. See Kellner, pp. 103–4.

43. *CT*, pp. 9c, 30d.

44. Supra, pp. 101–102, 103.

45. *CT*, p. 2c.

46. See references supra, p. 198 n. 5.

NOTES TO CHAPTER SEVEN

1. It seems that Gersonides meant his commentaries to be read according to the order of the biblical text.

2. *CT*, pp. 17c, 22b, 77c, 208c, 209c–d to. 5; C. *I Kings* 11 to. 24, 22 to. 28.

3. Touati, p. 449. A number of studies have been done on medieval Jewish conceptions of the land of Israel. See, for example, the essays in Aviezer Ravitzky and Moshe Hallamish (eds.), *The Land of Israel in Medieval Jewish Thought* (in Hebrew) (Jerusalem: Yad Yitshak ben Tsevi, 1991), and Lawrence Hoffman (ed.), *The Land of Israel: Jewish Perspectives* (Notre Dame: University of Notre Dame Press, 1986); see also Moshe Idel, "Some Conceptions of the Land of Israel in Medieval Jewish Thought," *A Straight Path: Studies in Medieval Philosophy and Culture: Essays in Honor of Arthur Hyman*, Ruth Link-Salinger, ed. (Washington, D.C.: Catholic University of America Press, 1988), pp. 124–141.

4. *CT*, p. 77c.

5. Supra, p. 85.

6. Deut. 30:20. I have departed from the NJPS translation in order to capture Gersonides' understanding of the passage.

7. The term *tov*, which Gersonides uses here, is understood throughout this entire passage as referring to material well-being as opposed to spiritual well-being.

8. In the Hebrew, *ha-ḥayyim ha-hem* refers to *ha-ḥayyim ha-niẓḥiyyim*, or 'eternal life,' which has just been mentioned before these remarks.

9. *CT*, p. 241a. The same point is made on p. 210a–b to. 11.

10. *CT*, pp. 75c, 98b, 109d. The differences between the structure of Solomon's Temple and that of the original Tabernacle are of great interest to Gersonides. In a lengthy passage in his *Commentary on I Kings*, Gersonides explains the differences in a detailed exposition showing that each new element in the design of Solomon's Temple is meant to teach a valuable philosophical lesson. See C. *I Kings* 11 to. 18.

11. Gersonides contrasts this system of worship with the customs of the idolaters who worship a host of deities in any number of locations (*CT*, pp. 104a–b to. 3, 107c, 160b; Touati, pp. 526–7).

12. This phrase from Hosea 9:11 is consistently used by Gersonides to describe the superiority of the Levite tribe as a whole. See, for example, *CT*, p. 247c to. 4.

13. *CT*, p. 107d.

14. *CT*, p. 191 to. 15.

15. I depart here from the NJPS translation which renders *shomer ha-berit ve-ha-ḥesed* as ". . . who keeps His covenant faithfully." My translation more accurately captures Gersonides' understanding of the passage as will be evident below.

16. See previous note.

17. Zeph. 3:9.

18. Gen. 15:19–21.

19. Literally, "the Torah attempted to give Israel only seven nations. . . ." See Deut. 7:1.

20. Deut. 19:8–9.

21. *CT*, p. 213d to. 19. See also pp. 213b, 214a, 215d to. 1; *C. Dan.* 9:4, 12 to. 8; *C. Neh.* 9:8, 13 to. 13; *C. I Chron.* 16:15–20.

22. Gen. 15:19–21.

23. Deut. 7:1.

24. Deut. 19:8–9.

25. In addition to *CT*, p. 213d to. 19, Gersonides also develops these proofs in *CT*, pp. 226c, 227c to. 9. In *CT*, p. 226d, another proof is added that does not appear in the passage presently under consideration. Gersonides quotes I Kings 11:39, in which God tells Jeroboam just before the split in the Israelite kingdom, "I will chastise David's descendants . . . though not forever." Gersonides takes the last phrase to mean that eventually David's descendants will again rule over a unified monarchy. Since this has not yet occurred, this verse must be making reference to the messianic period in which the Davidic line will be restored.

26. Compare, for instance, our discussion of the redemption from Egypt which, according to Gersonides' reading, did not proceed as predicted in Abraham's prophecy (supra, p. 71). The high level of perfection of the Israelites delayed the onset of the slavery, and their unusually harsh treatment at the hands of the Egyptians required that the redemption occur earlier than predicted.

27. *CT*, p. 25b. In this passage, Gersonides cites *Bereshit Rabbah* as the source of this idea. See supra, p. 122, for the argument presented in Gersonides' commentary on Deuteronomy.

28. Gen. 15:16.

29. See Gersonides comments on this passage, *CT*, p. 25a.

30. II Kings 13:23.

31. Gersonides' comments on this passage will be taken up later in this chapter.

32. I have departed from the NJPS translation by translating the phrase *be-aḥarit ha-yamim* as "in the end of days," rather than "in the end." The former meaning better captures the eschatological meaning of Gersonides' reading.

33. Deut. 4:29–31.

34. Lev. 26:41–2. The same thoughts are reiterated in Lev. 26:43–5.

35. Deut. 4:30–31; CT, p. 209a–b.

36. See also Gersonides' exegesis of Lev. 26:41–5 in CT, p. 176b, where the same interpretation of the predicted exile and redemption are given. There are also a number of passages in the biblical text discussing the possibility of future punishment and reconciliation with God, but they do not mention the covenant of the Patriarchs. All such passages are interpreted by Gersonides according to the eschatological framework described here. See CT, pp. 240a–241a on Deut. 30:1–11; CT, p. 234b–d on Deut. 32:36–43.

37. Again, we depart from the NJPS rendering of *shomer ha-berit ve-ha-ḥesed* in order to capture Gersonides' understanding of the phrase.

38. C. Neh. 13 to. 18; supra, pp. 119–20. See also Gersonides' interpretation of Dan. 9:4, in which the same phrase is assumed to refer to the Patriarchal covenant.

39. CT, p. 227d to. 10.

40. In fact, the source of the principle described in this citation is Deut. 19:18–9, the same biblical passage regarding the cities of refuge that Gersonides uses to show that the covenant extends past the conquest. See CT, pp. 226c–d, 227c to. 9, and supra, pp. 121–2. To qualify as one of the *pinnot ha-torah*, the notion that observance brings full implementation of the covenant must surely be based on more than the single text in Deuteronomy 19. Gersonides undoubtedly formulates this doctrine with a number of other biblical passages in mind in which the redemption from future exile is conditional upon obedience to the commandments. Many of these passages, such as those in Lev. 26 and Deut. 4, have already been cited in the course of our discussion.

41. *Bereshit Rabbah* 44:23, vol. 1, pp. 445-7 and parallel sources in Albeck's notes; JT Ḥullin 32a; Maimonides, *Mishneh Torah, Hilkhot Roẓe'aḥ,* 8:4; Naḥmanides on Deut. 12:20 and 19:9.

42. JT *Sanhedrin* 10:1, 27d; *Va-Yikra Rabbah*, M. Margulies, ed. (Jerusalem: Wahrmann Books, 1953–8), 36:5, p. 851. Even though R. Aḥa expresses his opinion in terms of "ancestral merit" and not "covenant," in Gersonides' mind there would be little distinction between the two. We noted earlier that Gersonides probably derives the concept of inherited providence in part from the rabbinic doctrine of ancestral merit (supra,

pp. 35–6). Moreover, even R. Aḥa himself seems to have seen no distinction between ancestral merit and covenant. The biblical source he cites to support his point refers to the Patriarchal covenant, even though he casts his view in terms of ancestral merit.

43. Supra, pp. 120–1. Other examples abound; see, for example, *CT*, p. 176b (cited immediately below), 209b.

44. *CT*, p. 176b in explication of Lev. 26:44–5.

45. Deut. 31:17.

46. Deut. 32:35.

47. *CT*, p. 241d to. 15.

48. *MH*, p. 182; *WL* 2, pp. 201–2 supra, pp. 20–1.

49. The previous citation from Gersonides' commentary on Leviticus also implies the very same point. The Patriarchal covenant is depicted as a factor that saves the Jews in Gersonides' own day from destruction at the hands of their enemies, but apparently does not put an end to their suffering altogether.

There are only two other passage in the biblical commentaries, to my knowledge, in which Gersonides makes reference to *hester panim*. In *CT*, p. 241a, Gersonides informs us that *hester panim* was the state of affairs "immediately after the death of Joshua and the Elders who followed after him." Also, in his commentary on I Kings 13, Gersonides uses this doctrine to explain the death of the Judean prophet who disobeys God's command by accepting an invitation from a prophet from the kingdom of Israel to dine together (*C. I Kings* 13:18, 22 to. 9).

50. *Supra*, pp. 58, 61–2.

51. II Kings 13:23 and supra, p. 124.

52. *C. II Kings* 25 to. 2.

53. II Kings 14:26–7.

54. *C. II Kings* 25 to. 1.

55. Esther 4:13–14.

56. *C. Esther*, p. 46b to. 32.

57. See Gersonides' glosses scattered throughout his commentary on both *tokheḥah* portions in *CT*, pp. 175b–d and 238d–239a. A similar correlation between events predicted in the biblical text and actual historical events can be found in Gersonides' commentary on Deut. 32.

58. *CT*, pp. 175b, 238d.

59. Literally, "the blessing."

60. Literally, "the curse."

61. The reference here is to Deut. 28:16.

62. I have adopted the reading of F here: *mi-kol ha-pe'ulot she-ya'asem ha-'adam tamid.*

63. *CT*, p. 239a.

64. In fact, the punishments intensify according to Gersonides if the Israelites insist on attributing their misfortune to chance events (*CT*, p. 176a–b). This idea is anticipated in Maimonides' *Guide* III:36, pp. 539–40.

65. Is. 1:5.

66. *CT*, p. 175d. Cf. *CT*, pp. 238c–239c; *C. Neh.* 13 to. 18. In a passage in book four of the *Wars*, Gersonides explains why the providential punishments in Leviticus 26 proceed in this manner. His comments are focused on the threat in Lev. 26:18 in which God warns that if the Israelites do not respond initially to punishment, He will discipline them "sevenfold" for their sins:

> . . . when God reproves them with these afflictions, and they are not chastised but persist in their crimes, it is proper that He chastise them seven times for their sins. The chastisement of someone who is only superficially implicated in some evil is not comparable to the chastisement of someone who is so deeply involved in it that this evil trait becomes "second nature." For a man who is deeply enmeshed in sinful action cannot be extricated from it except through severe chastisements (*MH*, pp. 181–2; *WL* 2, pp. 200–1).

67. *CT*, p. 178d to. 1.

68. See Josh. 6:26, I Kings 16:34, and Gersonides' comments ad loc.

69. I Kings 17:1.

70. A reference to the events in I Kings 18.

71. See I Kings 20:1f.

72. I Kings 20:26f.

73. Ahab is eventually killed in battle in I Kings 22. *C. I Kings* 22 to. 15.

74. See *C. II Kings* 12 to. 3, in which Gersonides also explains events in the first chapter of II Kings along similar lines.

75. Supra, p. 132.

76. Lev. 26:31.

77. Lev. 26:38.

78. Gersonides is referring here to the expulsion of the Jews from France in 1306. According to Yosef Hayim Yerushalmi, this passage is one of the only references to this expulsion in Jewish texts of this period. See Yosef Hayim Yerushalmi, *Zakhor: Jewish History and Jewish Memory* (Seattle and London: University of Washington Press, 1983), p. 59.

79. *CT*, p. 176b.

80. *MH*, pp. 172–3; *WL* 2, pp. 186 –7; supra, p. 21.

81. Lam. 5:7.

82. Touati and Feldman both translate the phrase *hashgaḥah nifla'ah* as "miraculous providence." The phrase in their view is a specific reference

to miracles (*WL* 2, p. 187 n. 13). I prefer the translation, "extraordinary providence," because of evidence in the *Commentary on the Torah* which supports this understanding of the phrase. In *CT*, p. 41d to. 5, Gersonides clearly uses this expression to refer to individual providence in general, not just miracles. The problem centers on the term *nifla'ah* which can mean either "extraordinary" or "miraculous."

83. The reference here is to providential suffering which is described in a later section in the *Wars*.

84. *MH*, p. 173; *WL* 2, p. 187.

85. *CT*, pp. 76a, 115a; *C. Josh.* 7:1; cf. *C. I Kings* 8:46.

86. In reference to the destruction of the first Temple.

87. This is Gersonides' rendering of the cryptic phrase *shavu'im shiv'im* in Dan. 9:24. According to Gersonides' calculation, the second Temple stood 490 years, a period of time predicted in this verse. See Gersonides' remarks ad loc.

88. *C. Dan.* 12 to. 2.

89. Cf. *BT 'Avodah Zarah* 4a.

90. Ibn Ezra's position is stated in his commentary on Gen. 27:40. A superb study of this issue is Gerson Cohen's "Esau as Symbol in Early Medieval Thought," *Jewish Medieval and Renaissance Studies*, Alexander Altmann, ed. (Cambridge, MA: Harvard University Press, 1967), pp. 19–49.

91. *CT*, pp. 35d–36b. Gersonides is deeply troubled about how to explain these blessings philosophically. After a lengthy discussion, he concludes that they are, in fact, prophetic predictions of events to come. The problem with this interpretation is that Isaac tells Esau after he realizes that Jacob has stolen his brother's blessing, "Your brother came with guile and took away your blessing" (Gen. 27:35). If the blessing was a prophetic prediction, how is it that Jacob "took away" Esau's blessing? Gersonides' solution is that the prophet has an effect on the outcome of a prophetic prediction. While he certainly cannot change what is foreordained altogether, he can accentuate the good features of a prophetic prediction on behalf of the recipient. In the case we are dealing with here, Isaac accentuated Jacob's blessing by including within it the prediction that he would have dominion over this brother. It was in this sense that Jacob "took away" Esau's blessing.

92. Here Gersonides applies a principle which we encountered in our analysis of his interpretation of Genesis 15. A prophetic prediction promising benefits over a lengthy period of time is conditional upon the recipient being worthy of individual providence. See our discussion supra, p. 44.

93. Gen. 27:40.

94. Gen. 6:4.

95. Cf. Jer. 1:17.

96. Cf. Is. 1:26.

97. II Kings 19:23, Is. 37:24.

98. *CT*, p. 72b, incorrectly labelled p. 71 in the printed Venice editions.

99. In some medieval Jewish sources, Christendom is specifically identified with Amalek, not just the descendants of Esau in general; see Ginzberg, *Legends of the Jews*, vol. 6, p. 24 n. 21. Gersonides, however, seems to stop short of making this identification in this passage.

100. This passage is absent in *F*. In *EVE*, it is circled with a note in the margin indicating that the passage is not found in the other, more complete family of manuscripts (*'ein zeh be-nusaḥ 'aḥarinah*).

101. *C. Dan.* 7:25, 11:36–7. Like many medieval Jewish thinkers, Gersonides identifies Rome and its heir, Christian Europe, with the fourth kingdom predicted in Dan. 7:23–5. Gersonides believes that the Islamic Empire was also part of this fourth kingdom but later split from it. See *C. Dan.* 2:41–5; Touati, p. 529.

102. The prophetic predictions in Isaac's blessing regarding the descendants of Esau would still apply to others who are clearly identified with Esau's offspring. We have, for instance, the Edomites, whose relationship to Esau is established in Gen. 36:1 and 36:8. Their rivalry with the Israelites is attested to throughout the historical books of the Prophets. Most important are the Amalekites, who crop up in a number of episodes in the biblical history. In several passages, Gersonides also takes the traditional position that Haman was a descendant of Amalek. For Gersonides' views on the Amalekites, see *CT*, p. 72a–b; *C. II Sam.* 1 to. 8; *C. Esther*, pp. 42d, 48d to. 50.

NOTES TO CHAPTER EIGHT

1. Touati deals with this material in a brief chapter devoted to Gersonides' interpretation of the messianic era; see Touati, pp. 528–32. Besides Touati's discussion, the only other study that has dealt with Gersonides' conception of the messianic period is Menachem Kellner's "Gersonides on Miracles, Messiah and Resurrection of the Dead," *Daʿat* 4 (1980): 5–34. Kellner's study, like ours, focuses exclusively on the philosophical aspects of Gersonides' views.

2. This commentary is referred to in *CT*, pp. 197c, 227b; *C. II Kings* 19:25. See also Touati, p. 70.

3. This scenario is not discussed by Kellner—although, in all fairness, the focus of his study is more on the miracle of resurrection than on the messianic era. Touati briefly discusses the relationship between the Pa-

triarchal covenant and the messianic period but does not comment on the significance of this relationship. See Touati, p. 536.

4. Supra, p. 124f.

5. The same year was the focus of messianic speculations by other medieval Jewish thinkers—including Rashi, Abraham bar Ḥiyya, and Naḥmanides; see Kellner, p. 7 n. 15, and Touati, p. 531 n. 19.

6. Supra, pp. 126–7.

7. Supra, pp. 137–8.

8. Is. 60:22. C. Dan. 12 to. 8. Cf. BT Sanhedrin 98a.

9. Note, however, Gersonides' emphatic assertion in CT, p. 226c, that "if the Israelites were to keep all of the commandments, they would immediately be redeemed." This statement would suggest that the Jews have a greater impact on the timing of the Messiah's arrival than the passage in the Commentary on Daniel would suggest.

10. Supra, pp. 77–8, 80–1.

11. Deut. 34:10.

12. Deut. 34:12.

13. Is. 52:13. CT, p. 248b to. 19.

14. Is. 52:13.

15. See Yalkut Shim'oni, chapter 476.

16. Zeph. 3:9.

17. CT, p. 198b. Cf. CT, p. 247a. See also a similar explication in MH, pp. 452–3. This latter passage is the only one in the Wars that deals with the messianic era.

18. Deut. 30:6.

19. Literally, "the faith."

20. CT, p. 241c to. 7. The last reference to the prophets is probably to the celebrated passage in Jer. 30:31-3, in which the prophet declares that in the future a new covenant will be made with the Jewish people that will effectively replace the covenant the Israelites made with God upon leaving Egypt. Gersonides may also have another celebrated passage in mind. In Ezek. 36:24-8, the prophet utilizes imagery that appears to draw from the verses in Deuteronomy upon which Gersonides is commenting in the above passage.

21. Incidentally, it is intriguing to note that according to this interpretation Gersonides attaches no intrinsic worth to the resurrection event. Its sole function is to impress the non-Jewish nations so that they will worship the God of Israel. Thus, the implication is that any extraordinary miracle could have accomplished the same purpose. This approach is in marked contrast to most other Jewish thinkers. According to ibn Ezra and Saadiah, for instance, the resurrection serves the specific function of allowing the righteous people of all generations to enjoy the life in the future

messianic world. See Saadiah's *Book of Beliefs and Opinions*, Samuel Rosenblatt, trans. (New Haven: Yale University Press, 1948), 7:10, p. 434; ibn Ezra's commentary on Deut. 23:39 and Dan. 12:2.

22. In this passage Gersonides enumerates a number of *pinnot hatorah* that emerge from I Chron. 16.

23. I Chron. 16:31.

24. See Gersonides' remarks on I Chron. 16:31.

25. Zeph. 3:9. *C. I Chron.* 29 to. 6.

26. Is. 2:1–4.

27. I Sam. 2:6.

28. *C. I Sam.* 7 to. 21. The verse, I Sam. 2:6, which is the basis of Gersonides' *pinnah*, is widely cited in rabbinic sources as proof for the resurrection. See, for example, *BT Rosh Hashannah* 17a; *Sanhedrin* 92b. This interpretation is inspired by the sequence in Hannah's description of God's activity, in which God first "deals death" and then "gives life."

29. *C. I Chron.* 29 to. 6. There are no other passages, to my knowledge, in which Gersonides uses the phrase *pinnot ha-'emunah*.

30. *CT*, p. 245b to. 14. This verse is also widely accepted in rabbinic sources as a reference to the future resurrection. See, for example, *BT Pesaḥim* 68a; *Sanhedrin* 91b, 104a.

31. *C. Dan.* 12:2–3, 12 to. 6. For examples of rabbinic sources that read these verses in connection with the resurrection, see *BT Rosh Hashannah* 16b; *Sanhedrin* 92a.

32. See appendix, pp. 192–3.

33. For more details about the doctrine of resurrection in Gersonides' commentaries, consult Touati, pp. 532–6.

34. The central passage in which this covenant is formulated is II Sam. 7:13–17. See also II Sam. 23:5; I Kings 3:6, 9:4, 11:4, 14:8, 15:3.

35. Literally, "all of the days that the world would exist."

36. II Sam. 23:5.

37. Ibid.

38. Is. 11:1.

39. II Sam. 22:51 and Ps. 18:51.

40. II Sam. 23:5. *C. II Sam.* 24 to. 11.

41. Cf. *C. II Sam.* 21 to. 35, 36; *C. I Kings* 11 to. 40.

42. I Kings 11:13.

43. *C. I Kings* 11:13.

44. *C. Dan.* 12:2, 12 to. 7. For Maimonides' view on this matter, see *Hilkhot Melakhim* 12:1–2. Both Maimonides and Gersonides echo the naturalistic view of the messianic period expressed by Shemu'el in *BT Berakhot* 34a.

NOTES TO CHAPTER NINE

1. Gersonides' tendency to describe divine activity in personal terms does not pose a philosophical problem when he is dealing with the content of prophetic visions. As we have already pointed out on several occasions, the prophet will often experience a personal interaction with God in a vision as the result of the images supplied by his imagination. Thus, in Abraham's vision in Genesis 15, God carries on a lively dialogue with Abraham, responds to Abraham's concerns about his descendants, and then seals a covenant with him. The philosophically adept reader would certainly not mistake these descriptions as a portrayal of actual divine activity.

2. *CT*, pp. 70b to. 3, 71d to. 2.

3. *CT*, p. 57b to. 4.

4. *CT*, p. 56c to. 14.

5. *CT*, p. 59b.

6. My translation is somewhat awkward due to the awkwardness of the Hebrew.

7. Read with *EVE* and *F: she-yasur.*

8. *CT*, p. 59c to. 1.

9. Similar assertions about God's capacity to do whatever He wishes are repeated in *CT*, pp. 56c to. 12, 70a, 72a, 79b to. 1.

10. *CT*, p. 58b to. 3. Other examples of this sort abound in the biblical commentaries. See, for instance, *CT*, pp. 53c to. 1, 54a to. 2.

11. *CT*, p. 68b on Ex . 14:19.

12. *CT*, p. 69a to. 6 on Ex. 14:21.

13. Read with *EVE: ve-hu᾿ mah she-᾿amar le-ha᾿amin.*

14. Ex. 20:2.

15. According to *EVE* and *F*, the printed editions are missing a section here that discusses the importance of the commandment to believe in God. I have omitted it because it is not relevant to the point being made here.

16. Read with *EVE* and *F: takhlitit.*

17. Read with *EVE* and *F: be-᾿ishey min ha-᾿adam.*

18. *CT*, p. 79b to. 1.

19. The notion that God "upsets the order" (*mevalbel ha-siddur*) determined by the stars is particularly striking. This is an obvious reference to miracles. What is remarkable about this terminology is that precisely the same phrase is used by Gersonides in the *Wars* to describe man's capacity to contravene the order of nature when exercising free will; see *MH*, p. 97; *WL* 2, p. 36.

20. Touati also makes this point in a brief remark. See Touati, p. 71 with n. 103.

21. *MH*, pp. 181–2; *WL* 2, pp. 200–1, with adjustments to the translation.

22. *MH*, pp. 163–4; *WL* 2, pp. 172–3; cf. *MH*, p. 182; *WL* 2, p. 201, for a similar passage in which the anthropomorphic language is just as strong.

23. *MH*, p. 174; *WL* 2, p. 188, with some adjustments to the translation.

24. Supra, p. 158.

25. Ex. 10:1–2.

26. *MH*, p. 183; *WL* 2, p. 203.

27. Supra, p. 159.

28. Helpful for the following discussion were Harry Wolfson's article, "Maimonides and Gersonides on Divine Attributes As Ambiguous Terms," in *Studies in the History of Philosophy and Religion*, vol. 2, Isadore Twersky and George H. Williams, eds. (Cambridge, MA.: Harvard University Press, 1977), pp. 231–47, and Touati's discussion, pp. 108–128.

29. *MH*, pp. 132–7; *WL* 2, pp. 107–15.

30. *MH*, pp. 136–7; *WL* 2, pp. 114–5.

31. *MH*, pp. 278–85. With regard to this second list, Gersonides also explains why each attribute is appropriate for God. His general approach is to show that each term is implied by his conception of God, which is worked out in the discussion immediately preceding this list in book five of the *Wars*.

32. Supra, p. 159.

33. The verb *razah* was translated by me as "willing" in Gersonides' list of attributes in book three (supra, p. 164). Of course, this verb as applied to God is the focus of much speculation in medieval philosophy. For Gersonides, it is a particularly problematic term. The exercise of divine will appears to refer only to the implementation of the laws of the natural order. As we have noted many times, God cannot experience a change of will. A comprehensive study of Gersonides' conception of divine will is a desideratum.

34. Touati, pp. 118–19. *MH*, p. 137; *WL* 2, p. 115.

35. Touati states that he is unable to find a reason for the omission of the attribute "willing" in the second list in book five of the *Wars* (Touati, p. 127). Our observations here may provide an answer to this question. If Gersonides saw some of these attributes as synonymous, the attribute of will may very well be implied in the final three attributes that are listed together in the second group: "strong", "governing", and "powerful."

36. II Sam. 16:10. This prooftext is from a statement made by King David in reaction to the curses of Shimei ben Gera who hurls insults at him as he retreats from Jerusalem during the rebellion of Absalom. When one of David's men volunteers to kill Shimei, David asserts that he should go unpunished, because "the LORD told him to abuse David." This passage

supports Gersonides' contention that human actions are attributed to God, even though divine influence on human action is indirect.

37. *MH*, p. 450.

38. In book four of the *Wars*, similar reasoning is alluded to by Gersonides to justify passages in the Bible that describe God as directly punishing the wicked. Punishment by means of chance events from the constellations is "ultimately attributable to God (may He be blessed), since all things are caused by Him" (*MH*, pp. 183–4; *WL* 2, p. 203).

39. Further discussion of the problems we have raised here would have to proceed in a number of directions. First, one would have to conduct a thorough examination of Gersonides' interpretation of Moses' Song at the Sea in Exodus 15 (*CT*, pp. 69b–70c). There Gersonides takes a more restrictive position on the question of anthropomorphic language than that which has emerged in our discussion. It would appear that Gersonides is reacting to the corporeal descriptions of God in that section of the biblical text. Furthermore, as we pointed out in the introduction to this chapter, one would also have to examine all the passages in Gersonides' biblical commentaries in which he comments on divine attributes that appear in the biblical text. For instance, Gersonides frequently employs the talmudic statement, "the Torah speaks in the language of men," when encountering divine attributes, a dictum used frequently by Maimonides in his discussion of anthropomorphisms in the *Guide*. A discussion of Gersonides' attitude towards anthropomorphic language would have to examine when and how this dictum is employed.

NOTES TO CHAPTER 10

1. Supra, p. 126–7.

2. See supra, pp. 58, 62, 129–30.

3. *BT Shabbat* 156a.

4. Passages where this dictum appears or is alluded to include *CT*, pp. 197a, 197c, 209a, 240a to. 8.

5. A succinct summary of this research is Delbert Hillers' *Covenant: the History of a Biblical Idea* (Baltimore: Johns Hopkins Press, 1969).

6. Supra, p. 96.

7. See Gersonides' remarks on these passages ad loc.

8. Supra, pp. 153–5.

9. The concept of the *amr ilāhi* is first introduced in *Kuzari* I:39–42, and is referred to consistently throughout the rest of the treatise.

10. The only instances in which Gersonides attributes the inheritance of divine providence to internal genetic factors are God's decision to choose the Levites as the tribe which would serve in the Tabernacle, and

God's preference for Aaron's family over that of Moses for the priesthood (supra, pp. 118–9).

11. See Herbert Davidson, "The Active Intellect and Hallevi's Theory of Causality," *REJ* 131 (1972): 385–7, with references cited therein.

12. *Kuzari* I:43, I:95, II:14.

13. *Kuzari* I:39–42.

14. Menachem Kellner in a recent study *Maimonides on Judaism and the Jewish People* (Albany: State University of New York Press, 1991) has attempted to construct Maimonides' position on Jewish chosenness by bringing together and analyzing scattered references in his writings which are relevant to this theme.

15. Supra, pp. 123–4.

16. Supra, p. 35.

17. Supra, pp. 19, 26–7.

18. Touati claims that in Gersonides' thinking prophecy in general is a faculty unique to the Jews (pp. 451–2). This claim cannot be sustained. According to Gersonides, there are a number of instances of prophecy among non-Jews. God's conversations with Noah throughout the flood story are treated as prophetic communications. The messengers who visit Abraham in Gen. 18 bearing the prediction of Isaac's birth are prophets (*CT*, p. 26c). The messenger who rescues Hagar in Gen. 21:17 is a prophet according to Gersonides' reading (*CT*, p. 30b). Gersonides also accepts Balaam as a genuine prophet—even though Balaam's actions demonstrate how non-Jews often misuse their prophetic gifts (*CT*, p. 198 to. 2).

19. Supra, p. 92.

20. What we are saying here applies to natural science as well. In his introduction to his *Commentary on the Torah*, Gersonides groups metaphysics and natural science together under the rubric *ḥokhmat ha-nimẓa'ot*, "the science of existents," in his description of the third and most important category of philosophical material that is found in the Torah; see supra, pp. 91–2. However, the majority of the material that the *Wars* and the biblical commentaries share in common is in the area of metaphysics.

21. In addition to book four which deals directly with providence, book two which discusses prophecy, and book three which is concerned with divine knowledge, are also relevant to the question of providence. In fact, books two through four could be seen as a unit culminating in the discussion of divine providence in book four. The discussion in book six on miracles is, of course, also concerned with the question of providence.

22. We were perhaps more successful with the subject of Mosaic prophecy than we were with the question of the present exile.

NOTES TO APPENDIX

1. Supra, pp. 82–3, 126–7.

2. Touati, pp. 484–5.

3. This portion of our discussion reiterates earlier remarks, supra pp. 92–3.

4. *MH*, pp. 6–7; *WL* 1, p. 98.

5. See *Guide* II:25, pp. 327–8, where Maimonides affirms this position. We will be discussing this passage below.

6. *MH*, pp. 6–7; *WL* 1, p. 98.

7. *MH*, p. 6; *WL* 1, p. 98; see also *MH*, p. 441.

8. *MH*, pp. 6–7; *WL* 1, p. 98; Gersonides repeats his position on the relationship between philosophy and Scripture in a later passage in the *Wars*, p. 419; see also *C. Prov.* 30:4.

9. See sources in *MH* and *WL* 1, ibid.; Touati, pp. 94–5.

10. *MH*, pp. 418–41.

11. *MH*, pp. 441–2.

12. *MH*, p. 10; *WL* 1, p. 104. Feldman translates *ha-pinnot ha-toriyyot* here as "basic principles of the Torah." For the sake of consistency, I have substituted "fundamental principles of the Torah," since that is the coinage I will be using throughout this discussion.

13. *MH*, p. 6; *WL* 1, p. 97.

14. *MH*, p. 150; *WL* 2 p. 136. Later on in this chapter, we will be discussing Gersonides' relationship to Maimonides and the passage to which he alludes here.

15. Prov. 22:17.

16. Ibid.

17. Here, Gersonides uses the term *yesodot ha-torah* which is occasionally used as an alternative form for *pinnot ha-torah* (see infra, n. 20). It would appear that Gersonides sees God as the speaker in this passage.

18. Touati, pp. 484–5. According to Touati, *pinnah* is a translation of the Arabic term, *qāʿida*, which often refers to a fundamental dogma or belief.

19. Touati's list includes the following beliefs: God's existence, creation, miracles, prophecy, ultimate joy is in being close to God, all nations will eventually worship God, and resurrection of the dead.

20. While the term, *pinnah*, is the most common designation for these principles, it is not the only one. Gersonides occasionally refers to a principle as a 'root,' *shoresh* (*CT*, pp. 104c, 213c to. 1; *C. I Kings* 11 to. 3) and more rarely as a 'foundation,' or *yesod* (*CT*, p. 34c to. 3; *C. Prov.* 22:17).

21. *CT*, pp. 171c, 211b to. 2.

22. This concept is referred to explicitly in *CT*, p. 213b to. 2, and then identified as one of the *pinnot* in to. 4.

23. *CT*, p. 71d to. 3; *C. I Chron.* 29 to. 6. Gersonides appears to be inconsistent with regard to this principle. We noted earlier that Gersonides specifies creation as one doctrine he would be willing to reject if reason could prove that the universe is eternal. Yet, if creation is one of the fundamental principles of the Torah, presumably it would take priority over any of the conclusions arrived at through philosophical speculation.

24. *CT*, p. 71d to. 3.

25. *CT*, p. 104d.

26. *MH*, p. 149; *WL* 2, p. 135; *C. I Kings* 22 to. 24; *C. II Chron.* 21:12.

27. *C. Esther*, p. 49a to. 51.

28. *CT*, pp. 69a to. 6, 79b to. 1; *C. I Chron.* 29 to. 6.

29. *CT*, p. 213c to. 10.

30. *C. I Kings* 22 to. 37.

31. *CT*, pp. 9a, 48d; *C. Dan.* 7 to. 9.

32. *MH*, p. 149; *WL* 2, p. 135; *CT*, pp. 25b, 26c to. 4, 37a to. 6, 104c; *C. I Kings* 11 to. 3; *C. I Chron.* 29 to. 6.

33. *C. I Chron.* 29 to. 6.

34. *CT*, p. 182a.

35. *C. I Chron.* 29 to. 6.

36. This command is referred to in *CT*, p. 213b to. 3 and is then identified as one of the *pinnot* in to. 4.

37. *CT*, p. 240d.

38. *CT*, p. 211c to. 4. I am deliberately using the term, 'everlasting,' and not 'eternal.' The latter would imply that the Torah was co-existent with God from creation—which is not Gersonides' intent. The Torah is everlasting in that, once given at Sinai, it will never be revoked.

39. *C. II Chron.* 19:10.

40. *CT*, pp. 240c, 241c to. 5.

41. *CT*, p. 227d to. 10. In this passage the messianic age is not specifically mentioned. However, this *to'elet* is based on a passage in *CT*, p. 226c–d, where the messianic age is definitely part of the formulation.

42. *C. I Chron.* 29 to. 6.

43. *C. I Sam.* 7 to. 21. It is unclear whether Gersonides sees resurrection as one of the *pinnot ha-torah*. See our discussion supra, pp. 152–3.

44. See, for example, *CT*, p. 194a, where the notion of immortality is referred to in this way.

45. See, for example, *CT*, pp. 104d, 213c to. 10; *C. I Chron.* 21:12.

46. Supra, p. 187.

47. The thirteen articles of faith and some of the terminology that we are analyzing here are discussed in Menachem Kellner's comprehensive study, *Dogmas in Medieval Jewish Thought* (Oxford: Oxford University Press, 1986), pp. 10–66.

48. *Guide* II:25, pp. 327-9. Pines tends to translate *qawāʿid al-shariʿa* as "foundations of the Law." We will be using this phrase interchangeably with "fundamental principles of the Law."

49. These observations may help explain why Maimonides in the *Guide* will sometimes refer to foundations of the Law which have nothing to do with the thirteen articles of faith. Thus, Maimonides in *Guide* II:2, p. 253, sees the existence of angels as one of the fundamental principles of the Law, a concept not enumerated in *Perek Ḥelek*. Other doctrines that are termed foundations of the Law in the *Guide* and are not included in the thirteen articles are listed by Kellner in *Dogmas*, p. 53. Whether these concepts are seen by Maimonides as serving the same function in philosophical discussion as miracles, reward, and punishment is a question that is worthy of separate study.

50. The complexity of Maimonides' position cannot be dealt with here. An analysis of the foundations of the Law in Maimonides' thought would involve a thorough discussion of how this concept is used throughout his writings.

51. *CT*, p. 20c to. 1.

52. *C. I. Kings* 22 to 24.

53. *Guide* III:18, p. 475; in the Ibn Tibbon translation, *hu pinnah mipinnot ha-torah ve-ʿaleha binyanah* (p. 27a, standard editions).

54. This metaphor is applied most frequently to prophecy; see *CT*, pp. 25b, 26c to. 4; *I Chron.* 29 to. 6. See also the complete passage in the previous reference.

55. *C. I Chron.* 29 to. 6.

56. *CT* pp. 104d–105a. The notion that the oneness of God is one of the *pinnot ha-torah* needs no justification. The Maimonidean notion that the Torah was given to teach the oneness of God and to stamp out idol worship is a doctrine that permeates Gersonides' thought.

57. *CT*, p. 182a.

58. Gersonides makes this connection in *CT*, p. 9a. Why Gersonides sees the belief in creation as necessary for the belief in miracles is a very complex issue that deserves separate treatment. Touati argues that Gersonides' discussion of creation in book six of the *Wars* precedes the discussion of miracles because of the intimate connection between the two (pp. 163–4). The key issue is how Gersonides views divine will, especially with regard to creation. See Touati, pp. 205–7; Menachem Kellner, "Gersonides on the Problem of Volitional Creation," *HUCA* 51 (1980): 111–28.

59. *CT*, p. 71d to. 3. The commandment to love God is also one of the *pinnot ha-torah*. The reason for its inclusion is obvious. In several places, Gersonides emphasizes that the entire Torah is designed to inculcate love

of God. See, for instance, *CT*, p. 227d to. 10. Thus, the entire set of divine directives is tied up with this particular commandment.

60. *Guide* III:45, pp. 576–7. The existence of the Separate Intellects, which are identified with angels in Maimonides' thought, is referred to as one of the fundamental principles of the Torah in *Guide* II:2, p. 253. Prophecy is identified as one of the fundamental principles in *Guide* III:24, p. 502.

61. *CT*, p. 104c. In several other places, Gersonides emphasizes that the Torah would collapse without the belief in prophecy; see *CT*, p. 25b, 26c to. 4; *I Chron.* 29 to. 6.

62. One might also see the belief in miracles in this way. That belief may also be a prerequisite for accepting the revelation at Sinai, since Gersonides describes Mosaic prophecy in some passages as nothing less than a miracle. See *CT*, pp. 209d–210a to. 8 and our discussion, supra, pp. 79–82.

63. *CT*, p. 241c to. 5.

64. A practical concern for safeguarding the proper observance of biblical and rabbinic law also seems to have been the motivation for Gersonides' view that the appointment of judges is a fundamental principle of the Torah.

65. See *MH*, p. 149; *WL* 2, p. 135; in this reference Gersonides is referring to the doctrine that there are contingent events in the world. Since the only contingent events are the result of free will in Gersonides' philosophy, his comments are effectively directed at this latter issue.

It is also interesting to note which doctrines are not referred to as *pinnot ha-torah* in Gersonides' writings. The most notable exception is the doctrine of immortality. To my knowledge, Gersonides never refers to immortality as one of the *pinnot ha-torah*, even though he reads several passages in the Bible—especially the Garden of Eden story—as referring to immortality. See *MH*, pp. 438–9; *CT*, pp. 33a, 4a to. 18, 210a–b to. 11.

66. Hasdai Crescas was probably the first to have insight into this problem. For Crescas's conception of *pinnot ha-torah*, see Kellner, *Dogmas*, pp. 108–39.

Bibliography

GERSONIDES' PRINTED WORKS

Bible commentaries on Joshua, Judges, I & II Samuel, I & II Kings, Job, and Proverbs. In standard rabbinic Bibles (*Mikra'ot Gedolot*). (Cited by chapter, verse, and *to'elet*, as applicable.)

Bible commentaries on Ezra, Nehemiah, and I & II Chronicles. In *Nakh 'im Malbim*. New York: M. P. Press, 1973. (Cited by chapter, verse and *to'elet*, as applicable.)

Ḥamishah Ḥumshey Torah 'im Be'ur ha-Ralbag (*Commentary on the Torah*). Edited by Eli Freiman and Baruch Braner. Ma'aleh Adumim: Ma'aliyyot, 1993. (So far, only Genesis has appeared in print.)

Perush 'al ha-Torah (*Commentary on the Torah*). Venice: D. Bomberg, 1547. (Cited by page, column and *to'elet*, as applicable.)

Perush 'al ha-Torah (*Commentary on the Torah*), with handwritten emendations. Venice: D. Bomberg, 1547; National Library, Jerusalem; call number, R79 A6661 MS 94.

Perushey Ralbag 'al ha-Torah (*Commentary on the Torah*). Edited with notes by Yaacov Leib Levi. Jerusalem: Mossad ha-Rav Kook, 1992. (So far, only Genesis has appeared in print.)

Perush 'al Ḥamesh Megillot (*Commentary on the Five Scrolls*). Riva di Trento, 1559/60; reprint, Konigsberg: Gruber and Longrien, 1860. (Cited by page, column and *to'elet*, as applicable.)

Perush 'al Sefer Dani'el (*Commentary on Daniel*). In *'Oẓar ha-Perushim*, vol. 2. Tel Aviv, 1966. (Cited by chapter, verse and *to'elet*, as applicable.)

Perush 'al Shir ha-Shirim (*Commentary on the Song of Songs*). Introduction edited by Menachem Kellner, *Da'at* 23 (1989): 17–26.

Sefer Milḥamot ha-Shem. Leipzig: C. B. Lorck, 1866; reprint, Berlin, 1923. (Cited by page.)

GERSONIDES' WORKS IN MANUSCRIPT

Perush 'al ha-Torah (Commentary on the Torah). Or. 42, Biblioteca Medicea-Laurenziana, Florence, Italy.

GERSONIDES' WORKS IN TRANSLATION

Bleich, J. David. *Providence and the Philosophy of Gersonides* (Translation and notes, book four of *The Wars of the Lord*). New York: Yeshiva University Press, 1973.

Feldman, Seymour. *The Wars of the Lord.* 2 volumes (third volume, forthcoming). Philadelphia: Jewish Publication Society, 1984–87.

Kellerman, Benzion. *Die Kämpfe Gottes von Lewi ben Gerson.* 2 volumes. Berlin: Mayer and Müller, 1914–16.

Kellner, Menachem. " 'Introduction to the *Commentary on the Song of Songs* Composed by the Sage Levi ben Gershom'—An Annotated Translation." In *From Ancient Israel to Modern Judaism: Intellect in Quest of Understanding: Essays in Honor of Marvin Fox,* vol. 2. Jacob Neusner, Ernest S. Frerichs, and Nahum M. Sarna, eds., pp. 187–205. Atlanta: Scholars Press, 1989.

Lassen, Abraham. *The Commentary of Levi ben Gershom on the Book of Job.* New York: Bloch, 1946.

Samuelson, Norbert M. *Gersonides on God's Knowledge* (Translation and notes, book three of *The Wars of the Lord*). Toronto: Pontifical Institute for Mediaeval Studies, 1977.

Silverman, David W. *The Problem of Prophecy in Gersonides* (Translation with analysis, book two of *The Wars of the Lord*). Ph.D. diss., Columbia University, 1975.

Touati, Charles. *Les Guerres du Seigneur: Livres III et IV.* Paris: Mouton, 1968.

OTHER PRIMARY SOURCES

Aristotle. *The Works of Aristotle.* Translated under the editorship of W. D. Ross. 10 volumes. Oxford: The Clarendon Press, 1908–31.

Averroes. *Kitāb Faṣl al-Maqāl.* Edited by George Hourani. Leiden: E. J. Brill, 1959.

————. *On the Harmony of Religion and Philosophy*. A translation of *Kitāb Faṣl al-Maqāl* with introduction and notes by George Hourani. London: Luzac, 1961.

Babylonian Talmud. Standard edition.

Bereshit Rabbah. Edited with notes by J. Theodor and Ch. Albeck. 3 volumes. Jerusalem: Wahrmann Books, 1965. (Cited by chapter and paragraph, then volume and page.)

Halevi, Judah. *Kitāb al-Radd wa-'l-Dalīl fī 'l-Dīn al-Dhalil* (*Kuzari*). Edited by David H. Baneth. Jerusalem: Magnes Press, 1977.

————. *Sefer ha-Kuzari*. Translated into Hebrew with introduction and notes by Yehudah Even-Shmuel. 2d ed. Jerusalem: Dvir, 1972.

Ibn Ezra, Abraham. *Ḥamishah Ḥumshey Torah ʿim Ḥamesh Megillot* (*Pentateuch with Five Scrolls*). With supercommentary of *Meḥokekey Yehudah* on ibn Ezra. New York: Reinmann Seforim Center, 1975.

————. *Perushey ha-Torah* (*Commentary on the Torah*). 3 volumes. Edited with notes by Abraham Weiser. Jerusalem: Mossad ha-Rav Kook, 1976.

Jerusalem Talmud. Standard edition.

Kimḥi, David. *Perush R. David Kimḥi ʿal ha-Torah* (*Commentary on the Torah*). Edited with notes by Moshe Kamelhar. Jerusalem: Mossad ha-Rav Kook, 1970.

Maimonides. *Dalālat al-Ḥaʾirīn* (*The Guide of the Perplexed*). Edited by I. Joel. Jerusalem: Junovich, 1929.

————. *The Guide of the Perplexed*. Translated with introduction and notes by Shlomo Pines. Chicago: University of Chicago Press, 1963. (Cited by book, chapter, and page.)

————. *Maimonides' Treatise on Logic*. Edited and translated by Israel Efros. New York: American Academy of Jewish Research, 1938.

————. *Maimonides' Treatise on Resurrection*. Edited by J. Finkel. *PAAJR* 9 (1939).

————. *Mishneh Torah*. Standard edition.

————. *Moreh ha-Nevukhim* (*The Guide of the Perplexed*). Translated into Hebrew by Samuel ibn Tibbon. Standard edition.

Mekhilta de-R. Ishmael. Edited by H. S. Horowitz and I. A. Rabin. Frankfurt: J. Kauffmann, 1931. (Cited by *massekhta*, chapter, and page.)

Midrash Rabbah. 2 volumes. Vilna, 1878; reprint, Jerusalem, 1975. (Cited by chapter and paragraph.)

Midrash Tehillim. Edited by S. Buber. Vilna: Rom Press, 1891. (Cited by chapter and page.)

Naḥmanides. *Perushey ha-Torah* (*Commentary on the Torah*). Edited by C. Chavel. 2 volumes. Jerusalem: Mossad ha-Rav Kook, 1975.

Rashi. *Pentateuch with Rashi's Commentary*. Translated by A. M. Silbermann. 5 volumes. Jerusalem: Feldheim, 1973.

———. *Rashi ʿal ha-Torah*. Edited by Abraham Berliner. Frankfurt: J. Kauffmann, 1905; reprint, Jerusalem: Feldheim, 1970.

Saadiah Gaon. *Al-Mukhtār fī ʾl-Amānāt wa-ʾl-ʾIʿtaqādāt (Beliefs and Opinions)*. Arabic text with Hebrew translation by Yosef Kafiḥ Jerusalem: Sura, n.d.

———. *The Book of Beliefs and Opinions*. Translated by Samuel Rosenblatt. New Haven: Yale University Press, 1948.

———. *Perushey R. Saʿadiah Gaʾon li-Breʾshit (Saadiah's Commentary on Genesis)*. Edited with Hebrew translation by Moshe Zucker. Jerusalem: Jewish Theological Seminary, 1984.

———. *Saadiah on Job*. Translated with notes by Lenn Goodman. New Haven: Yale University Press, 1988.

Tanḥuma. Edited by S. Buber. 2 volumes. New York: Sefer, 1946. (Cited by page.)

Targum Onkelos. In standard rabbinic Bibles (*Mikraʾot Gedolot*).

Va-Yikra Rabbah. Edited by M. Margulies. 3 volumes. Jerusalem: Wahrmann Books, 1953–58. (Cited by chapter, paragraph, and page.)

SECONDARY SOURCES

Bacher, Wilhelm. *Die Bibelexegese der jüdischen Religionphilosophen des Mittelalters vor Maimuni*. Strassburg: Trübner, 1892.

———. *Die Bibelexegese Moses Maimunis*. Budapest: Landes Rabbinerschule, 1896.

Baron, S. W. *A Social and Religious History of the Jews*. Volumes 6–12. New York: Columbia University Press, 1958.

Cohen, Gerson. "Esau As Symbol in Early Medieval Thought." In *Jewish Medieval and Renaissance Studies*, Alexander Altmann, ed., pp. 19–49. Cambridge, MA: Harvard University Press, 1967.

Dahan, Gilbert, ed. *Gersonide en son temp*. Louvain: Peeters, 1991.

Davidson, Herbert. "Alfarabi and Avicenna on the Active Intellect." *Viator* 3 (1972): 109–178.

———. "The Active Intellect and Hallevi's Theory of Causality." *REJ* 131 (Fall 1970): 351–96.

Davies, W. D. *Paul and Rabbinic Judaism*. Philadelphia: Fortress Press, 1980.

Dienstag, Jacob I. "The Biblical Exegesis of Maimonides in Jewish Scholarship." In *The Samuel K. Mirsky Jubilee Volume*, Simon Bernstein and Gershon Churgin, eds., pp. 151–90. New York: Jubilee Committee, 1970.

Eisen, Robert. "Reason, Revelation and the Fundamental Principles of the Torah in Gersonides' Thought." *PAAJR* 57 (1991): 11–34.

Emery, Richard W. *The Jews of Perpignan in the Thirteenth Century*. New York: Columbia University Press, 1959.

Encylopedia Judaica. Jerusalem: Keter, 1972.

Fakhry, Majid. *A History of Islamic Philosophy*. New York: Columbia University Press, 1970.

Feldman, Seymour. "Gersonides' Proofs for the Creation of the Universe." *PAAJR* 35 (1967): 113–37.

———. "Platonic Themes in Gersonides' Cosmology." In *The Salo Whittmayer Baron Jubilee Volume*, pp. 383–405. Jerusalem: American Academy for Jewish Research, 1975.

———. "Gersonides on the Possibility of Conjunction with the Active Intellect." *AJS Review* 3 (1978): 99–120.

———. "The Binding of Isaac: the Test-Case of Divine Omniscience." In *Divine Omniscience and Omnipotence in Medieval Philosophy*, Tamar Rudavsky, ed., pp. 105–135. Dordrecht: D. Reidel, 1985.

———. "Gersonides and Biblical Exegesis." Appendix in *The Wars of the Lord*, vol. 2, pp. 213–47. Philadelphia: Jewish Publication Society, 1987.

Fox, Marvin. *Interpreting Maimonides*. Chicago: University of Chicago Press, 1990.

Freiman, Eliyahu. "A Passage from Gersonides' *Commentary on the Torah*" (in Hebrew). *Me-ʿAley ʿAsor* (Yeshivat Birkat Mosheh Tenth Anniversary Volume), B. Braner, O. Kafiḥ and Z. Shimshoni, eds., pp. 162–89. Maʿaleh Adumim: Maʿaliyot, 1988.

Freudenthal, Gad, ed. *Studies on Gersonides—A Fourteenth Century Jewish Philosopher-Scientist*. Leiden: E. J. Brill, 1992.

Friedlaender, M. *Essays on the Writings of Abraham Ibn Ezra*. London: Society of Hebrew Literature, 1877; reprint, Jerusalem: Metsahef, 1963.

Ginzberg, Louis. *Legends of the Jews*. 7 volumes. Philadelphia: Jewish Publication Society, 1962.

Goldstein, Bernard R. "Preliminary Remarks on Levi ben Gerson's Contribution to Medieval Astronomy." *Proceedings of the Israel Academy of Sciences and Humanities* 3 (1969): 239 –5.

———. "Astronomical and Astrological Themes in the Philosophical Works of Levi ben Gerson." *Archives Internationales d'Histoire des Sciences* 29 (1976): 221–24.

Greenberg, Moshe, ed. *Jewish Biblical Exegesis: An Introduction* (in Hebrew). Jerusalem: Magnes Press, 1983.

Guttmann, Julius. *Philosophies of Judaism*. Translated by David Silverman. New York: Schocken Books, 1973.

Heinemann, Yitshak. *The Reasons for the Commandments in Jewish Literature* (in Hebrew). 4th ed. 2 volumes. Jerusalem: World Zionist Organization, 1954.

Herring, Basil. *Joseph ibn Kaspi's Gevia' Kesef*. New York: Ktav Publishing Co., 1982.

Hillers, Delbert. *Covenant: The History of a Biblical Idea*. Baltimore: Johns Hopkins Press, 1969.

Hoffman, Lawrence, ed. *The Land of Israel: Jewish Perspectives*. Notre Dame: University of Notre Dame Press, 1986.

Husik, Isaac. *A History of Medieval Jewish Philosophy*. Philadelphia: Jewish Publication Society, 1958.

Idel, Moshe. "Some Conceptions of the Land of Israel in Medieval Jewish Thought." In *A Straight Path: Studies in Medieval Philosophy and Culture: Essays in Honor of Arthur Hyman*, Ruth Link-Salinger, ed., pp. 124–141. Washington, D.C.: Catholic University of America Press, 1988.

Kasher, Rimon. "Miracles, Faith and Merit of the Fathers: Conceptual Development in the Sages' Writings" (in Hebrew). *Jerusalem Studies in Jewish Thought* 5 (1986): 15–23.

Kellner, Menachem. "Gersonides, Providence and the Rabbinic Tradition." *Journal of the American Academy of Religion* 42 (1974): 673–685.

———. "Gersonides and his Cultured Despisers: Arama and Abravanel." *Journal of Medieval and Renaissance Studies* 6 (1976): 269–96.

———. "Maimonides and Gersonides on Mosaic Prophecy." *Speculum* 52 (1977): 62–79.

———. "R. Levi ben Gerson: A Bibliographic Essay." *Studies in Bibliography and Booklore* 12 (1979): 13–23.

———. "Gersonides on Miracles, the Messiah and Resurrection." *Da'at* 4 (1980): 5–34.

———. "Gersonides on the Problem of Volitional Creation." *HUCA* 51 (1980): 111–28.

———. *Dogmas in Medieval Jewish Thought.* Oxford: Oxford University Press, 1986.

———. *Maimonides on Judaism and the Jewish People.* Albany: State University of New York Press, 1991.

Klatzkin, Jacob. *A Dictionary of Philosophical Terms and a Philosophical Anthology* (in Hebrew). 2 volumes. New York: Feldheim, 1968.

Klein-Braslavy, Sarah. "Gersonides on Determinism, Possibility, Choice and Foreknowledge" (in Hebrew). *Da'at* 22 (1989): 5–53.

Kreisel, Howard. "Miracles in Medieval Jewish Philosophy." *JQR* 75, no. 2 (October 1984): 99–133.

———. "Veridical Dreams and Prophecy in the Philosophy of Gersonides" (in Hebrew). *Da'at* 22 (1989): 73–84.

Marmorstein, Arthur. *The Doctrine of Merits in Old Rabbinical Literature.* London: Oxford University Press, 1920.

Mesch, Barry. *Studies in Joseph ibn Caspi.* Leiden: E. J. Brill, 1975.

Nehorai, Michael. "Maimonides and Gersonides: Two Approaches to the Nature of Providence" (in Hebrew). *Da'at* 20 (1988): 51–64.

Pines, Shlomo. "Scholasticism after Thomas Aquinas and the Teachings of Hasdai Crescas and His Predecessors." *Proceedings of the Israel Academy of Sciences and Humanities* 1:10 (1967): 1–101.

———. "Saint Thomas et la pensée juive médiévale: quelques notations," *Aquinas and Problems in His Time,* G. Verbeke and D. Verhelst, eds., pp. 126–28. Louvain: University Press and The Hague: Martinus Nijhoff, 1976.

———. "Appendix: Problems in Teaching Gersonides," appended to "On Certain Subjects Included in the Book *Ezer ha-Dat* by Isaac Polkar and Parallels to them in Spinoza" (in Hebrew). *Studies in Kabbalah, Jewish Philosophy and Ethical Literature in Honor of Isaiah Tishby* (in Hebrew), pp. 447–57. Jerusalem: Magnes Press, 1986.

Ravitzky, Aviezer, and Hallamish, Moshe, eds. *The Land of Israel in Medieval Jewish Thought* (in Hebrew). Jerusalem: Yad Yitshak ben Tsevi, 1991.

Renan, Ernst. *Averroes et l'averroisme*. Paris: Calmann-Lévy, 1852.

Renan, Ernst and Adolph Neubauer, *Écrivains juifs français du XIVe siècle*. Paris: Imprimerie nationale, 1893.

Rosenberg, Shalom. "On Biblical Interpretation in *The Guide of the Perplexed*" (in Hebrew). *Jerusalem Studies in Jewish Thought* 1 (1981): 85–157.

———. "The Concept of *Emunah* in Post-Maimonidean Jewish Philosophy." In *Studies in Medieval Jewish History and Literature II*, Isadore Twersky, ed., pp. 273–309. Cambridge, MA: Harvard University Press, 1984.

Rudavsky, Tamar. "Divine Omniscience and Future Contingents in Gersonides." *Journal of the History of Philosophy* 21 (October 1983): 513–536.

———. "Divine Omniscience, Contingency and Prophecy in Gersonides." In *Divine Omniscience and Omnipotence in Medieval Philosophy*, Tamar Rudavsky, ed., pp. 161–181. Dordrecht: D. Reidel, 1985.

Samuelson, Norbert M. "On Knowing God: Maimonides, Gersonides and the Philosophy of Religion." *Judaism* 18 (1969): 64–77.

———. "Philosophic and Religious Authority in the Thought of Maimonides and Gersonides." *CCAR Journal* 17 (1969): 31–43.

———. "The Problem of Free Will in Maimonides, Gersonides and Aquinas." *CCAR Journal* 17 (1970): 2–20.

———. "Gersonides' Account of God's Knowledge of Particulars." *Journal of the History of Philosophy* 10 (1972): 399–416.

Sanders, E. P. *Paul and Palestinian Judaism*. Philadelphia: Fortress Press, 1977.

Sarachek, Joseph. *Faith and Reason: The Conflict over the Rationalism of Maimonides*. Williamsport: Bayard Press, 1935.

Schechter, Solomon. *Aspects of Rabbinic Theology*. New York: Schocken Books, 1961.

Segal, M. H. *Biblical Exegesis* (in Hebrew). 2d ed. Jerusalem: Kiryat Sefer, 1952.

Septimus, Bernard. *Hispano-Jewish Culture in Transition: The Career and Controversies of Ramah*. Cambridge, MA: Harvard University Press, 1982.

Shatzmiller, Joseph. "Suggestions and Addenda to *Gallia Judaica*" (in Hebrew). *Kiryat Sefer* 45 (September 1970): 607–610.

———. "Gersonides and the Jewish Community of Orange in his Day" (in Hebrew). *University of Haifa Studies in the History of the Jewish People and the Land of Israel* 2 (1972): 111–26.

———. "Some Further Information about Gersonides and the Orange Jewish Community in his Day" (in Hebrew). *University of Haifa Studies in the History of the Jewish People and the Land of Israel* 3 (1972): 139–43.

Silver, Daniel J. *Maimonidean Criticism and Maimonidean Controversy 1180–1240*. Leiden: E. J. Brill, 1965.

Sirat, Colette. *A History of Jewish Philosophy in the Middle Ages*. Cambridge: Cambridge University Press, 1986.

Staub, Jacob J. *The Creation of the World According to Gersonides*. Chico, CA: Scholars Press, 1982.

Steinschneider, Moritz. *Die Hebraïsche Übersetzungen des Mittelalters*. Berlin, 1893.

———. "Levi ben Gerson." In *Gesammelte Schriften* 1, pp. 233–70. Berlin: H. Poppelauer, 1925.

Strauss, Leo. *Philosophy and Law*. Translated by Fred Baumann. Philadelphia: Jewish Publication Society of America, 1987.

Talmage, Frank. "R. David Kimhi as Polemicist." *HUCA* 38 (1967): 213–35.

———. "David Kimhi and the Rationalist Tradition." *HUCA* 39 (1968): 177–218.

———. "David Kimhi and the Rationalist Tradition II: Literary Sources." In *Studies in Honor of I. Kiev*, C. Berlin, ed., pp. 435–70. New York: Ktav Publishing House, 1972.

———. *David Kimhi: The Man and His Commentaries*. Cambridge, MA: Harvard University Press, 1975.

———. "Apples of Gold: the Inner Meaning of Sacred Texts in Medieval Judaism." In *Jewish Spirituality*, vol. 1, Arthur Green, ed., pp. 313–356. New York: Crossroad, 1988.

Touati, Charles. "Les idées philosophiques et théologiques de Gersonide (1288–1344) dans ses commentaires bibliques." *Revue des sciences religieuses* 27 (1954): 335–67.

———. "Le problème de l'inerrance prophétique dans le théologie juive du Moyen Age." *Revue de l'histoire des religions* 174 (1968): 169–187.

———. "La lumière de l'intellect, création du Premier Jour: l'éxegèse de Genèse 1:1–3 chez Gersonide." In *In Principio: Interprétations des premiers versets de la Genèse*, pp. 37 –45. Paris: Presses Universitaires de France, 1973.

———. *La pensée philosophique et théologique de Gersonide*. Paris: Les Editions de Minuit, 1973.

Twersky, Isadore. *Rabad of Posquières*. Cambridge, MA: Harvard University Press, 1962.

———. "Aspects of the Social and Cultural History of Provençal Jewry." In *Jewish Society Through the Ages*, H. H. Ben Sasson and S. Ettinger, eds., pp. 185–207. New York: Schocken Books, 1971.

———. *Introduction to the Code of Maimonides*. New Haven: Yale University Press, 1980.

Urbach, Ephraim E. *The Sages: Their Concepts and Beliefs*. Translated by Israel Abrahams. 2d ed. Jerusalem: Magnes Press, 1979.

Vajda, Georges. *Introduction à la pensée juive du moyen age*. Paris: J. Vrin, 1947.

Ventura, Moïse. "Belief in Providence According to Gersonides" (in Hebrew). In *Minḥah le-Avraham*, pp. 12–21. Jerusalem, 1959.

Wolfson, H. A. "Maimonides and Gersonides on Divine Attributes as Ambiguous Terms." In *Studies in the History of Philosophy and Religion*, vol. 2, Isadore Twersky and George H. Williams, eds., pp. 231–47. Cambridge, MA.: Harvard University Press, 1977.

Yerushalmi, Yosef Hayim. *Zakhor: Jewish History and Jewish Memory*. Seattle and London: University of Washington Press, 1983.

Index